Stranger in My Own Country

Stranger in My Own Country

A JEWISH FAMILY IN MODERN GERMANY

Yascha Mounk

FARRAR, STRAUS AND GIROUX   NEW YORK

Farrar, Straus and Giroux
18 West 18th Street, New York 10011

Grateful acknowledgment is made for permission to reprint an excerpt
from "What Has to Be Said," copyright © 2012 by Günter Grass,
originally published on April 10, 2012, as "Was gesagt werden muss,"
Süddeutsche Zeitung. Translation by Yascha Mounk.

The Library of Congress has cataloged the hardcover edition as follows:
Mounk, Yascha, 1982– author.
    Stranger in my own country : a Jewish family in modern
Germany / Yascha Mounk. — First edition.
        pages cm
    ISBN 978-0-374-15753-1 (hardback)
        1. Mounk, Yascha, 1982–   2. Jews—Germany—Biography.
    3. Holocaust, Jewish (1939–1945)—Germany—Influence.
    4. National characteristics, German.   5. Germany—Biography.
    I. Title.

DS134.42.M68 A3 2014
305.892'4043092—dc23
[B]
                                                2013032996

Paperback ISBN: 978-0-374-53553-7

Designed by Jonathan D. Lippincott

Farrar, Straus and Giroux books may be purchased for educational, business,
or promotional use. For information on bulk purchases, please contact the
Macmillan Corporate and Premium Sales Department at 1-800-221-7945,
extension 5442, or write to specialmarkets@macmillan.com.

www.fsgbooks.com
www.twitter.com/fsgbooks • www.facebook.com/fsgbooks

P1

To Leon and Ewa and Bolek and Mila

Contents

Stranger in My Own Country

Prelude: An Unlikely Refuge

I never thought to question why my family might be so small, or so scattered. In Munich, there was my mother—Ala—and me. Relatively close by, in Frankfurt, there was my grandfather Leon. Far away, in southern Sweden, there was my grandmother Ewa, my uncle Roman, and my cousin Rebecka. There was also my great-uncle, a man by the name of Herrmann, but he lived even farther away, in San Francisco. As I was told whenever his name came up, he was, in any case, not much of a family man. I saw him just twice in my life.

That was it. Six of us. Seven, if you counted generously.

It seemed natural to me, of course, just as most children, even those who grow up in circumstances they later recognize to be unusual or downright bizarre, think that their reality is normal, natural, even inevitable. I simply assumed that families everywhere come in small sizes, that a reunion of three full generations never amounts to more than seven people.

Only much later did I understand that none of this was natural; that, on the contrary, it was the result of historical forces I might be tempted to call abstract, had they not had such a tangible effect on the world I grew up in.

No, it was not natural that my family was so small, for Leon and Ewa should have had parents who might still have been alive when I was born. Leon should have had seven siblings, not just

Herrmann. Ewa should have had an older sister, as well as many cousins, aunts, and uncles. Even Roman and Ala should, I eventually learned, have had a big brother.

Nor was our dispersal, a good two decades after the death of so much of my family, natural. It was the result of a second man-made tragedy—a much smaller tragedy, to be sure, but one that, in its own way, dispensed with my grandparents' lifelong hopes and aspirations in just as comprehensive a manner.

Ever since they were teenagers, Leon and Ewa had devoted their lives to an ideology that promised to rid the world of ethnic persecution: communism. But, in the event, the Communist government of Poland ended up throwing them—its most loyal aides—out of their homeland for no better reason than that they were Jews. It was in the wake of this second tragedy that my family dispersed to the United States, to Israel, to Sweden—and to Germany, where I was to grow up.

•

Leon first considered moving Ewa, Ala, and Roman out of Poland in 1956.

With an unprecedented speech to the Soviet Communist Party, Nikita Khrushchev had just denounced the terrible abuses of Stalinism. In Poland, the effects of this speech were immediate. The hard-line policies of the last years softened a little, making it much easier for Jews to obtain exit visas. At the same time, a significant part of the population used their newfound political freedom to give voice to the same old anti-Semitism.

A prominent political faction, the so-called Natolin Group, publicly stoked the anti-Semitic mood of the day with thinly veiled attacks on "Zionist traitors" who supposedly remained at large in Poland. Even Władysław Gomułka, the newly appointed secretary general of Poland's Communist Party, began to flirt with anti-Semitic sentiments, encouraging anybody who wanted to stick to his Jewish identity—anybody who expressed solidarity with Israel, or merely wore a yarmulke in public—to leave the country.

Not surprisingly, many Polish Jews proved unwilling to sacrifice their identity in so radical a way. Between 1956 and 1958, half of the seventy thousand Jews who still remained in Poland fled the country. But Leon was not one of them.

Leon had been born on Christmas Day, 1913, in Kolomea, a little shtetl in the easternmost stretches of the fading Austro-Hungarian Empire. The faces of his childhood are the faces you see in those old photographs that chronicle the lost world of traditional Eastern European Jews: bearded men in dark jackets; women in modest, flowing robes; joyful children, momentarily forced to sit stock-still, visibly impatient to escape the photographer's lens and get back to playing.

Leon grew up in just such a traditional family, together with his parents and grandparents and seven brothers and sisters. But he found his shtetl's way of life outmoded and considered its poverty a terrible injustice. And so he was particularly receptive when older children started to talk to him about the ideals of communism—about a world in which all the prejudice of tradition would be done away with, a better world in which everybody would be equal and nobody would have to go hungry. When he was no older than sixteen, he ran away from Kolomea.

The Communist movement became his home and his educator. Leon moved to nearby L'vov, where he found work as a printer's apprentice—the most intellectual of manual jobs, for it consisted of reading texts and then setting them in type, letter by letter. But his main interest was his after-hours work as an organizer for the Polish Communist Party, an illegal activity for which he was even prepared to go to jail. Far from discouraging him, his repeated stints behind bars only made him a more fervent activist.

And so, when the Nazis broke their pact with the Soviet

Union and moved on L'vov in late June of 1941, it was only natural that Leon should turn east for help. In double danger—because he was a Jew *and* a Communist—he managed to flee L'vov on the last train for Russia before the Germans arrived. For the rest of the war, he was put to work in a makeshift ammunitions factory in Siberia, where he performed dangerous tasks for interminable hours, subsisting on scraps.

That harsh treatment made Leon the luckiest member of his family. Both his parents perished in the gas chambers or were shot dead in some Eastern European ditch. Of his eight brothers, only one, my great-uncle Herrmann, survived.

With most of his family dead, Leon, like so many others in the same situation, must at times have thought it impossible to go on. In those desperate moments, it was his faith in communism that provided a bridge between his prewar and his postwar self. He now thought it more imperative than ever to create a new, better kind of society.

As the Iron Curtain descended upon Europe and Poland found itself under Soviet hegemony, Leon's political dream finally came true: the new Poland would be Communist. The contacts Leon had made in a lifetime of political activism now stood him in good stead. After a few years in Lodz, where Ala, his first daughter, was born in 1947, he moved to Warsaw, quickly rising through the ranks of the Communist regime to become the technical director of RSW Prasa, postwar Poland's largest printing conglomerate.

But even though Leon had been a Communist his whole adult life, and was now a moderately important man, he wasn't blind to the injustices of the Eastern bloc. One sunny afternoon in March of 1953, when Ala was five, she came home from school crying.

"What happened, Alushka?"

"It is father Sta—" Ala had trouble speaking between sobs. "It is Father Stalin. Father Stalin has died."

Leon's face hardened. "You, my daughter," he demanded, "will not shed a single tear for that swine."

Leon was, after all, nothing if not a good man. Like his wife, Ewa, he had become a Communist out of idealism, not opportunism. And yet his fervently held ideals made him doggedly loyal to a regime whose cruelty was getting more apparent by the day. Like the tormented, self-delusional intellectuals described in Czesław Miłosz's *The Captive Mind*, Leon had, for a long time, contorted his conscience, ultimately tolerating far too much.

There were the severe Stalinist repressions that swept Poland during much of the postwar era. There were the political show trials. There was the all-encompassing censorship, of which, as the technical director of RSW Prasa, Leon must have been keenly aware.

All of that he had tolerated. In his mind, giving up on his beliefs because Communist reality didn't yet match Communist ideals would have meant abandoning a lifelong commitment. Better, he concluded, to keep the faith.

And so, when Gomułka asked Polish Jews to shed their identity, Leon did what he had gradually grown accustomed to doing. Grudgingly, he obeyed.

In the years after 1957, open hostility against Poland's Jews briefly subsided. Superficially, my family's situation improved.

But beneath the surface, the most fervently anti-Semitic members of the Communist regime were busy preparing the ground for an even bigger pogrom. In 1960, General Wojciech Jaruzelski, the highest-ranking political operative in Poland's Ministry of Defense, compiled a list of "racially unclean" military officers. In 1964, the Ministry of Internal Affairs followed suit, amassing a list of all Jews still in Poland—a few of them religious; most, like my family, merely of Jewish ancestry.

These preparations bore their poisonous fruit in the late 1960s, when the leaders of the Communist regime found themselves in a rapidly deteriorating position. Abroad, Czechoslovakia's Alexander Dubček was promising to institute a form of "socialism with a human face" that would largely dispense with government censorship and allow more private economic initiative. At home, Poland's planned economy was stagnating. Moderates within the party, emboldened by Dubček's success, were pushing for liberalizing reforms. Popular discontent with the regime was growing palpable.

Then, on March 8, 1968, 1,500 students took to the streets of Warsaw to protest repressive government policies like the recent suspension of *Forefathers' Eve*, a patriotic play by Adam Mickiewicz that included allusions to Russian domination of Poland. Within a few days, the protests exploded in size and spread to universities all over the country. A general strike loomed.

Challenged in their orthodoxy both at home and abroad, Gomułka and his men were gripped by fear. Their hold on power seemed to be slipping. To diffuse popular resentment and rescue their authority, they settled on a classic political ploy: divert the attention of the population from real grievances to imagined enemies within the country. Poland's remaining Jews were quickly scapegoated. In a clever top-down campaign, the population's latent anti-Semitism was whipped up into open hostility.

First, government propaganda seized upon the fact that many of the leaders of the student protests, like Adam Michnik, had Jewish ancestors: "Jews," leaflets handed out at the University of Warsaw emphasized, "have no right to teach Poles patriotism." Show trials against Michnik and other Jewish protest leaders were hastily arranged. A state-controlled newspaper dutifully reported that, at their trials, "the accused behaved with the insolence typical of people of Jewish extraction."

Then, with the help of the Interior Ministry's list of Polish Jews, a campaign of systematic harassment commenced in earnest. In a state-run economy, most livelihoods could easily be destroyed by a directive from above. Within a few months, Jews were purged from positions in the civil service, the Communist Party, and the army. Jewish doctors, academics, and schoolteachers were also fired. So, too, were some simple workers. All four of my grandparents were booted out of their jobs.

Acts of intimidation, some planned by public officials, others carried out with impunity by ordinary citizens, were a daily feature of this bleak time.

One cold winter day, in the early months of 1968, Ala was walking home to the apartment she shared with Leon, Ewa, and Roman when she saw a car parked on the street. In the car, she could make out three plainclothes police officers. On the car's roof, there was a searchlight that was shining a bright beam straight at her family's apartment. It was to remain lit, day and night, for close to a week.

A few weeks later, Ala—who was only twenty years old at the time—was on her way to Warsaw's Music Conservatory. As usual, she was running late for class. She rushed up seven steps, pushed the conservatory's heavy doors open, glanced at a huge banner in the atrium, kept running toward the classrooms, suddenly stood still, returned her gaze to the banner, then stared at it, aghast. It read: GOTTLIEBS, WEINS, COHENS: LEAVE FOR ISRAEL! (Her surname was Gottlieb.)

All of this sent one message loud and clear. Jews, even those who had long since abdicated their Jewish identity, were no longer welcome in Poland. By 1970, nearly all of them had left the country.

Though the Polish authorities brutally encouraged Jews to leave, they contrived to make emigration as costly as possible.

Those who wished to gain permission to exit the country had to run a Kafkaesque gauntlet designed to ensure that they would leave the bulk of their meager belongings behind. In a particularly perverse move—designed to prove to the outside world that the government's actions were not anti-Semitic—they would even be forced to declare that they were Zionists who freely chose to renounce Polish citizenship out of a desire to move to Israel.

Despite the intense worries they had for their family's future, livelihood, and safety, this perfidious requirement stung my grandparents more painfully than anything else. All their lives, Leon and Ewa, as well as Bolek and Mila (the parents of my father, whom I didn't meet until I was a teenager), had championed communism, enchanted by its promise to free the world from religious hatred and ethnic chauvinism. After 1945, they had decided to stay in Poland to share in the burden of building a Communist society, even though so many of their relatives had perished on Polish soil. When their children were born, they gave them Polish names like Roman and Alicja and Andrzej and Wiktor and Helena. They raised them, just as Gomułka had demanded, as Poles and Communists; so far as possible, they even avoided mentioning to their children that they were Jewish. But now, as they were being thrown out of their homes, they were forced to declare that they wanted to leave Poland to move to a faraway country whose policies they viewed with considerable skepticism.

It was not until that point that my grandparents' dream of contributing to the realization of Communist ideals—the dream to which they had devoted the better part of a lifetime—was irrevocably dashed. Serious misgivings about the Socialist regimes of Eastern Europe had reared their head much earlier. Only now did they come to the unbearable realization that their seemingly noble ideals would likely never be realized: communism hadn't just been held back by Stalin or Gomułka; the causes for its failure were much more fundamental.

My grandparents' disenchantment, which overcame them when they were already in their fifties, would mark them for the rest of their lives.

By the time I was old enough to talk to him about politics, Leon had turned into a soft-spoken retiree who had long since traded in the fervent convictions of his youth for a moderate form of social democracy. Embracing a cautious yet passionate humanism, he now put personal virtues above abstract political goals.

"More than anything else," he demanded of me in German, "you must stand upright and remain true to yourself."

It was a wonderful, moving piece of advice. I took it very seriously. But not until much later did I realize the extent to which Leon, when he was exhorting me to remain "*aufrichtig*," might really have been addressing his former self; the self that, in whatever limited way, tolerated Stalinist repressions in his role as the technical director of Poland's printing business; the self that, in 1957, promised to give up all vestiges of a Jewish identity, turning himself, even more than before, into nothing but a Pole and a Communist.

As for Bolek, my father's father—who, as the head of the Communist Party's political training academy, had ascended to an even more senior position within the regime—I remember him sitting in his little flat on the outskirts of Copenhagen. Already in his nineties by then, he was waving a cigarette about in one of his inimitable gestures, energetic yet melancholy.

"I'm jealous of you," he told me.

I looked at him in surprise.

"I still don't believe that capitalism has got it right. But neither has communism. I know that now."

"I'm not sure I follow."

"One day, you'll see, something else, something new, will come along. I'm too old. I won't be around to see what that might be. But you will, Yascha. You will, and that's why I'm jealous of you."

Heartbroken, Leon and Ewa, their children in tow, agreed to sign whatever sheet of paper was thrust in front of them. Their Polish citizenship was revoked before the signatures on the enforced Zionist declaration had dried. Then they were issued a travel document that would allow them to exit Poland, pass through Czechoslovakia, and enter Austria. Once they crossed the border, their predicament became official: they were stateless.

My mother, uncle, grandfather, and grandmother—thrown out of the country they had always considered home—suddenly found themselves stranded in Vienna. Where could they go?

It would have been easy for them to move to Israel. Jewish refugee organizations were providing free transport to the Jews' new homeland; upon their arrival, they would have been presented with Israeli passports, instruction in Hebrew, and a little money to make a start in their new life. But Leon wasn't keen. Despite the Polish regime's efforts to portray him as such, he was no Zionist.

With their parents still unsure of what to do, Roman and Ala decided to go to Sweden.

An acquaintance of theirs had some distant family there. When it became clear to him that he would have to flee Poland, he applied for a Swedish visa. Unexpectedly, he got it. Overjoyed, the Swede-to-be told his friends. His friends told their friends. They all applied for visas, too. Within months, hundreds of young Polish Jews were on their way to Sweden—all, as it later turned out, on the initiative of one sympathetic mid-level diplomat.

My mother and my uncle were among the many Polish Jews who were issued Swedish visas in this way. Shortly after arriving in Austria, they began to make their travel arrangements. They were to leave Vienna together, by night train, on the evening of February 13, 1969, Roman's eighteenth birthday. The local Jewish community was to send somebody to pick them up upon their arrival in Malmö. Roman and Ala had even bought the train tickets.

But then, just a few days before their departure, their plans were suddenly called into doubt. Ala, who had been studying to become a sound engineer for the past two years, had written to the Royal Academy of Music in Stockholm to enquire about relevant courses. When the Royal Academy finally sent its response, it contained bad news: in the whole of Sweden, it said, there was not a single program in which Ala could continue her studies. Devastated, she decided to remain in her Viennese state of limbo.

Roman, furious at Ala's change of heart, decided to leave for Sweden on his own. On the evening of his eighteenth birthday, armed with just a few dollars, a small backpack, a guitar, and the anticipation of an unknown country he would call his home for the rest of his life, he boarded a night train to Sweden.

When he arrived in Malmö, the representative of the city's Jewish community was nowhere to be found. After waiting at the foot of the platform for an hour, Roman shouldered his sparse belongings and walked, through a foreign city whose residents spoke a friendly, incomprehensible, singsongy language, in the direction of the Jewish community's offices. By the time he had located them, night had fallen—and the community center had closed down for the day.

Lacking sufficient funds for a hotel room, Roman was growing convinced that he'd have to spend the night on the street, in the freezing Swedish winter. Then he had an idea. Doing his best to forget the abuses he'd experienced over the past months, he nervously entered a police station. The policemen politely listened to his story—of which, Roman's Swedish being as nonexistent as their Polish, they understood precious little. In the end, one of the cops asked Roman to surrender his shoelaces. "In case you should try to hang yourself," he indicated by means of a little pantomime. Then he smilingly showed Roman to a prison cell, leaving its heavy door unlocked. That's where, strumming his guitar in a cell kindly lent him by the Swedish authorities, Roman, eighteen years and one day old, spent the first night in his new country.

Ala, still in Vienna, still without a plan, decided to study sound engineering at the local music conservatory. She entered the admissions office, was sent away ("Auditions are twice a year. No, we never make exceptions!"), then marched into the director's office and, with the benefit of surprise and chutzpah on her side, was granted a short interview.

Speaking in French, Ala inquired whether the conservatory had a course in *prise de son*. The director replied that it did. But, he explained, the course was restricted to students who spoke fluent German. Couldn't she audition for a different course and transfer to *prise de son* once she'd improved her language skills? Ala agreed. After playing an étude by Chopin on the Steinway in the director's office, she was admitted to the prestigious piano class.

Over the next months, Ala tried to settle in as best she could. Once her German had improved, she went back to the conservatory's director to change to the course in sound engineering. It turned out that there was none. With his limited French, the director had understood *prise de son* to mean electronic composition. If she was serious about sound engineering, Ala would have to leave Austria. The best course, she was told, was at a conservatory in Germany, in a small western town called Detmold. Student visas were not difficult to come by—although, without a German passport, it would probably be impossible to stay on beyond the duration of her course.

In a way, this made Ala's decision a little easier. To move to Germany forever was out of the question. To move there just for a degree, just for a few years, was something else entirely. Out of other options, she decided to give it a try.

By this time, my little family was well on its way toward implosion.

Leon and Ewa had never been a happy couple. Or at least they hadn't been a happy couple so long as Ala and Roman could remember; which is to say since the war; which is to say since the woman Leon had loved vanished, never to return.

Ewa must once have been an extremely courageous woman.

Her mother died in childbirth. Her father devoted his days to grief, vodka, and the Torah. He neglected to do so much for his daughter as to enroll her in school. So, when she was six years old, Ewa walked to the closest primary school in her part of L'vov and enrolled herself. When she started secondary school, she paid for the steep tuition fees by tutoring her classmates. But the cost of sitting for the final exam was more than she could afford. Forced to leave school, she drifted toward the Communist underground, where she met and later married Leon.

Like Leon, Ewa was willing to go to jail for her convictions. Later, when Hitler invaded, she, too, fled east, spending the war years in Gori, a small town in Georgia whose greatest contribution to world history it had been to witness Joseph Stalin's birth.

Her body survived the war, but her spirit did not. By the time she returned from Gori, she had, by all accounts, become a different person.

I, for one, never got to see so much as a flicker of her earlier personality. My most vivid memory of Ewa is that, on our yearly visits, every last inch of the kitchen table would be covered with food. In the center stood an epic mountain of my favorite meal, meat pierogi. I ate and I ate and I ate.

A few minutes after I finally capitulated in front of this seemingly interminable pile of food, Baba Ewa—with a desperate insistence that, even as a child, I found funny, infuriating, and spooky all at once—implored me: "You must be hungry! You haven't eaten for so long . . . Come, you *must* eat a few more pierogi, Yascha. Just a few more pieroshki."

When her pleas reached fever pitch, I dutifully accepted a small morsel of food—as much as I was physically able to force down. This bought me fifteen, ten, sometimes just five minutes of peace. Then she started again. "Yaschka, please eat. Please. Just a few pieroshki. You haven't eaten for so long . . ."

So it went, hour after hour, and year after year.

When I asked my mother why Baba Ewa was so obsessed with

food, she told me a story from her own childhood. One day, when Ala was about my age—ten or eleven years old perhaps—she forced open a locked drawer in her Warsaw apartment. It contained but one item: the framed photograph of a little boy.

The boy stared up at Ala from his photograph. Ala, disconcerted, stared back at his dark, pretty eyes. With his striking chin and melancholy brow, there was something handsome, even manly, about him. Yet the boy's face was a little too delicate for his age. Ala remarked that, even though he had altogether different features from her younger brother, Roman, they bore a striking resemblance.

Why did this small boy, whom she had never before seen, look so strangely familiar? Why had his photograph been placed in a locked drawer? Instinctively, Ala knew that she had uncovered an anxiously guarded secret.

Only when, digging deeper into the drawer, she found a crestfallen letter that Leon had written to Ewa upon hearing the terrible news did Ala come to understand the nature of the secret. The boy whose face she had been studying was that of her own brother: an older brother whose short life had painstakingly been hidden from her; an older brother who had been born during the war; an older brother who, a few months after posing for his one surviving photograph, about four years before his little sister was to see the light of day, had starved to death amid the chaos and deprivation of the war.

Leon and Ewa, like so many others who barely survived the Holocaust, were rarely able to talk about their murdered siblings, parents, and grandparents. They never talked about their eldest son. The knowledge that this little boy had once existed remained. So, as long as she lived, did Ewa's desperate desire to feed her family. Everything else about him is lost.

The death of her firstborn son helps to explain why, half a century later, Ewa force-fed me, her grandson, delicious meat pierogi with spooky devotion. But it cannot bring back to life the woman Ewa must once have been. To Roman and Ala and Rebecka and me, she remains, in some ways, just as lost as her firstborn son.

In a way, that made it easier on us.

Unlike Roman and Ala, Leon did remember what his wife had once been like. To him, Ewa's transformation was a daily torment. Much as he tried to marshal patience and sympathy for her, their relationship was doomed to failure. They liked each other less and less. In their last years in Poland, they rarely spoke.

So when Ewa decided that she wanted to move to Israel, Leon announced that he would not go with her. She resolved to go anyway, and that was that. Leon and Ewa saw each other only two or three more times in their lives.

In Israel, Ewa tried to build a new life for herself in the small coastal town of Ashkelon. But her life in the Promised Land quickly turned out to be disappointing. Her Hebrew remained minimal. Her skills and education were not exactly custom-tailored to her new surroundings. She was deeply unhappy.

A few years later, Roman gained Swedish citizenship—and, with it, the right to sponsor his parents for immigrant visas. Without much hesitation, Ewa left Israel to join her son in southern Sweden.

With his soon-to-be ex-wife on her way to Israel, Leon, newly single, cast around for other options. The United States had already refused him a visa because he'd long been a Communist. Sweden, where his son was headed, only accepted young refugees at that time. Leon would have liked to stay in Austria, where, thanks to the German he had learned in childhood, he had already been offered a good job. But there was no way of getting a work visa. Since his daughter was, at least temporarily, headed for Germany, Leon finally decided to seek asylum there as a political refugee.

Leon was likely to be granted asylum if only he could manage to reach German territory. But as a stateless person he wasn't actually allowed to enter the country. If he was to accompany Ala to Germany, he had to find a way to cross the border illegally.

The task seemed impossible at first, but with a little luck Leon soon found a solution. The father of a school friend of Ala's had until recently been the Polish ambassador to Austria. From that time, he remained in contact with Bruno Kreisky, a leader of the Austrian Social Democrats who was about to be elected the country's head of government. The friend's father phoned Kreisky, and (it seems unlikely, but this is the story I've always been told) Kreisky passed on the contact details of a devoted party member, a simple comrade who worked as a conductor on the night train from Vienna to Frankfurt.

One Tuesday evening, when few passengers were expected, Leon carried the bag containing his sparse belongings to Vienna's Westbahnhof and boarded a train headed to Germany. The conductor locked Leon into a compartment, drew the curtains, and told him to keep quiet. When German border guards entered the train in the early morning hours, this loyal comrade, perhaps reliving some services he had performed for his party in more perilous times, told them that the compartment containing Leon was empty. It worked. Leon had once taken the last train out of L'vov to escape the approach of the Wehrmacht. Now, with the help of an aging Austrian comrade, he successfully smuggled himself *into* Germany.

Once in Frankfurt, Leon was put into a squalid asylum seekers' home. Long months passed—difficult months during which he was neither allowed to work nor to travel more than a few miles. When his papers were finally approved, he already had a job offer. As the technical director of RSW Prasa, he had often purchased machinery from a company in Wiesbaden, near Frankfurt. The head of that company now offered Leon a comfortable position as a mid-level manager.

But after all the transformations he had undergone in his life—from shtetl-dweller to a partisan of the Communist underground; from partisan of the Communist underground to high functionary of the regime; from high functionary of the regime to asylum seeker—this last proposed switch, from asylum seeker to capitalist, proved one too many for Leon. He thanked his former colleague for his generosity, declined the managerial position, and asked whether he might not be able to work as a simple printer instead. And so he spent the rest of his working life in the same position he had taken on in L'vov as a teenage runaway: setting the next day's paper letter by letter.

•

As the cruel 1960s drew to a close and a new decade dawned, my family found itself scattered across the globe, with Ala in Detmold, Leon in Wiesbaden, Roman in Malmö, and Ewa in Ashkelon. As they struggled to make new lives for themselves in the places fate had temporarily assigned to them, their futures remained uncertain. Could they grow accustomed to their new surroundings, or would they soon decide to move again?

Ala's future seemed particularly unpredictable. She had, after all, neither the right nor, really, the intention to spend the rest of her life in Germany. Even so, thanks in part to the strange story of another family—one that has only the most tenuous of links to my own life yet explains why I was to be born in Germany—she did end up staying on.

Back in Warsaw, Ala had had a stormy romance with Christian Skrzyposzek, a young writer well respected for his early literary work and notorious for his attacks on the Communist regime. Christian came from a German-Polish family in Silesia. His mother, Margarete, was a fervent nationalist who prided herself on being German. A relative of hers had even become a high-ranking Nazi functionary—according to some accounts, an SS officer. When her hometown came under the control of the Nazis, Margarete was overjoyed.

Christian's father, Wilhelm, had a more complicated identity. Despite his Polish surname, he seems to have had some German ancestors; at any rate, he signed a declaration that he was ethnically German, a so-called *Volksdeutscher*. This allowed him to avoid being drafted for immediate military service and to continue his studies at the university. Within a few years, he rose through the ranks of a local branch of Deutsche Bank to become its director.

Unbeknownst to his own wife, however, Wilhelm soon grew disgusted with Nazism. Identifying less and less with his German heritage, he turned into a fervent Polish patriot. Even as he feigned loyalty to the Third Reich and continued to work at the Deutsche Bank, he joined the Polish resistance movement.

Superficially, life for Wilhelm and Margarete seemed strangely ordinary in those early war years. But below the surface, Wilhelm's work for the resistance was placing him in ever more danger. And, sure enough, one sunny day, while Margarete was pregnant with a baby boy, the veneer of normalcy dissolved in one ugly hour: the Gestapo arrested Wilhelm. He was transported to Auschwitz, and later transferred to the labor camp at Mauthausen.

Margarete was afraid for Wilhelm's life and did what little she could to rescue him. But she was also disgusted by her husband's actions. That he could have betrayed her beloved fatherland seemed unfathomable to her. When her son was born a few months later, she took her revenge. The newborn German-Polish boy was to carry a decidedly Germanic name: *Christian Berthold Wilhelm*.

What a name: Christian Berthold Wilhelm . . . *Skrzyposzek*. According to a family story (beloved by Christian but probably apocryphal), his birth caused much hilarity at Mauthausen. One day, at one of the camp's sadistic roll calls, a guard called out the number tattooed on Wilhelm's forearm.

"Inmate! Your wife gave birth to a healthy son by the name of Christian Berthold Wilhelm Skr— . . . er, Christian Berthold Wilhelm Skrzrzp . . ."

The first inmates started giggling.

"*Ordnung!* By the name of Christian Berthold Wilhelm Skrzprprk . . ."

By now, an unlikely fit of laughter—part indefatigable juvenile humor, part muted act of political bravado—had conquered the inmates' emaciated faces.

"By the name," the guard bellowed, menacingly rolling his *r*'s in the style of Hitler's speeches, "of Chrrristian Berrrthold Wilhelm . . . *Shi . . . posh.*"

Against the odds, Wilhelm survived both Auschwitz and Mauthausen. Soon after the Allies liberated him, he was reunited with his wife and saw his son for the first time. Though the trauma of the camps marked him to the end of his days, he was able to build a new life for himself and his family, giving Christian and his siblings a patriotic Polish education.

As Christian grew up, he imbibed Wilhelm's Polish patriotism. He also inherited his father's courageous indignation at injustice, and grew to hate the Communist regime. By the time he got to know Ala, Christian's uncompromisingly public criticisms of the regime had attracted the attention not only of numerous admirers but also of concerned government officials. When Ala was forced into exile, and as his own situation grew ever more precarious, Christian decided to follow her to Detmold. Though he knew that his request might well be denied, and would almost certainly lead to all kinds of payback, he requested an exit visa. To his surprise, it was quickly granted. As it turned out, the regime, keen to rid itself of a prominent detractor, was only too happy to see him go.

But while Christian was granted permission to leave Poland rather more easily than he'd imagined, permission to settle in

Germany turned out to be much more difficult to come by. Christian had simply assumed that he'd easily be able to claim German citizenship. After all, a strong component of German blood flowed in his veins, and German citizenship law, with its exclusive focus on jus sanguinis, certainly stressed ethnic origin. But when he arrived in Germany, Christian found that neither his German mother nor his German first names were sufficient to establish his Germanness.

"A German mother is irrelevant for the purposes of your application, Herr Skrrk . . . Herr Shikosh. You are German if your father, not your mother, is German. In *our* country, you see, citizenship descends in a purely patrilineal fashion," a civil servant at the *Ausländeramt*, or Foreigners' Office, told him.

"Furthermore," the bureaucrat continued, "according to documents from Auschwitz, your father was classified as a Polish inmate." Christian Berthold Wilhelm's petition for German citizenship, he announced with the pleased air of a mathematician writing *QED* under an impeccable proof, would be denied.

Christian appealed the decision, and started some research of his own. Eventually he managed to unearth a single document on which his father's nationality was specified as German. Was it Wilhelm's declaration that he was a *Volksdeutscher*, made in 1939 to avoid being drafted to fight for the Nazis? Or could it really have been, as Christian used to insist, a medical document from Mauthausen?

According to Christian's version, Margarete, despite being shocked by Wilhelm's treason, begged her relative, the SS officer, to do anything in his power to save her husband; and indeed Margarete's relative did intervene to make sure that Wilhelm would be transferred from Auschwitz to Mauthausen. At one point, he even helped procure a medical examination and some desperately needed drugs for Wilhelm—whose nationality, being a relative of a German SS officer who bestowed such favors on him, was naturally assumed to be German. It was, Christian said, his

"*Sanitätskarte*," the record of his medical history at Mauthausen, that indicated his father's citizenship as German and ultimately vindicated his own claim to German citizenship.

With Christian finally winning the right to stay in Germany, he and Ala embarked on their new life together in Detmold. Their relationship was going strong, and in February of 1970 they married.

Professionally, too, life in Germany was turning out well. Ala had quickly realized that her creative urge was too strong for her to remain a sound engineer. Though women were virtually unheard of in her new profession in those days, she decided to embark on a career as a conductor. Before long, she was able to celebrate her first successes. With her professional prospects looking good, her father working in Wiesbaden, and her husband living in Detmold with her, it seemed natural that, for now at least, Ala should remain in the country.

But while Ala had made her peace with staying in Germany for the time being, she was ambivalent about settling there for good, and downright opposed to the idea of taking on German citizenship. After her love for Poland had been so cruelly dashed, she no longer felt that she belonged to any particular country—certainly not the country that was responsible for the death of so many of her family members. In theory, being stateless suited her just fine.

In practice, however, the lack of a real passport created constant problems. Perhaps worst of all was that it hugely complicated international travel. When Ala moved to West Berlin—which was then an island of sorts in the middle of East German territory—it even made it frustratingly difficult for her to do so much as leave the city.

All of these inconveniences Ala was willing to endure. But when she tried to extend her residence permit, she was told that there were only two options. Either she could take the German passport to which she was entitled as Christian's wife; or she'd have to return to Austria in the middle of the semester to begin an uncertain wait for a new visa. Unhappily, Ala gave in to the inevitable: she applied for German citizenship.

The story of Christian's family, then, explains not only how Ala ended up staying in Germany, but also how I came to be a German citizen.

In keeping with a 1975 law, which for the first time enabled citizenship by way of matrilineal descent, I inherited my German citizenship from my mother. My mother, in turn, had a right to German citizenship thanks to her ill-fated marriage to Christian (a marriage that was dissolved long before I was born). And Christian, apparently, owed *his* German citizenship to the intervention of an SS officer, or perhaps to Mauthausen's meticulously kept archives, as consulted by an official of the German Federal Republic in 1970.

All of this foreshadowed a lesson I would learn over and over again as I grew up. As a German Jew, you don't have to make a special effort to remember the past. The past, usually in manners most surreal, will find a way of imposing itself on you.

PART I

The Past Lingers

I tell ya, life ain't easy for a boy named Sue.   —Johnny Cash

ONE

A Boy Named Jew

I was born in 1982 as the citizen of a democratic, forward-looking, peaceful Germany. I've lived all over the country, growing up in reasonably idyllic places like Munich, Freiburg, Kassel, Maulbronn, Laupheim, and Karlsruhe, until I left to go to college in England at age eighteen. German is, and will forever remain, the only language I speak without an accent.

My family's Jewish identity, meanwhile, has never been strong. While the fact that they are Jews shaped the lives of my grandparents, and even those of my parents, in deeply tragic ways, they are neither religious nor traditional. As for me, I never celebrated my bar mitzvah, and feel far more comfortable on a soccer field or at the library than in a synagogue.

Even so, as I grew up, I came to feel more and more Jewish—and less and less German.

In July 1990, when I had just turned eight, Germany faced Argentina in the final of the World Cup. After eighty-four long minutes, Roberto Sensini brought down Rudi Völler, the referee awarded a penalty kick, and Andreas Brehme scored the only goal of the match. Germany took the world championship and I was ecstatic, waving a little German flag, and chanting "Deutschland, Deutschland, Deutschland" at the television.

But by 2010, when Germany faced Spain in the semifinals of the same tournament, I felt more ambivalent. Yes, Germany's team was younger, more skilled, even more diverse than ever before. Yet when the chips were down, I found myself rooting for the Spanish team. And the real reason why I was glad, or perhaps *relieved*, when, in the seventy-third minute of play, Carles Puyol headed the ball into the net for Spain's winning goal, wasn't even that I liked the Spanish team. The real reason—I feel embarrassed to admit this, but it is true—was that I simply couldn't bring myself to support the German team.

At some point in those two decades—somewhere between 1990 and 2010, between the ages of eight and twenty-eight—I had stopped rooting for the German team, or identifying with Germany, or thinking of myself as German.

Until today, I'm not quite sure why this happened.

•

When I was fourteen, Klaus, a regular at my chess club, tried to turn me into a Nazi. Klaus wasn't threatening and he wasn't a skinhead—he was a middle-aged, middle-class, mid-level manager at BMW. Actually, we were friends, of sorts.

One evening, over a game of speed chess—or *Blitz*, as it's called in German—Klaus told me that, some ten years earlier, on a trip to Paris, two black men had mugged him. The experience, he said, had opened his eyes to the moral superiority of the Aryan race. He now realized that politically correct opinions were a bunch of lies. Germans should be proud of their race and country. It was high time for the German nation to assert itself again. So Klaus explained, calmly, taking another sip of his *Weissbier*.

"You won't convince me, of all people," I said.

"Sure I will," he responded. "Everyone resists at first. It's not what we're supposed to think. Goes against all the indoctrination. But it's obvious Germans are superior to others. If you think about it with an open mind, you'll agree."

"You don't understand," I said cautiously. "I'm not exactly . . . well, I'm not . . . Aryan, you see."

"You aren't?" Klaus smiled a good-natured smile at me. "You mean because you're short and have dark hair? Don't be silly. Not every Aryan is tall and blond. Just look at Hitler! No, no, you're Aryan all right."

There was, I realized, only one way out of this conversation. But I was nervous about it—just as I was nervous anytime I had to tell somebody this simple fact about myself.

"I'm Jewish."

Klaus might have expected for me to be any number of things: a Trotskyite, an anarchist, perhaps even a Jehovah's Witness. The one thing that had never occurred to him—that much was obvious from his frozen face—was that I might be a Jew. He did not know what to say, perhaps because there were too many phrases that could have expressed his disbelief—the kind of phrases I typically heard when I mentioned that I was Jewish. "But . . . you speak such good German." Or: "But . . . you don't *look* Jewish."

Klaus remained sheepish, almost stricken, for ten, twenty, thirty seconds. When he finally began to stutter a reply, I got up and walked away.

My encounter with Klaus shouldn't have come as a surprise. In today's Germany, there is a dark underbelly of lingering, even resurgent, anti-Semitism. Neo-Nazi organizations like the National Democratic Party (NPD) have at times been able to celebrate considerable electoral successes. And most neo-Nazis aren't as civil as Klaus. In 2011, 811 anti-Semitic crimes, ranging from defaced tombs in Jewish cemeteries to a few violent assaults, were registered in Germany. (Only five arrests were made.)

As former government spokesman Uwe-Karsten Heye admitted, there are some places those who are visibly non-Aryan do well to avoid. In some areas of contemporary Germany, sporting a yarmulke, or being black, makes trouble likely.

Sociologists suggest that anti-Semitic attitudes are even widespread among seemingly ordinary, law-abiding people—and have been on the rise in recent years. According to a 2012 study, over 40 percent of Germans partly or strongly agree with the notion that Jews "always sow disharmony with their ideas," or that they have "too much influence" in Germany. Even more give credence to the notion that Jews have too much power on Wall Street. A study commissioned by the German government concluded that, all things considered, about a fifth of Germans can be considered "latently anti-Semitic."

Hatred of immigrants is even more widespread than anti-Semitism. Thirty-seven percent of Germans either fully or strongly support the notion that Germany is *überfremdet*, or "over-foreignized"; another 27 percent partially agree and partially disagree with this idea. Worse still, a staggering 58 percent believe that "freedom of religion should be significantly curtailed" for some religious groups, especially Muslims.

Despite all of these glaring facts, German politicians and journalists have long played down the threat posed by Germany's far right. Between September 2000 and April 2006, nine small-business owners with foreign roots—eight Turkish and one Greek—were murdered in cold blood. Police and the media quickly jumped to a convenient conclusion: it must, they suggested, have been a matter of score-settling among Turkish gangs.

When it turned out that the assassinations had been carried out by a terrorist organization calling itself the National Socialist Underground—an organization whose members had long enjoyed considerable support from German secret service organizations hoping to cultivate them as informers—journalists colored themselves shocked at the revelation. Even so, many of them continued to apply their original name to the attacks. Because two of the murdered businessmen had run Turkish fast-food joints, even highbrow German papers referred to these tragic events as the *"Döner-Morde,"* or kebab murders.

(In the remainder of Part I, I describe how an eerie silence about the Nazi past reigned supreme in the early postwar years. This helps to explain why xenophobic and anti-Semitic views remain widespread. It also brings to life how difficult it was for those few Jews who, like Leon and Ala, ended up taking refuge in postwar Germany to make the country a true home for themselves.)

•

A cavalier attitude toward the radical right remains a real problem in today's Germany. But, for me at least, the threat of anti-Semitic violence has always remained distant and abstract. When I was growing up, a fear of neo-Nazis came to me in sudden bursts, like on the rare occasions when I saw a group of them milling about. On the whole, though, it no more defined my childhood than the vague fear of being mugged would define the childhood of a kid growing up in an affluent American suburb.

So it wasn't violence or hatred that made me feel that I would never be a German.

It was benevolence.

Far from being openly anti-Semitic, most Germans I met were so keen to prove to me that they weren't anti-Semitic that they treated me with the kind of nervous niceness usually reserved for the mentally handicapped or the terminally ill. Driven by misplaced guilt and embarrassment about the unspeakable things their ancestors had done to mine, they ended up feeling limitlessly sorry for me. The effect of their pity and their virtue was to leave both of us with the sense that I couldn't possibly have anything in common with them.

This was made worse by their understandable, yet deeply alienating, fear of making a misstep.

It is a fear that can make the simplest interaction between Jew and Gentile degenerate into a politically correct comedy of errors. A friend, assuming that I must speak Hebrew at home, goes into panegyrics about how beautiful a language it is. Another friend conspiratorially informs me that her "family people" are "one-seventh" Jewish. And an acquaintance, with genuine empathy, tactfully inquires whether I find the word "Jew" offensive.

At times, this compulsive niceness manifests itself in the least likely situations. Even Klaus, ever since that evening when he'd told me about the superiority of the Aryan race, was strangely friendly to me. Perhaps he was too polite—or perhaps, secretly, he was too ridden by collective guilt—to reiterate his neo-Nazi talking points. In any case, once he was faced with a "real-life Jew," Klaus, despite claiming to be a virulent anti-Semite, tried to prove to me how tolerant and considerate he was.

As I realized when, at age seventeen, I found myself in the waiting room of a recruitment center of the Bundeswehr, this selfsame fear of offending a Jew now even suffices to scare the German army.

I had been summoned for my *Musterung*, a compulsory army physical, which, for those unfortunate enough to pass muster, was followed by a year's military service. I'd only been waiting for five minutes when a fresh-faced soldier in uniform, not more than a few years older than me, marched up to my chair and stiffly extended his hand. "How do you feel about committing to a career in the Bundeswehr, Yascha?"

The young soldier—Thomas, he informed me with imperious friendliness—was good at his job. Before I had a chance to answer, he launched into an account of the advantages of patriotic service.

"You get twelve years of guaranteed employment," Thomas said. "But that isn't all. The army will train you. Wouldn't you love to learn how to fly a bomber?"

I said that I would not. "Actually," I told him, playing my trump card with a thumping heart, "I would like to apply for an exemption of indeterminate length from compulsory military service."

Now that it was I who was launching into a prerehearsed little spiel, he seemed less self-assured. "A what?"

"An exemption from compulsory military service."

"But . . . why?"

"Article 12a of the Constitution specifies that individuals can be exempted if military service would induce 'special hardship,'" I recited. "According to an administrative directive issued by the Defense Ministry, such special hardship pertains if a person's direct ancestors were persecuted by the Third Reich on grounds of their ethnicity. This applies to me. I'm . . . Jewish."

Thomas couldn't have turned whiter if he'd known my family's history in all its tragic detail. "Oh, of course. Of course. I'm so sorry. I'm just here to recruit people. You'll have to speak to an administrator. Please, why don't you just, just sit down and I'll go get somebody to talk to you as soon as they possibly can . . ."

Within minutes, Thomas was back. Lost for words, he silently led me to the table of a middle-aged woman, a civilian who looked as though she would have been uncomfortable even under less vexing circumstances.

"I've heard about your proble—" Having pronounced all but the last consonant, she decided that the word was vastly inappropriate. "I mean, about your . . . situation. Could you just explain your request again?"

I did, in greater detail than before. But after listening in silence, my interlocutor told me that she only worked part-time. "Really, unfortunately, sincerely," she did not know what to do. I was sent to someone yet more senior.

Herr Weiland, another civilian, seemed to feel a little more comfortable in his own skin. As I entered his second-floor office, which was adorned with a poster of Mallorca, a plastic palm tree, and a Bundeswehr calendar featuring soldiers smilingly displaying their latest weaponry, he vigorously shook my hand. Then, sitting me down near his desk, from where I enjoyed a full view of his computer screen, he calmly went about searching his hard drive for a template order that might apply to my case. Special hardship because the potential recruit's labor is indispensible on the family farm—no. Special hardship because two elder brothers have already served—no. Special hardship because a relative has died in the service of the army—not quite.

Apologetically, he turned to me: "I'd love to give you the official document now, but I'll have to come up with the right formulation. You could wait around. Or else, I promise we'll have it sent to you by Christmas."

Now Herr Weiland, too, turned white. "I mean, by Chanu—" Panicked, he gave up a heroic attempt to remember not only the name but even the pronunciation of Chanukah. "By the twenty-fourth of December. Definitely. I promise."

Those words, uttered less than thirty minutes after I'd arrived for my *Musterung*, ended my adventures with the German army. The usually so methodical bureaucrats even forgot to make me take the army physical—in theory a legal requirement, special hardship or no special hardship. On December 24 of that year, the state's Christmas present duly arrived in the form of a letter officially informing me that, "due to his very special family circumstances, the potential recruit shall be granted an exemption of indeterminate length from compulsory military service."

Sometimes, Germany's philo-Semitism has its advantages. I wouldn't have liked to waste a year performing the mindless tasks that made up Germany's compulsory military service even if I weren't Jewish. Nor would it have been particularly fun to strip naked in front of a military commission so that the Bundeswehr could assess the potential usefulness of my physical constitution for war.

Even so, in my experience, all of these forms of special treatment ultimately add up to an overall feeling of alienation. The very mention of a simple fact about me—a fact I'm not prepared to hide away in shame, however little importance it might have to me in my daily life—now suffices to make me a strange and exotic creature. I fear that so long as this remains the case, I will always feel estranged from my nominal compatriots.

(Part II will trace how, from the 1960s all the way through the 1980s, a younger generation of Germans forced the country to face up to its past. Their radical challenge to their elders helped make Germany more thoroughly democratic. But the ensuing fashion for all things Jewish also led to serious excesses and confusions; in some ways, it had the perverse effect of making Germany's Jews feel even more like outsiders.)

•

When I was growing up, the feeling that, as a Jew, I could never truly be German was further compounded by a spreading sense of resentment against the country's supposed obsession with the past—a resentment that is voiced especially loudly by younger Germans.

One beautiful Saturday morning in the fall of 2006, at 11:00 a.m., I went to Munich's Oktoberfest with a large group of friends and acquaintances. We had arrived this early to beat the crowds to one of the coveted tables inside the massive tents. Our first beer—the only acceptable drink, no matter the time of day—had just been served. As is customary, the mugs in front of us contained *eine Maß*, or just over two pints of freshly brewed Bavarian lager.

"How do you fit two hundred Jews into a small car?" Stephanie, a petite woman in her late thirties, asked us as she peeped over the rim of her giant beer mug.

"Stephanie," one of her friends chided her, more teasing than angry. "We haven't even had a sip yet. I propose a toast to—"

As though on command, the oompah band, a jolly brass combo in lederhosen, started playing. It proposed, in song, a traditional Bavarian toast: *"Ein Prosit! Ein Prosit! Auf die Gemüt . . .*

lich . . . keit!" (A toast! A toast! To conviviality!) We gathered up our mugs, clinked, put the mugs down again in a nod to local tradition, lifted them up a second time, and finally imbibed. A contented sigh escaped my lips.

"Now that you've all had a sip, go ahead and take a guess," Stephanie said. "How do you fit two hundred Jews into a Volkswagen Beetle?"

"Knock it off, will you. This is not appropriate," Hans, a big-boned, folksy friend of mine said.

"Why should I?" Stephanie shot back, her earlier guise of provocative playfulness giving way to anger. "Because you tell me to shut up? Because they tell me to shut up? Come on, it's just a joke!"

"I doubt it'll be funny," Hans said.

"Not funny? Have a sense of humor! Why can't a joke about the Jews be funny? It's 2006. The Holocaust happened sixty years ago. We *should* tell jokes about the Jews again!"

"Look," Hans said, "you know as well as I do that Germans have a special responsibility to be sensi—"

"A special responsibility? I'm not even forty! No, no. I won't stay silent any longer. Here's how you fit them in. You gas them. You incinerate them. You stuff them in the ashtray. That's how you do it."

Stephanie's joke was anti-Semitic. But, even as her bad taste and provocative demeanor repelled me, I realized that her reasons for telling it were not anti-Semitic, at least not in a straightforward sense. Stephanie does not hate Jews as such. Rather, she hates standard conceptions of what Jews, and her country's past, should mean to her. In this sense, Stephanie is not just another neo-Nazi. She is part of a fast-spreading movement.

Unnoticed by much of the outside world, Germany's attitudes about its past—and about the role that past should play in the present—are changing. Since the 1990s, a mood of "enough is enough" has taken hold of the country. Advocates of the so-called *Schlussstrich* want to draw a "finish line" underneath Germany's preoccupation with World War II. After sixty-odd years, they argue, it is time to make remembrance of the crimes committed by the Third Reich a less prominent part of public life.

According to a recent study, a majority of the population endorses these views. More than a third of Germans say that they are "fed up with hearing about Germany's crimes against the Jews again and again." Another quarter "partially agrees and partially disagrees" with that sentiment.

I have real sympathy for young Germans who want to move beyond the hysterical philo-Semitism of their elders. In particular, their avowed desire to treat Jews the same as anybody else is commendable.

For all its good intentions, however, I fear that the "finish line" movement now runs the danger of being counterproductive. I'd love nothing more than to be treated as just another German. But many people my age are so determined to demonstrate that they won't treat me any differently just because I'm a Jew that, all too often, they end up treating me very differently indeed.

(In Part III, I describe how calls for a finish line became increasingly mainstream over the course of the 1990s and 2000s. These changes had an immediate impact on relations between Jews and Gentiles. As my encounter with Stephanie illustrates, German Jews now find themselves cast as extras in the country's increasingly aggressive attempt to prove that it has finally left the past behind.

As described in Part IV, many Germans have also come to believe that an earlier generation of politicians had been so determined to apologize for the past that they were easily cowed into submission, whether by other nations or by minorities within the country. That's another respect in which many Germans are now intent on reversing course. This helps to explain Germany's rapidly changing foreign policy, which has already made Berlin a less reliable partner to both its European neighbors and the United States. It also sheds light on why policies toward the country's ethnic and religious minorities are becoming increasingly restrictive.)

•

All of these different attitudes—the lingering anti-Semitism, the embarrassed philo-Semitism, and of course the growing resentment against Jews—combine to make me feel like a stranger in what should be my own country. Once, there was such a thing as a German Jew. Then the Holocaust happened. Today, there are Jews and then there are Germans. The two categories, in the German even more so than in the Jewish imagination, no longer overlap.

Charlotte Knobloch, a former chairwoman of the Central Council of Jews in Germany, has a story to tell about this. Knobloch is a German Jew, born and bred. She survived the Holocaust, in hiding, with a Catholic peasant family in Franconia who passed her off as their own daughter, and has never lived outside the country. She even speaks with the jolly, lilting accent of Germany's south. One day, she was lunching with a friend, a cosmopolitan, philo-Semitic German.

"Are you coming to the reception at the Israeli embassy tonight?" she asked him.

"Yes," he answered. "Yes, I'll see you later on at your ambassador's."

It is, Knobloch laments, a familiar sort of occurrence.

Her friend meant no harm, of course. But it is not a mistake that would ever happen to a Brit or an American—or has any reasonable American ever thought that Michael Bloomberg or Jerry Seinfeld are really, deep down, Israelis?

If I ask my New York cousins, whose parents have the same background of forced emigration from Poland in the late 1960s as mine do, whether they feel American, they barely understand the question. "What do you mean?" they ask, honestly baffled. "I *am* American."

But me, in what should be my own country? I look German enough. I sound German. When I talk to a stranger or a shop assistant, they naturally assume that I am German. I may have an unusual first name, but there are many innocuous explanations for that—most likely, my parents, guilt-ridden about the country's past, have chosen the most exotic name they could think of. Nothing wrong with that.

The instant I mention a certain fact about myself, however, ordinary human communication becomes difficult. One minute, people are free to like or dislike me; to treat me well or badly; to offer warmth or disdain. But once I pronounce these four letters— *J-u-d-e*—I become, for all intents and purposes, a boy named Jew. Their attitude toward me turns into a political statement, and a seemingly unbridgeable divide opens up between us.

Writing this book is my attempt to understand my place within the strange world I was thrown into at birth. It contains copious elements of personal memoir, family saga, and political history. Nonetheless, it is neither a conventional memoir about my childhood, nor a straightforward account of the story of my family, nor even a traditional history of German-Jewish relations since 1945. It is, rather, an attempt to ruminate on the questions I was unable to answer back when I still lived in Germany.

Why do I hesitate to call myself a German? What does my experience say about modern-day relations between Jews and Gentiles? And what light can it shed on the character of modern Germany?

All of these topics, in turn, raise issues that should be of interest well beyond Germany's borders. To truly come to terms with my own experience, I will have to understand the varied stages in the slow, arduous process of reconciliation between (the descendants of) perpetrators of injustice and (the descendants of) their victims. Perhaps, then, the strange twists and turns in the relationship between Germans and Jews will prove to be of interest to other societies struggling with reconciliation today: to those far afield, in Rwanda or South Africa or Chile; but also to us here in the United States, where we are still trying to understand how best to overcome the legacy of slavery and Jim Crow.

TWO

The Remnant

"Welcome, and best of luck for the coming years," Herr Weiss, our teacher, greeted us on the first day of middle school. A tall man in his forties with a pronounced regional accent and a proud talent for scaring students, he had little time for ceremony. "Before we begin our math lesson, we need to take care of a few formalities. Let's have a look at the student list. Allsbach, Lisa. Are you Protestant or Catholic?"

"What?"

"Concentrate, people. I have to sign you up for either Catholic or Protestant religion classes. So, Lisa?"

"Catholic."

"Good. Bach, Klaus?"

"Protestant."

"Emmerle, Johannes?"

The list went on. Soon, I realized, Herr Weiss would get to M. And I still didn't know what to say—in part out of an instinctive understanding that I would be marked out; in part because, not being religious, really, I didn't quite know the right answer.

"Mo . . . Mo-unk. Ya . . . How do you pronounce that name, boy?"

"Yascha."

"Sascha?"

"Yascha. Like Sascha, but with a Y."

"All right. So—Protestant or Catholic, Yascha?"

"Well, I guess I'm sort of . . . Jewish."

I had expected any number of reactions, but not the one I got. The whole class laughed. Uproariously.

"Stop making things up," Johannes Emmerle, a Protestant, shouted as the hilarity ebbed. "Everybody knows that the Jews don't exist anymore!"

Herr Weiss reprimanded Johannes. "Don't talk unless I call on you. We must have order. Okay, Sascha. You'll have a free period when the others take religion. There's a Turk in another class, I think. You two can keep each other company."

Then he added, as an afterthought, "And, Johannes, you are wrong, as a matter of fact. There are a few Jews. Again."

•

Nearly 600,000 Jews lived in Germany when Adolf Hitler took power on January 30, 1933. Two-thirds of them escaped the Nazi terror before Germany invaded Poland in September 1939. During the war, 170,000 German Jews were murdered. By the time of the Third Reich's unconditional surrender on May 8, 1945, a mere 15,000—having survived the Holocaust in hiding or as the spouse of an Aryan—remained in German territory. Only a minority within that tiny minority intended to stay on. Johannes, my classmate, might very nearly have been right: German Jews, it seemed, would soon be extinct.

But, though this extinction was anticipated—and at one point even desired—by both Germans and Jews, it never came to pass. Quite to the contrary, in the immediate postwar years there was an unexpected flowering of Jewish life on German soil.

When the Allies conquered the Third Reich, they also liberated hundreds of thousands of Eastern European Jews from forced-labor and concentration camps. Many of them wished to return to their old homes. But during their absence, Jewish settlements had been destroyed, and Jewish houses confiscated. Those few liberated Jews who attempted a return experienced acute anti-Semitism and even renewed pogroms. A return to their shtetls in Eastern Europe proved impossible for most survivors. They had been freed from the camps, but they were not free to go anywhere in particular. In the parlance of the day, they were "displaced persons" (DPs).

In all, over 200,000 Eastern European Jews had survived the Holocaust but now had nowhere to turn. They found a temporary home in DP camps erected by the Allied powers. Most of these were located in the U.S. occupation zone—on German territory.

The hopes of most DPs quickly turned toward making a new life for themselves outside Europe, far from the places where so many of their relatives had been murdered. But that wasn't easy. The State of Israel hadn't been founded yet. The British, who held the colonial mandate over Palestine, capped the number of available immigrant visas at 1,500 a month. For all but a lucky few, the "promised land" could be reached only in illegal, and often perilous, ways.

The United States, too, had tight quotas for immigration. Congress at first proved unwilling to create a special program that would allow a greater number of DPs to come to the country. On December 22, 1945, President Harry S Truman issued a directive that required existing immigrant quotas to be filled solely by DPs. As a result, over 15,000 Jewish DPs were given the chance to start a new life in the United States. But that wasn't nearly enough. For most DPs, the United States, too, remained inaccessible.

The majority of Eastern European survivors, then, continued to await their uncertain futures in places like Bergen-Belsen (in the military barracks attached to the former concentration camp), Fürth (a few miles from Nuremberg, the city where the Nazi Party had held its bombastic rallies), or Munich (the "capital of the Nazi movement"). In the aftermath of the catastrophic crimes perpetrated in the name of the German nation, they were anxiously whiling away the months—in Germany, yet largely separated from their German environs by the machine guns of U.S. soldiers; liberated, yet still living in camps. Never in the history of the Jews can the meaning of the diaspora, the dispersion and life of Jews among the Gentiles, with all its overtones of homelessness and menace, have been more intense.

This bleak period, however, also saw an unlikely renaissance of the culture of traditional Eastern European Jewry—grieving and temporary, but vibrant. Most DPs hailed from deeply religious, Yiddish-speaking settlements in Eastern Europe. These shtetls had now been destroyed forever. With them, at least in their original setting, a rich culture, grown over centuries, had also perished. But for a few years, before the DPs managed to emigrate to Israel or to the United States, where they would swap Yiddish for Hebrew or English, it was reincarnated in the DP camps. Shielded from public view, a fascinating Yiddish cultural life flourished in Germany. As Ruth Gay writes,

> this became an unexpected moment in Jewish history, a final irony, as the last flowering, the last living moment of Polish Jewish culture, played itself out in the D.P. camps in Germany . . . With substantial populations sometimes reaching 7,000 or 8,000, the displaced persons camps became Jewish villages where for the last time Yiddish was still a working language. What emerged spontaneously and powerfully were original music, poetry, theater, and literature. A brilliant flicker of life before the culture of Polish Jews disappeared.

At the same time as traditional Eastern European Jewish culture enjoyed its very "last flowering," many DPs braved a new beginning of a rather different kind. Most of them had lost parents, siblings, wives, and children in Nazi concentration camps.

But, somehow, they had to go on living, and so—like my grand-parents back in Poland—they were keen to found their families anew.

In Auschwitz, Jewish children who were too young to be ex-ploited for Hitler's war machine had been mercilessly gassed upon arrival. Now, a year or two after the end of World War II, new-born babies became a joyous symbol that Hitler's "final solution" had failed. A whole new generation of Jews saw the light of day in Germany's DP camps. So powerful was the desire for a new beginning in those postwar years that the birthrate among Jewish DPs was, according to some estimates, the highest in the world.

Then, at long last, the state of anxious limbo between past and future ended. On November 29, 1947, inmates of DP camps all over southern Germany erupted into chants of joy as they heard the news that, four thousand miles to the west, the Second Session of the UN General Assembly, in Flushing Meadows, New York, had approved the partition of Palestine. The end of their forced stay in Germany, the DPs now knew, was nigh.

The State of Israel was founded on May 14, 1948. It immedi-ately opened its borders to all Jews, whoever they were. That same year, finally heeding the wishes of President Truman, the U.S. Congress also made possible additional immigration by DPs, al-lowing eighty thousand Jews to leave Germany's DP camps for the United States. In the following months and years, a great ma-jority of displaced persons left Germany.

By 1953, the Israeli consulate in Munich had fulfilled its pri-mary task: to facilitate a swift emigration of Germany's displaced persons to Israel. As the Jewish state saw no other reason to main-tain a diplomatic presence on German soil, the consulate shut-tered its doors. In his farewell speech, the parting consul, Chaim Yachil, reaffirmed his expectation that the remaining Jewish communities in Germany—mostly composed of those too old or too frail to travel overseas—would soon die a natural death. German-Jewish history had, to all appearances, come to an end.

—

In the evocative description of Amos Elon, the German-Jewish relationship began in 1743 when, coming from the east, a fourteen-year-old boy entered Berlin through the Rosenthaler Gate, which was then reserved for Jews and cattle. Over the following years, he was to gain fame and acclaim as the philosopher Moses Mendelssohn, the first of many Jews who'd make a significant contribution to German cultural life.

For Elon, the tragic end of this special German-Jewish relationship was symbolized less than two hundred years later when another German-Jewish philosopher, Hannah Arendt, fled Nazi Germany. She left her home country on an eastbound train that passed through the very same Rosenthaler Gate.

The strange history of Jewish DPs adds a peculiar coda to Elon's melody. It has the same logic and displays the same sad symmetry. From 1945 onward, as the concentration camps were liberated, Jews once more came to Germany from Eastern Europe. Starting in 1948, when the Jewish state was officially recognized, they were heading back east in great numbers, finding a permanent home in Israel. By the early 1950s, when most DP camps were being dissolved, the last notes of this coda promised to mark a definitive end to the entire piece.

At the time, most Jews, and likewise most Germans, welcomed this definite disentangling of their lives. The expected extinction of Jewish life in Germany, however, never came to pass. In retrospect, we perceive that the melody—transposed into a stranger, more timid mode—was quietly carrying on: despite the expectations of their coreligionists, both inside and outside the country, some Jews stayed on in Germany.

In the 1950s, most of these Jews were so-called *Hängengebliebene*—DPs who, though they had never really chosen to stay in Germany, had somehow "gotten stuck" there.

During their period of waiting for an unforeseeable future, these hangers-on had procured good employment, founded a business, or fallen in love with a Gentile. For the moment they couldn't leave, but—so they used to repeat to themselves— Germany would never become a permanent home to them. "Our bags," went the ubiquitous refrain in those first years, "are always packed." It is not a coincidence that the organization founded in 1950 to represent the remaining Jewish communities was named Zentralrat der Juden in Deutschland—the "Central Council of Jews *in* Germany," rather than the "Central Council of German Jews."

Most of the Jews who remained in Germany after the war, then, were recent immigrants from Eastern Europe. But there were also some Jews whose families had lived in Germany for much longer. There was that tiny minority within that tiny group of fifteen thousand remaining German Jews who, having survived the Holocaust in the heart of the Third Reich, decided to stay on in the land of their murdered fathers. This can't have been an easy decision for any of them. But German was their native tongue. Many had been married to a Gentile for decades. Despite the traumas of twelve long years under Hitler, it seemed to them more realistic to stay on than to start a completely new life in a foreign land.

And then there were also those German Jews who had fled the Third Reich in the 1930s but now returned in the hope of shaping a better future for Germany. Distinguished intellectuals like philosophers Theodor Adorno and Max Horkheimer or theater director Fritz Kortner returned to West Germany from the United States for political reasons: they aspired to contribute to a lively cultural life that might help to consolidate liberal democracy. Others, like Fritz Bauer, perhaps the most important public prosecutor of Germany's postwar era, even resumed careers in law or the civil service. In the postwar era, these "remigrants" were by far the most visible subgroup of Jews. But they were also the fewest in number.

At the end of 1951, some 21,500 Jews were living in West

Germany, fewer than 5 percent of the number there had been two decades before. Unlike the handful of prominent intellectuals who had decided to return, most of them had no German roots at all.

•

While some Jewish luminaries returned to West Germany to build a democratic society, nearly as many returned to East Germany to help the "other Germany" develop.

At the war's end, the four Allied powers had divided Germany into four zones of occupation—the American Zone in the southeast; two small, barely contiguous French Zones in the southwest; the British Zone in the northwest; and the Soviet Zone in the northeast. (Berlin, which was precariously situated in the middle of the territory occupied by the Red Army, was itself divided into four "sectors.") These demarcations were originally intended to serve military and administrative purposes. But in the context of the incipient Cold War, they quickly mutated into a permanent political border. By March 1946, Winston Churchill, speaking in Fulton, Missouri, recognized that "from Stettin in the Baltic to Trieste in the Adriatic an iron curtain has descended across the Continent." This Iron Curtain ran right through the middle of Germany. On May 23, 1949, the American, British, and French zones merged to form the Federal Republic of Germany. A few months later, on October 7, 1949, the Communist German Democratic Republic (GDR) was founded on the territory of the Soviet Zone, including East Berlin.

Marxist intellectuals like philosopher Ernst Bloch, writer Arnold Zweig, and literary scholar Hans Mayer now moved to East Germany in the hope of contributing to the cultural life of the GDR. One of them, the composer Hanns Eisler, even set to melancholy music the GDR's self-reflective new anthem ("From the ruins risen anew / To the future turned we stand").

In the early years of the GDR, the handful of Jews who decided to move to East Germany had high hopes for a peaceable future. Their faith derived, in part, from the political leadership of the early GDR. It not only consisted of many men who themselves had suffered grave persecution at the hands of the Third Reich; it even seemed willing to deal with Germany's past in an honest manner.

East German authorities punished Nazi war criminals with far more vigor than their West German counterparts. Official Communist pronouncements even indicated outright opposition to the commonly accepted notion, defended at the highest political levels in the West, that those participants in criminal activities who had merely followed orders could not possibly be guilty. As the Central Committee of Germany's Communist Party acknowledged in June of 1945, a "share of the guilt is borne by all those German men and women who, without the will to resist, watched as Hitler claimed power for himself, smashed all democratic organizations, especially workers' organizations, and locked up the best Germans, martyred them and beheaded them."

But the ruling clique of the GDR—in its early years, as throughout its existence, a most keenly ingratiating lapdog of the Soviet hegemon—soon took a lead from the anti-Semitic Stalinist purges. In the early 1950s, Communist leaders all over Eastern Europe were stepping up their speeches against "rootless cosmopolitans" and instituting "anti-Zionist" measures in a thinly veiled display of anti-Semitism. They even staged show trials—most famously in Czechoslovakia, against Rudolf Slánský—against prominent Jews who had supposedly maintained contacts with rich capitalists, or harbored secret loyalties to Israel.

By 1953, the same process was taking place in East Germany. There was only one pernicious difference. The leaders of the GDR were conscious of the international outcry that a bogus show trial against a Jew would have provoked so short a while after Auschwitz. The most prominent defendant put on trial by them was not Jewish. As the historian Mario Kessler has recognized, "even in a show trial with an anti-Semitic component a non-Jew seemed predestined as the main defendant. Then it would be easier if necessary to reject the accusation of anti-Semitism."

So instead of picking on a Jew, the East German authorities went after Paul Merker, who, though not himself Jewish, had tried unsuccessfully in the late 1940s to persuade the Communist leadership to compensate Jewish victims of the Third Reich living outside the GDR. Now he was being derided as a collaborator with the "U.S. Finance Oligarchy," and as the "King of the Jews."

In the aftermath of the Merker trial, anybody who had survived World War II in Britain or the United States came under special suspicion of sympathizing with capitalism. For obvious reasons, many Jews were among that group.

Prominent Jewish intellectuals were now attacked as *Westemigranten*, and quickly marginalized. Arnold Zweig, for example, was forced to retire as president of the Academy of the Arts in 1953; at about the same time, the leading East German paper, *Neues Deutschland*, called Hanns Eisler's libretto for a modern opera on the Faust theme "a slap in the face of German national feeling."

In January 1953, Julius Meyer, an Auschwitz survivor and the president of the Association of Jewish Communities in the GDR, fled to the West along with a majority of the country's Jewish leaders. Many of his coreligionists soon followed. When the Berlin Wall was built in 1961 only 1,500 Jews remained in the GDR; by the time the Wall fell, in 1989, their number had dwindled to 400. (In part for that reason I will, for the rest of this book, concentrate on the experiences of Jews in West Germany.)

•

By 1970, when Leon and Ala joined the ranks of those who had somehow gotten "stuck" in West Germany, 30,000 Jews were living there. A little less than two decades later, when I started school, that number remained more or less unchanged; altogether, Jews comprised about 0.05 percent of the West German population.

So, when I was growing up, German Jews, we strange creatures, no longer seemed headed for extinction. But neither had we been domesticated. Nobody thought that we belonged: not the Germans, not the Jews abroad, not even we ourselves. Being in Germany was strange for us, and dealing with us was strange for the Germans.

Some of this strangeness was surely inevitable. But, especially in those first postwar years, long before I was born, it was rendered that much worse by a persistent, widespread, and even self-righteous silence about the past.

THREE

Silence, Reverberating

If the leaders of postwar Germany were to be believed, 1945 constituted "zero hour." The Third Reich's unconditional surrender had, they thought, insulated the present from the past—canceling old debts, moral and material, just as jubilee years had done in biblical times. Those lone voices who insisted on talking about the Nazi era seemed, to them, to be distracting, disloyal, or even vindictive.

In the immediate postwar years, some sense of a radical rupture between past and present was perfectly natural. Within an astoundingly short period of time, Germany had gone from ruling most of Europe to being occupied by the Allies. The Third Reich's leaders, who had seemed all-powerful until so recently, had committed suicide, fled to Latin America, or were sitting in the dock at Nuremberg. German soldiers, who were used to seeing the trembling and the desperate of innumerable countries plead with them for their lives, had now returned home in ignoble defeat or were whiling away their days in prisoner-of-war camps.

Even for German women and children, most of whom had stayed at home throughout the war, life changed radically within a few months. For most of World War II, the Nazi leadership had been able to avoid battles on German territory. At the cost of starvation everywhere else, the home front had been pampered with generous food rations. But in the war's last years, Allied bombing raids wreaked havoc on German cities. For the first time, Germans had to get used to severe food shortages. And then, of course, there were the millions of ethnic German refugees who settled all over the country when they were expelled from their former homes in Central Europe.

Talk of a zero hour did have some basis in reality, then. But as early as 1949, when the American, British, and French zones of occupation united into a West German state, it had metamorphosed from mere description to self-serving ideology. It now expressed not only the radical change in objective circumstances, but also the kind of attitude that the newly formed Federal Republic intended to cultivate toward the Third Reich. The message it conveyed was unambiguous: the new Germany would not accept any responsibility for the actions of the old Germany. Its implication for relations between Jews and Gentiles was just as clear: they would, for the time being, be built on a foundation of superficial politeness and deep-rooted distrust.

At first, it had looked as though Germany would not be allowed to move on from the past quite so quickly. In the weeks and months following the Third Reich's unconditional surrender, the Allies obsessively asked themselves how they could purge Germany of its militarism. Germany had started two disastrous world wars in less than three decades. To counteract any future German expansionism from the start, the Allies set out to effect no less than a complete transformation in the views both of future decision makers and the population at large.

The Nuremberg Trials were consciously designed to serve this purpose. Within months of Germany's surrender, twenty-four of the worst Nazi criminals were put on trial. In the city where, until so recently, vast masses had worshipped Hitler at the Nazi Party's gigantic rallies, judgment was now to be passed on the most prominent representatives of his regime.

The goal was not just to make the most heinous war criminals accountable for their actions; it was to expose the full extent of the Nazis' inhumanity to public view. This, the Allies hoped, would force Germans to make a clear break with their recent past—ideologically as well as politically.

The Nuremberg Trials were but one part of a much wider campaign for the denazification of German society. All Germans above the age of eighteen had to answer 131 questions concerning their past and their political views. In light of these answers, impromptu courts staffed with politically irreproachable Germans were to decide about the extent of each person's guilt, imposing sanctions ranging from the temporary withdrawal of voting rights to monetary fines and even prison terms.

During the first few years of occupation, many Germans were punished by these makeshift courts. But, compared to what transpired in the Soviet zone of occupation, the number of condemnations in the western zones was very low—in large part because most war criminals easily got off by producing affidavits of innocence written on their behalf by friends and family. The sentences were also far more lenient. In most cases, the courts exculpated the defendants as mere *"Mitläufer"*—people who had supported the Nazi regime to further their own careers but weren't deemed actually to have been blameworthy.

In any case, the Allies' political priorities soon changed radically. With the onset of the Cold War, the British and the Americans grew more concerned about the immediate threat posed by the Soviet Union, their recent ally, than about the potential threat posed by Germany, their recent enemy. Under the changed circumstances, a thorough cull of Germans implicated in Nazi atrocities came to look like an unaffordable luxury. A pragmatic solution now seemed more appealing: a bright future in the Federal Republic was to bribe former Nazi elites into loyalty to democracy.

Before long, denazification efforts all but collapsed. By the early 1950s, Allied involvement in bringing Nazi war criminals to justice had ground to a halt.

As for the German legal establishment—which was, in theory, charged with putting particularly inhumane Nazis on trial for criminal offenses like murder—it had been adamantly opposed to what it termed "victors' justice" from the very start.

In 1948, with denazification still high on the Allies' agenda, the German criminal justice system passed 1,819 guilty sentences for Nazi crimes. In the following years, as the United States and Britain gave the German legal system increasingly free rein, the number of cases dwindled rapidly. By 1955, German efforts to bring Nazi war criminals to justice had become so lax that there were no more than twenty-one convictions. And even in those few trials that did take place after the Federal Republic was founded in 1949, the punishments were increasingly laughable. As Devin Pendas, a historian who has studied postwar Germany, once said to me: "Tell me the year in which a war criminal was tried and I'll tell you how the court sentenced him. The rule of thumb is perfectly simple: the later the trial, the shorter the prison term."

Just as the legal establishment refused to punish former Nazis, so public opinion more broadly refused to accept that Germans might have done anything wrong. Both stances relied heavily on the notion that no individual guilt could derive from the misdeeds of a collectivity. The ascription of collective guilt, so the perfidious, self-serving argument went, was the domain of the Nazis; in an individualistic democracy, no collective responsibility for the crimes of the Third Reich could exist. To portray Germans as perpetrators was to unfairly victimize them. In holding Germans responsible for the Nazis, the Allies had, for all intents and purposes, themselves turned into Nazis.

The argument against collective guilt does, of course, have a certain force: it goes without saying that a specific blameless individual is not personally guilty just because his countrymen, or his relatives, have committed horrific acts. But this argument all too easily glosses over more complicated ways in which individuals might have a special responsibility for actions of a collectivity with which they identify: for example, if you insist on your right to feel proud at your country's achievements, it is only natural that you should also be prepared to feel shame at its failings.

In any case, in the context of the postwar years, the argument that Germans were being victimized by some kind of draconian form of collective punishment rang particularly hollow. After all, most Germans did not even want those compatriots of theirs who had actually, personally, committed horrible war crimes to be punished. Many among them even refused to acknowledge that the Third Reich itself had done anything particularly wrong.

This became painfully obvious in 1953, when Konrad Adenauer, Germany's first postwar chancellor, agreed to reparation payments to the State of Israel. Though Adenauer may privately have conceived of the reparations as an act of genuine contrition, publicly he justified them as a prudent step made necessary by Jewish animosity against Germany. As he curtly put it, echoing Nazi propaganda about a Jewish world conspiracy, "the world's Jewry is a great power." (As late as 1965, when he was asked why he had advocated reparations, Adenauer first talked about a moral obligation, but then quickly added: "The power of the Jews, even today, and especially in America, should not be underestimated— and that is why, very strategically and very consciously, I have worked with all my power to achieve, as best as possible, a reconciliation between the German and the Jewish peoples.")

Even though he was willing to stoop to such populist rhetoric in order to get the Bundestag, the Federal Republic's parliament, to agree to the reparations, Adenauer suffered a rare near-defeat. Many members of his own party flat-out refused to vote in favor of reparations. In the end, the motion was carried only because numerous opposition politicians voted in its favor.

Public opinion, meanwhile, remained resolutely opposed to the reparations: a mere 11 percent of West Germans were in favor; 24 percent agreed with the idea in principle but thought that the agreed sum was "too high"; 44 percent considered reparations altogether "superfluous." Average Germans clearly felt that the Third Reich had not done anything wrong—at least not anything particularly noteworthy.

Over the next years, barriers of entry for politically or administratively useful personnel with a dark past were dismantled almost completely. Hundreds of thousands of former Nazis ascended to positions of power and influence again. To cite but one statistic, three out of every five bureaucrats appointed to leading positions in federal ministries between 1950 and 1953 had been members of the Nazi Party. In the judiciary the situation was, if anything, even worse. Evidently, the old elites continued to shape the political and administrative habits of postwar Germany.

Hans Globke is perhaps the most shocking case of personal continuity between the Third Reich and the early years of the Federal Republic. Globke had been a leading lawyer during the Nazi regime. He had even authored the "*Gesetzeskommentar*" for the Nuremberg Race Laws of 1935, an official commentary that courts used in applying the laws. (In the name of Aryan purity, they forbade marriages and sexual intercourse between Jews and Aryans; stripped Jews of their German citizenship; and painstakingly distinguished between "full Jews," who had at least three Jewish grandparents, "crossbreeds of the first degree," who had one Jewish parent or two Jewish grandparents, and "crossbreeds of the second degree," who had only one Jewish grandparent.)

Regardless, in 1953 Globke was appointed director of the Federal Chancellery—roughly equivalent to the White House chief of staff. He continued to serve as Adenauer's right-hand man for the next ten years.

Globke's case is revealing. His activities in the Nazi era had been perfectly public all along, and yet he could rise to a position of inestimable personal access to, and influence on, the all-powerful Adenauer. There can be only one conclusion: the reason why Globke could have a stellar career in the Federal Republic wasn't that his past lay in the dark; it was that his past, of which everybody was well aware, was not considered grounds for concern.

Unsavory though it was, the across-the-board accommodation of the former Nazi elite that was carried out in the name of zero hour had one simple thing to recommend itself: it succeeded.

Adenauer, who ruled the Federal Republic in nearly autocratic fashion until he retired in 1963, proved particularly masterful at convincing former Nazis to accept democracy, in great part by using communism as a counterfoil.

In these early postwar years, the most pressing issue for many Germans was reunification. Quite a few nationalists may even have been willing to accept Germany's neutrality between East and West if only it could assure national unity. This included some on the right as well as many on the left, like Kurt Schumacher, the leader of the Social Democrats. But Adenauer stood firm against his critics. Time and again, he argued that Germany's integration into the club of Western democracies was of paramount importance as a bulwark against the Soviet Union. By firmly anchoring Germany in the Western alliance, Adenauer wedded the fight against communism to an adherence to democratic values and the tacit toleration of the territorial losses suffered at war's end.

Meanwhile, though Adenauer vilified Hitler and a few prominent Nazi leaders, he restyled most other Germans as valiant resistance fighters against the tyrannical hordes of the Red Army, no questions asked. With the help of this ingenious rhetoric, he drew upon the virulently anticommunist strand of National Socialist ideology to convince old Nazi sympathizers that the goals of the Federal Republic were not wholly antithetical to their own aspirations. In that respect, Adenauer dressed up his own foreign policy as but a continuation of Hitler's foreign policy by other means. Old Nazis were told that democracy was the way to hold at bay the enemy they claimed to have been fighting all along—and he topped off the offer with the implicit promise that, if only they paid minimal lip service to democracy, they would gain silent absolution for their past crimes.

As a result, many former Nazi sympathizers came to see democracy as the lesser evil. Every four years, Adenauer, invoking this spirit, won reelection with a simple slogan: *Keine Experimente,* "No Experiments."

The Weimar Republic—Germany's first, tragically failed, attempt at democracy in the interwar years—had never managed to convince conservative and nationalist power elites to embrace democratic values. The Federal Republic, by contrast, managed to win over the hearts and minds of most of its citizens. By 1976, only 20 percent of Germans were dissatisfied with the way democracy worked in their country. (In Great Britain, the equivalent figure stood at 46 percent. In Italy, a staggering 80 percent were unhappy.)

There were, no doubt, many reasons why the Federal Republic proved so popular. In part, the economic miracle of the 1950s and 1960s, which more than doubled the income of average Germans in less than two decades, was to thank for turning average Germans into "consumption democrats." But an equally important reason was Adenauer's success in turning anticommunism into the overarching ideology of postwar Germany. Since the high offices of the Federal Republic were staffed by former Nazis, it was little wonder that there were few Nazis left who overtly attacked democracy.

In short, most of those who initially governed postwar Germany had either been Nazis or were still influenced by Nazi ideology (or both). Yet they managed to found a stable and popular democracy. Strange as that may seem, many of the successful founders of the Federal Republic were "Nazi democrats."

—

Politically, the disingenuous myth of the zero hour proved to have real benefits. But just as it allowed old Nazis to pretend that they had never done anything wrong, so, too, it allowed a large share of the population to hold tight to most of their long-standing social and cultural attitudes.

Most Germans were willing to admit that the Third Reich had had its flaws. But, the general consensus held, on the whole, the regime had not been all that bad. Hitler and his leading men had done some nasty things. And, yes, sure, the SS had probably committed some serious war crimes. As for the Wehrmacht, however, most Germans never doubted that simple soldiers—and even a great majority of their officers—had acted honorably. In fact, the spirit of camaraderie and the courage of soldiers were constantly held up as examples to be followed in the newly founded Federal Republic.

Uwe Timm, a German novelist, has movingly described the eerie atmosphere of his childhood years in a searching memoir about his big brother, an SS soldier who was killed during the war:

> Father could not permit sorrow, only anger. But because fortitude, duty and tradition were inviolable to him, this anger was directed not against its causes, but against amateurish military men, against deserters, against traitors. That's what he talked about with other comrades. They came in the evenings, sat together, drank cognac and coffee, and talked about the course of the war. Looked for explanations why the war had been *lost*. Battles were fought one more time, orders corrected, incompetent generals sacked, the military command taken away from Hitler. It is nearly impossible to imagine today that these topics could fill whole evenings for that generation.

Even on the printed page, the war's positive sides were freely celebrated. Erwin Rommel's account of his exploits in the African desert, written in 1943 and shrewdly titled *War Without Hatred* when it was published in 1950, was an instant success. Another big bestseller, by the name of *Lost Victories*, was written by Erich von Manstein, a field marshall of the Wehrmacht during World War II. In his lament, von Manstein (who had been sentenced to eighteen years in prison by a British court in 1949 but was released after serving less than five) argued bitterly that Germany could have triumphed on the Eastern Front if only Hitler had taken the advice of generals like himself. That von Manstein would have considered such a German victory in World War II an unmitigated good went without saying.

The cultural life of the 1950s was characterized by a similarly forgetful mood. All the most popular films of the epoch were studiedly apolitical. They depicted heartwarming love stories set in the idyllic countryside. Judging from the plots of these blockbusters, the primordial German landscapes they depicted had been free from dramatic political events since the dawn of time. The only big movies to break this mold starred Germans going on amusing colonial adventures in exotic lands. Veit Harlan, who had directed the infamous anti-Semitic propaganda movie *Jud Süß* in 1940, now reinvented himself as a master of these genres. In the 1950s and '60s, he directed works with names like *Es war die erste Liebe* ("First Love") and *The Maharajah's Blonde*.

Fifteen whole years after the war, the reception afforded Marlene Dietrich when she first returned to Germany shows how little sympathy most Germans had for those compatriots of theirs who had chosen to fight against the Nazis. Dietrich, perhaps the most famous German actress of the twentieth century, had fled the Third Reich and even—the audacity!—donned an American uniform in appearances for U.S. troops during the war. When she briefly returned to her hometown, Berlin, in 1960, angry crowds protested her concerts, one spectator egged her while she was onstage, and another spit at her. They all agreed with the slurs they had read in the local newspapers: to them, Dietrich was, quite simply, a traitor to her own country.

Germans, as yet unable to face the past, preferred, whenever possible, to remain silent about it. As Judit Yago-Jung, who grew up as the child of Holocaust survivors in a midsize German town in the postwar years, puts it:

> My teachers simply avoided the subject because they themselves were too directly implicated in the events. For them, history books ended in 1933. In history class we would spend half a year treating the Weimar Republic in detail only to end up racing through the "modern" history from 1933–1945 with a kind of vague nostalgia in the last class before the summer vacation. After the vacation it was Konrad Adenauer and the post-war miracle.

From my own teenage years I remember a document that, even a good five decades after zero hour, still perfectly embodied this convenient view of history. On a visit to a friend in Dachau, near Munich, I picked up a leaflet about the city's history. Not a word about the Dachau concentration camp appeared in the glossy publication: the historical account leaped, with impressive chutzpah, from the Weimar Republic straight to the postwar years.

•

In the spirit of zero hour, most Germans seemed to think that dealing with the past required nothing more of them than to excise the Third Reich from schoolbooks, remove a few swastikas, rename every Adolf-Hitler-Platz a Bonner Platz, and pay a little lip service to the horrors of totalitarianism. But the Jews who lived in postwar Germany were deeply aware of how shallow their countrymen's remorse for the past still ran. Many of them even felt personal shame at living in Germany. What excuse, after all, could there be for settling in a country that had killed so many members of their families—especially since most of the country's inhabitants didn't even seem particularly apologetic about their actions?

During the Third Reich, many Germans who were opposed to Hitler had chosen to withdraw into a kind of "internal exile": they didn't actively resist the Third Reich, but neither did they participate in public life. In the 1950s and '60s, a lot of German Jews—especially the former DPs—settled into a similar state of mind.

A majority of them lived in one of three cities: Munich, Frankfurt, or Berlin. Of necessity, they worked and shopped among Gentiles. Come nightfall, however, most would return to their own apartments, have dinner with other Jews, or attend an improvised cultural event at the small Jewish community centers they had formed. Better, they thought, to limit contact with mainstream society as much as possible under the circumstances.

Until the early 1970s, this icy tension between Germans and Jews thawed very slowly, if at all. Only at the official level did the German state and the leadership of the Jewish community strike an uneasy deal.

To prove to his potential Western partners that Germany had truly changed, Adenauer wanted to display—with minimal effort, and against the more complex reality on the ground—how well his country treated the Jewish community. Whenever a foreign dignitary came to visit, he needed a gracious, flesh-and-blood Jewish audience for his high-minded philo-Semitic remarks.

Heinz Galinski, the chairman of the Central Council of Jews in Germany, meanwhile, found himself internationally isolated. Organizations like the World Jewish Congress did not officially recognize Germany's Jewish community for much of the postwar era. They simply were not willing to invest precious relief resources to help their coreligionists make what they thought was the bizarre choice of staying in Germany, rather than migrating to Israel or the United States. As a result, the German-Jewish community, if it was to maintain a rudimentary religious life and provide its aging members with urgently needed social services, was in desperate need of money.

The horse trade tacitly agreed upon by Adenauer and Galinski was only logical, then. The German state would provide the country's Jewish communities with limited financial support, which allowed them to function at a basic level. In return, the leadership of the Jewish community would sing Germany's praises, smiling at the dissimulating philo-Semitism lavished upon them at convenient times (often by former Nazis), and explaining away any all too obvious eruption of anti-Semitism as a mere misunderstanding.

One of Galinski's successors, Werner Nachmann, was even more pliant. Over the course of his tenure, it became increasingly clear that Hans Filbinger, the popular prime minister of the state of Baden-Württemberg, had been a ruthless Nazi judge. Among his many terrible exploits was an episode from June 1, 1945, nearly a month after the Third Reich had tendered its unconditional surrender. In keeping with the Geneva Convention, the Allies allowed German POWs to administer justice among themselves. When a fellow POW took swastikas off his uniform, Filbinger had him imprisoned for six months. Still more shocking was Filbinger's complete lack of contrition. Asked to account for his past actions in 1978, he calmly replied that "what was just then cannot be unjust now." Even so, Nachmann—eager to play his accustomed role as the useful Jew—rode to Filbinger's defense, claiming that he was a "decent human being." (Filbinger, by the way, remains a popular figure in Baden-Württemberg. At his state funeral in 2007, one of his successors, Günther Öttinger, preposterously eulogized Filbinger as "an opponent of the Nazi regime.")

At the official level, then, all was reasonably well between

Jews and Gentiles even as early as the 1960s. But in reality, many German Jews resented Galinski's servility, calling him a "*Hofjude*"—an aspersion that translates literally as "court Jew" and is roughly equivalent to the American slur "Uncle Tom." In the minds of most German Jews, the behavior of official representatives like Nachmann and Galinski hardly changed the fact that Germany's stubborn attachment to the myth of zero hour made it impossible for Jews to feel at home there.

This was certainly how Leon and Ala felt when they first arrived in Germany. They did not just understand the nature of the postwar settlement on an abstract level; they also encountered it as a practical dilemma in their everyday lives.

How should Ala respond to a friend, only a few years her senior, who casually mentioned to her one day that, like her, he had been born in Lodz (his father, a senior Nazi, had been sent there to help govern the region)? How should Leon respond to coworkers who, like so many Germans of their generation, went on and on about the battles of Monte Cassino or Stalingrad? Or to colleagues who kept saying that Hitler hadn't really been all that bad? Or to those who bragged about their wartime exploits?

By and large, Leon and Ala, like most other Jews in Germany at the time, bit their lips and held their tongues. The role of the indignant protester who stands up and complains about a perceived injustice when nobody sees anything amiss is one that few people want to play. Nearly always, they kept *stumm* and bided their time. But on rare occasions, too much was too much.

One time, a colleague of Leon's went off on a particularly virulent anti-Semitic rant. My beloved *zaza*—that peace-loving old man who trembled with sadness whenever the TV brought news of yet another distant war, that soft-spoken optimist who left me an abject answering machine message the day Yitzhak Rabin was shot—asked, ever so politely, that his colleague stop the insults. His colleague doubled down on his rant, growing even more aggressive. This time, Leon, to his own surprise, lost his temper: he challenged the unrepentant Nazi to step outside with him.

When I asked Leon about this story, which had become the stuff of legend in our little family, he would not say anything beyond: "I won the fight, but I'm not proud of it."

I believe the first part of his statement. Though Leon was peace-loving and soft-spoken, he was extremely strong. (I still remember in horror how, at the sprightly age of eighty-three, Leon arm-wrestled his son. Roman is a very strong guy, but four, five, six minutes into the contest he still hadn't managed to best his octogenarian father. With Leon and Roman both red in the face, Ala had to shout hysterically to get them to agree to a draw and finally stop.)

But while the first part of Leon's statement rings true enough, I have trouble believing the second part, his claim that he wasn't proud that, for once, he'd lost his temper.

Like most Jews who lived in postwar Germany, he, I think, considered his everyday acquiescence with contemporary Germany a little shameful. Leon shared the guilt of so many survivors, the irrational yet stubborn shame of having escaped his parents', his siblings', his firstborn son's fate. He felt discomfort at his own strange choice of living in the "country of the perpetrators." And then, on top of all that, there was the daily humiliation of living among people who had been so thoroughly complicit yet remained so thoroughly unapologetic.

For Leon, as for many other German Jews of that era, any tiny escape from this impotence and dissimulation—any moment of rupture that allowed the myth of the zero hour to recede and the long-sublimated conflict to come to the fore—must have been a tiny, exhilarating moment of triumph.

•

By the time I was growing up, Germany had, in many ways, changed for the better. But, as I was to experience when I moved to Laupheim at the age of nine, in some places the postwar silence about the past still reigned supreme in the late 1980s and early 1990s.

I moved to Laupheim in 1991 because Ala had accepted the position of chief conductor at the opera house in nearby Ulm. A small town of 16,000 inhabitants, Laupheim was located in Germany's affluent southwest, about a third of the way between Ulm and Lake Constance. It featured a passable castle, a big military base, and persistent rumors that McDonald's was about to open a branch on the edge of town. (This, my classmates informed me, would really put us on the map.)

So far as I know, our arrival in Laupheim brought the town's Jewish population to a grand total of two: my mother and me. In that sense, it is hardly surprising that the attitudes of many of Laupheim's inhabitants seemed to be more typical of the postwar era than of the early 1990s.

Or perhaps it would be more accurate to say: it wouldn't have been surprising but for the fact that Laupheim, remote as it is, has an unusually long and rich Jewish history. To this day, the center of Laupheim contains a beautiful Jewish cemetery. In the middle of the nineteenth century Laupheim had been the largest Jewish settlement in the kingdom of Württemberg. At that time, one in five of Laupheim's inhabitants had been Jewish.

One of Laupheim's Jews, a certain Carl Laemmle, who was born in a small house just outside the town's Jewish ghetto before emigrating to the United States at age seventeen, became the founder and first boss of Hollywood's Universal Studios. Laemmle frequently returned to his hometown, even after he was rich and famous. In the Laupheim of the 1920s, he was a big philanthropist. He gave copious assistance to the local poor (Jewish or Gentile), donated vast sums after a flood had destroyed many homes, and built extensive sporting facilities for the town's high school. In recognition of his charitable activity, Laemmle was named an honorary citizen of Laupheim; the school he helped modernize was renamed Carl-Laemmle-Gymnasium.

But Laemmle did not remain a venerated guest for long. After Hitler gained power, the Nazis' terror reigned in Laupheim, too. On April 1, 1933, the Jewish department store Einstein (whose founders had likely been distant relatives of Albert Einstein) was damaged by SA troops staging a violent anti-Jewish boycott. Over the next months, Jewish businesses and homes were "Aryanized," which is to say, confiscated. For one last time, Laemmle played an important role: he underwrote the financial affidavits needed for over three hundred poor Laupheim Jews to obtain U.S. visas and escape the Holocaust. When World War II had run its tragic course, no Jews remained in Laupheim.

By the time I lived in Laupheim, it wasn't just the Jewish community that no longer existed. Its memory, too, had largely been wiped out.

In the spring of 1993, the (Aryan-owned) shop that had taken over the Einstein properties announced grand festivities for its sixtieth anniversary. Another local shop soon followed with its own announcement. Each and every month after that, it turned out that yet another establishment had its own, remarkably similar, milestone to commemorate. If this coincidence struck any of the locals as a little odd, they did their best to conceal their puzzlement.

As for the school I attended in Laupheim, it was in an eerie state of nameless limbo. No longer called Carl-Laemmle-Gymnasium—the Nazis had taken care of that—it was now variously referred to as "Laupheim's high school" or "the high school on Herrenmahd Road." It was in this nameless school that my classmates laughed uproariously when I nervously admitted to being a Jew—and where my teacher, Herr Weiss, had to explain to them that, yes, some Jews did in fact still exist.

I had been dimly aware of sort of being Jewish even before my first day as a student at the former Carl-Laemmle-Gymnasium.

But I probably didn't know all that much more about what it meant to be a Jew than did my classmates.

I knew I was Jewish because, every now and again, Ala and Leon would discuss whether this or that German celebrity might secretly be a Jew. I knew I was Jewish because, whenever somebody said the word *"Jude"* on the street, Ala shrunk into herself even as she craned her neck to hear what was being said. I knew I was Jewish because, sometime around when I was six or seven years old, after seeing a program on TV that mentioned these strange creatures, I asked Ala who the Jews were, and she said: "Us."

But if it was a fact that I was a Jew, that fact remained decidedly abstract. My being Jewish had no more significance to me than any number of other abstract facts I knew to be true of me— what hospital I was born in, for example, or how old I'd been when I said my first word; like these, it was a fact that would, I assumed, have no tangible impact on my life.

So while I had always dimly known that I was, in some sense at least, Jewish, I did not, for the first ten years of my life, know to what extent being Jewish would mark me out; nor did I think that being Jewish somehow stopped me from being German. Over the next several years, that was to change.

To the best of my memory and self-knowledge, this slow transformation was set in motion that day when, still unsure of myself, I first vocalized to a classroom full of strangers that I was a Jew. For a few seconds, while everybody laughed, I was simply confused. Like anybody who, setting out to say something in earnest, finds that he has inadvertently told a good joke—a joke everyone except the teller seems to find hilarious—I racked my brain to understand what had just happened. Are they laughing *at* me, because I'm a Jew? If so, is it funny to be a Jew? Or are they laughing *with* me, because I'm making fun of Jews? And if so, why is it funny that somebody would pretend to be a Jew?

But then the laughing stopped, and the reality sunk in. My classmates realized that I wasn't joking: I really was a Jew. Herr

Weiss realized (and didn't seem too pleased) that he really did have a rare specimen of that endangered species on his hands. And I, for my part, began to suspect that my being a Jew was no inconsequential abstraction after all.

It's not that my classmates grew hostile. Nor did they start hurling anti-Semitic slurs at me. What they did was subtler, though, over time, equally alienating: they came to see me as a strange and slightly mysterious outsider who wasn't bad, necessarily, but who also most definitely wasn't really a part of their community.

To mention that I was a Jew had been enough to make sure that I would never be one of them. I have no doubt in my mind that, had anybody asked my classmates on my second or tenth or five hundredth day at the former Carl-Laemmle-Gymnasium whether I was German, they would innocently have answered: "Yascha? No, he's no German. He's a Jew."

As I took in what a strangely powerful effect this one fact had on everyone around me, my self-conception began to change. Earlier, I had known that I was somehow Jewish, but I hadn't thought of myself as a Jew. Now I started to embrace that identity for myself in a much more self-conscious way. If I couldn't be a German, I supposed I'd have to be a Jew.

My reluctant embrace of being a Jew started to give way to defiant pride about half a year later. On a beautiful spring day, I went to see Ala conduct *The Marriage of Figaro* at the Ulm opera house. I had little musical training, but as a loving son I knew that it must have been a most accomplished performance. As soon as the final curtain fell, I exited the auditorium through a little side door, rushed up a staircase to the third floor, and skipped down a long corridor toward my mother's dressing room to congratulate her. When Ala finally came into view, I found myself glued to the spot.

"I am a German singer on German soil!" Bernd Kastaffer, one of the singers in the ensemble, was shouting at her. Even I could tell he was blind drunk.

"Perhaps we'd better talk about this tomorrow," Ala said. She sounded firm but looked a little scared. "Let me tell you this, though: if you ever turn up for a performance this drunk again, there will be consequences."

I watched in horror as Kastaffer staggered toward her, his operatic voice loudly projecting his slurs for the benefit of a quickly assembling crowd of bystanders. "You are a Jew. I am a German. You shouldn't be telling me anything."

There was a short pause while Kastaffer tried to think of a suitably impressive exit strategy. "A *German* singer. On *German* soil," he finally said. "Just go back to Israel, where you belong, will you?"

Satisfied with his finish, Kastaffer stomped off with the melodramatic flourish of a mediocre performer, careening down the long, brightly lit corridor in search of his dressing room.

Though I was a little shaken up by this experience, I did my best to forget all about it: Bernd Kastaffer, I told myself, was just a drunk guy saying crazy stuff.

But then, a month or two later, I returned home from school early to find Ala reading at the kitchen table, her face as white as the letter she held in her hand. When her eyes met mine, she immediately put the letter away and refused to answer any of my questions.

That night, after Ala had gone to bed—I must have been about as old as she herself had been when she'd opened that secret drawer back in Warsaw—I looked for the letter all over the house. Finally I found it. "German jobs are for Germans," it read. "You better go back to Israel—or *we* will dispose of this problem." Beneath it, I found more letters, older letters, some of them a good bit more vitriolic.

My first reaction was to be afraid. Who had written these letters? Might they try to do something to Ala? Shouldn't we move? Or hide?

But as I thought about Bernd Kastaffer, and about those

anonymous letters, I grew less and less fearful, and more and more defiant. My sense of actual danger receded, but my sense of injustice intensified. If we hadn't done anything bad, I thought, we shouldn't have to live in fear. Nor should we have to hide our identity, or to avoid confrontation, or to avoid acknowledging that we're Jews.

Henceforth, I resolved, I would be completely upfront about being Jewish. To call myself a Jew—to be open and honest about a fact my classmates seemed to consider so mysterious, and that some strangers seemed to find so hateful—now looked like an act of courage to me. If I was doomed to be an outsider, I would at least wear the mark of my difference with pride.

PART II

The Tyranny of Good Intentions

"Beware of Germans with good intentions!" cried someone at the back of the room.　　　　　　　　　　—Orhan Pamuk, *Snow*

As the tragedy had taken place, the satyr play now had to follow.
　　　　　　　　　　—Wolfgang Koeppen, *Death in Rome*

FOUR

Sweet Surrender

In the 1960s, a younger generation of Germans started to call attention to the serious injustices of the postwar era—to the hollow pretense that the Third Reich could blithely be forgotten; to the prominent Nazis who went on to occupy the Federal Republic's highest offices; to the general unwillingness to mourn the victims of the Third Reich. Rejecting the idea of 1945 as a radical rupture between past and present, they argued that talk of a zero hour had been little more than a convenient fig leaf.

This rebellion against the myth of zero hour transformed West Germany from the ground up. In the 1950s and 1960s, the Holocaust had been a well-heeded taboo. Today, public TV stations show one documentary about the Holocaust after another. Back when Ala and Leon arrived in Germany, they had often been confronted with unabashed anti-Semitism or undisguised nostalgia for the Third Reich. Today, most ordinary Germans are more likely to be given to excesses of philo-Semitism.

It is perfectly understandable, then, that prominent intellectuals like Jürgen Habermas are proud of the progress for which they have fought so hard. They take credit for inspiring a vast youth movement that changed the country's view of its own past and has helped to turn Germany into the stable and peaceful country we know today. For them, 1968 was a radical turning point in

German history. There is much truth to this story. Without a doubt, Germany has changed a lot.

Even so, I fear that this act of rebellion against the foundational myth of 1945 is now in danger of becoming a meta-foundational myth in its own right. Though it is never called by that name, and though it is said to have taken place in 1968 rather than in 1945, this new myth plays a strikingly similar role in the country's self-understanding: in the minds of many, 1968 and its aftermath has become the true zero hour. Just like 1945—that first, failed zero hour—it is thought to have cleansed away all the ugly debris of the Third Reich, finally insulating the present from the troubling past.

To be sure, this second zero hour is a lot less disingenuous than the first had been. It stems not from a lack of introspection but is claimed as the deserved reward for a painful process of unflinching self-criticism. And yet its implications are nearly as pernicious. Just as the first, false, zero hour blinded postwar Germans to their country's many problems, so this second zero hour exaggerates how perfect and inexorable Germany's progress toward liberal democracy has been. And just as the first zero hour made it difficult for Jews to feel at home in the country, so, too, this second supposed zero hour has done a lot to make German Jews feel that we will never truly come to be at home in Germany.

•

On May 11, 1960, a man by the name of Ricardo Klement was on his way home from his job as foreman at the Mercedes-Benz factory in Buenos Aires. Klement got off the bus at his usual stop, lit a cigarette, looked at his nondescript street—he could see a few men repairing a car, nothing extraordinary—and calmly set about walking the short distance to his home.

A few steps on, a man approached to ask Klement for a light.

Klement searched his pockets for some matches. Before he had the time to get them out, the man's accomplices—who had, he now realized, only been pretending to repair that car—jumped Klement. They tried to drag him into their vehicle. He resisted. One of the men knocked him out clean with a careful blow to his head. Then they stuffed Klement into the car and drove away at breakneck speed.

The men who kidnapped Klement were agents of Mossad, the Israeli secret service. As for Klement himself, his identity was a fake. Ricardo Klement's real name was Adolf Eichmann. He had been the logistical mastermind responsible for transporting Jews to their deaths in the concentration camps.

Israel was determined to bring Eichmann to justice. A few days after the Mossad agents got their hands on him, they sedated him and smuggled him out of Argentina in the guise of an El Al flight attendant.

The Eichmann trial took place the following year, from April to December 1961. It was a worldwide sensation. Interest in the case, during which Eichmann presented himself as an average and dutiful bureaucrat, was intense all around the world. Covering the proceedings for *The New Yorker*, Hannah Arendt was famously struck by the "banality of evil."

The trial was widely discussed in Germany as well. But though innumerable former bureaucrats who had committed war crimes were still at large on German soil, no comparable cases had ever been brought in the Federal Republic. Not only was the German legal profession, whose leading figures had themselves been deeply implicated in the administration of the Third Reich, passionately opposed to such trials. Even the legal basis for them was shaky. Especially so-called *Schreibtischtäter*—pencil-pushers-cum-war-criminals—could often escape prosecution by insisting, as Eichmann did, that they had merely been following orders.

—

Fritz Bauer was determined to change the well-nigh total impunity for former mass murderers still resident in Germany.

Born in Stuttgart a few years after the turn of the century, Bauer studied law in Heidelberg, Munich, and Tübingen. In 1930, at age twenty-seven, he was appointed a trainee judge in his hometown. He seemed to be on his way to a highly successful, if unremarkable, legal career. But Bauer was both Jewish and a Social Democrat. In May 1933, less than four months after Hitler had taken power, the Gestapo arrested him. For a few months, Bauer was interned at the Heuberg concentration camp. Though he was later released, he now knew the danger he was in and fled to Denmark in 1936.

Bauer, increasingly active in the resistance movement, stayed on in Denmark for seven years. Then, in the autumn of 1943, three years into the German occupation of the country, the SS moved to deport the 7,500 Jews who still remained on Danish territory. Luckily, Georg F. Duckwitz, a military attaché at the German embassy to Denmark, leaked word about these plans just in time. Alerted by Duckwitz, Danish authorities carried out an unparalleled rescue operation. In October 1943, ordinary fishermen secretly ferried thousands upon thousands of Jews—Bauer among them—across the Øresund strait from Denmark to safety in neutral Sweden. (Decades later, on our yearly visits to my grandmother Ewa, Ala and I would cross that same narrow strip of sea on a passenger ferry—invariably accompanied by drunk Swedes who had stocked up on inexpensive alcohol across the border to circumvent Sweden's steep liquor taxes.) Once in Sweden, Bauer became even more influential within the resistance. Among other activities, he cofounded the *Socialist Tribune* with fellow political exile Willy Brandt.

When, like a handful of other Jews, Bauer made the difficult decision to return to Germany in 1949, his motivation was political. One of the reasons for the downfall of the Weimar Republic had been the legal profession's utter lack of political neutrality. While left-wing political activism had been severely punished, extremists on the far right had frequently been treated like heroes. After the failed Beer Hall Putsch of 1923, for example, Hitler had to spend only a bare nine months in prison. The judge, as he freely expressed at the sentencing, had been impressed by Hitler's "German manner of thinking and feeling." (It was during this incarceration that, under luxurious conditions, Hitler composed *Mein Kampf.*) Bauer was now determined that the newly founded Federal Republic should not suffer from the same inability to punish right-wing enemies of democracy. And so he resumed his legal career.

Bauer's first big success came in a 1951 libel case that revolved around the question of whether or not foreign bribes had motivated the abortive revolt against Hitler staged by Claus von Stauffenberg in the last months of the war. As a result of the trial, at which Bauer served as chief prosecutor, Stauffenberg's attempted coup was officially recognized as an act of rightful resistance. Surviving coconspirators were fully rehabilitated. Even more important, the court's ruling followed Bauer's argument that the Third Reich had been an "*Unrechtsstaat*," an illegitimate political regime violating the rule of law.

Bauer's second big success came nine years later, when German government circles got wind that Eichmann was probably hiding in Buenos Aires. Bauer, worried that old brothers-in-arms would tip Eichmann off before he could be apprehended, informed the Israelis. It was only because of Bauer's swift intervention that the Mossad's agents got to Eichmann in time.

Then, in 1963, Bauer, who by this time had risen to the position of General Prosecutor for the State of Hessia, initiated the first big set of trials against Nazi war criminals since the founding of the Federal Republic. Constrained by the imperfections of German law, Bauer could not bring to justice masterminds of the Holocaust like Eichmann. What he could do, however, was to prosecute those who had carried out the "final solution" on the ground: men like Stefan Baretzki and Oswald Kaduk, whose sadism had gone well beyond the call of "duty" in humiliating, violating, and exterminating concentration-camp inmates.

As Bauer conceived of it, the point of these trials went beyond the punishment of the culprits themselves. Bauer's aim wasn't to imprison the greatest number of people; rather, Bauer hoped that the trials would elucidate the gruesome events at Auschwitz as thoroughly as possible, changing public perceptions of the Third Reich. That's why, of the thousands upon thousands of people who had helped to run the Auschwitz camp, only twenty-two sat in the dock.

To a certain degree, this strategy proved successful. The effect of the "Auschwitz trials" on the educated German public was considerable. Every day, as survivors in Bauer's Frankfurt courtroom gave detailed accounts of the horrors to which they had been subjected at Auschwitz, the nation's leading newspapers reported on them. It was a first step toward spreading awareness of the extent of Nazi crimes to the hitherto largely clueless public. At least for some influential intellectuals, it was a true moment of awakening.

One of these was German writer and novelist Martin Walser. After seeing the Auschwitz trials in person, he wrote a searching essay titled "Our Auschwitz." In it Walser fervently rejected the standard descriptions of Auschwitz in the mass media of the time—where the extermination camp was depicted, in vague terms, as the incarnation of some abstract, impersonal evil. "Auschwitz was not hell," Walser argued, "but rather a German concentration camp . . . The torturers were not phantastical devils, but human beings like you and me. Germans, or those who wanted to become Germans."

The Auschwitz trials were an important starting point for Germany's slow process of reckoning with the past. In Bauer's eyes, though, they were hardly an unmitigated triumph.

Only six of the twenty-two defendants in the Auschwitz trials were given life sentences. Eleven defendants were given much shorter terms, some as laughable as three or four years. Still others went home free men. Time and again, the claim that they had merely been following orders saved the former camp guards from harsher punishments.

Worse, it quickly became clear to Bauer that the trials had not transformed Germany's attitude toward the Holocaust nearly as profoundly as he had hoped. When, a few moments after their convictions had been handed down, the war criminals were led out of the courtroom, on-duty policemen respectfully saluted them. This was no isolated incident. The sympathies of many average Germans lay with the accused, not the accusers.

Victor Capesius, for example, was an SS *Sturmbannführer* who had decided the fate of thousands upon thousands of inmates at Auschwitz's selection ramp. Like other defendants, he was given a stunningly lenient sentence. By 1968, he was a free man. Upon his release from prison, Capesius attended a classical concert in his hometown, Göppingen. As he entered the auditorium, a hush of recognition spread among the audience. Moments later, long, enthusiastic applause erupted throughout the hall. The people of Göppingen were only too happy to welcome Capesius back into their forgiving fold.

Fritz Bauer was found dead in the bathtub of his apartment on July 1, 1968. The precise circumstances of his death remain unclear to this day. One hypothesis is that Bauer, losing hope that his judicial efforts could effect a real change of attitude in the German population, had committed suicide by taking an overdose of sleeping pills.

In retrospect, it is clear that the Auschwitz trials did not change most Germans' view of the Holocaust. Mass awareness of the true nature of the Holocaust still lay far in the future.

And yet the trials did help to set a transformation in motion. It was then that many young Germans who went on to shape the country's view of the Third Reich first began to grasp the true horrors of what had happened at Auschwitz. At least some among Germany's cultural and intellectual establishment were starting to demand an honest engagement with the past. When the radical student movement gained momentum in the late 1960s, it would draw on their ideas.

•

On May 27, 1967, Iran's ruler, Shah Mohammad Reza Pahlavi, and his glamorous wife, Empress Farah Diba, arrived in Germany for a state visit. Germany's tabloid press covered the occasion with breathless excitement. Press accounts of the meetings between the German political establishment and the Iranian court sounded like plot summaries from the blockbusters of 1950s German cinema—a real-life version of Veit Harlan's *The Maharajah's Blonde*. The suggestion, once more, was of a *"heile Welt,"* a beautiful, wholesome world where the Federal Republic's bourgeois respectability met the 2,500-year-old Persian monarchy under the admiring eyes of two carefree peoples.

Reality, however, was rather harsher, and not only in Germany. Even though the Iranian regime did have some accomplishments to its name—Shah Pahlavi had introduced moderate land reforms, improved universal education, exercised relative religious tolerance, and increased opportunities for women—it remained in power only thanks to the brutal suppression of all opposition. Pahlavi's opponents on both the radical left and the religious right were systematically persecuted, imprisoned, and tortured.

It is no surprise, then, that from the perspective of young, idealistic, left-wing Germans, the negative aspects of Pahlavi's rule seemed a lot more obvious than its achievements. The pomp and circumstance with which the Federal Republic greeted a repressive ruler seemed to them to indicate the secret sympathies and ambitions of their own political leaders. On June 2, 1967, when the Iranian guests were scheduled to attend a gala performance of Mozart's *The Magic Flute* at the Deutsche Oper in West Berlin, thousands of students assembled to protest the Shah's visit.

Some of the protesters were clearly misguided. The chant "Shah, SS, SA," with its reference to the most deadly aspects of the Third Reich, for example, was not only too extreme in its criticism of the Shah; it also showed how ignorant the sloganeers were about the history of their own country.

Yet the story of the day was one of senseless repression of legitimate democratic protests. While the protesters were awaiting the arrival of the state guests, about a thousand supporters of the Shah—many of them agents of the Iranian secret service—started to beat them up with wooden planks.

After standing idly by, the German police—a detachment on horseback—finally intervened. The protesters, who at first assumed the police were there to protect them, cheered them on. Only gradually did they realize that the gratuitous violence inflicted by the German police that night would prove worse than the beatings meted out by Iranian secret agents. Students were pursued into nearby streets and even the courtyards of private houses. In one case, three policemen continued to beat up a defenseless student for minutes on end before finally arresting him.

Then, at about 8:30 p.m., one gunshot changed the course of German history. Suddenly, Benno Ohnesorg, a largely apolitical literature student at West Berlin's Freie Universität, was lying on the ground, a bullet lodged in the back of his head. He was to die a few minutes later, in an ambulance, on the way to the hospital.

The precise circumstances of Ohnesorg's death remain murky to this day. Some witnesses reported hearing his last, desperate words: "Please, please, don't shoot!" Others claimed that Karl-Heinz Kurras, the policeman who shot Ohnesorg, immediately told his superior that he had not meant to fire his gun. (The mystery was only deepened a few years ago when, in another strange twist, historians discovered that Kurras had been a secret agent for the Stasi, the East German intelligence service.)

Some doubt remains about whether Kurras shot intentionally. There is no doubt, however, that panicked authorities conspired to conceal aspects of the student's death. The crime scene was never searched for evidence. A police report was compiled without any input from civilian witnesses. Most mysterious of all, the part of Ohnesorg's skull where the police bullet had entered his head went missing: somebody must have surgically removed it after his death. At his trial, Kurras claimed that he had fired his bullet in self-defense when he was attacked by up to ten knife-wielding protesters. Of seventy witnesses heard in the trial, only one supported this version of events. Even so, Kurras was acquitted.

The events surrounding Ohnesorg's death radicalized the German student movement. The murder of an innocent was shocking enough to them. But the subsequent handling by state authorities—as well as a savage media campaign blaming the student protesters for the violence—was worse. It seemed to vindicate the views of radical left-wingers who saw the Federal Republic as a fascist regime barely disguised under a veneer of democratic procedures. As a result, many young people who had previously been but mildly disgruntled with political realities in West Germany began to oppose the system wholesale. Over the next weeks and months, student protests spread to ever new cities and social groups.

Many participants in the student movement allowed themselves to be blinded by the false promises of radical ideologies. There were a few Stalinists. Some were Leninists. Many were Trotskyites. More still, Maoists. The resulting potpourri of idols would have been funny had it not been so misguided. One sunny day in 1968, for example, students of the Giselagymnasium, a rather bourgeois high school I was to attend some three decades later, marched down a central avenue in Munich chanting: "Ho- Ho- Ho Chi Minh! Che Guevara! Lenin!"

But while Vietnam or Cuba were on the minds of many, the real motivation for these protests lay closer to home. Germany's rebelling youth loathed what they perceived as the repressive and small-minded realities of the postwar era. Having grown up in peace and relative material affluence, they looked beyond the limited goals of their parents. Young men wanted more from life than a house, a car, a wife, and a few kids. Young women rebelled against the role traditionally assigned to them by the "three K's": *Kinder, Küche, Kirche* (children, kitchen, church).

The revolt of the "68ers," as they came to be known, soon turned against all forms of traditional authority: political, religious, social, economic, and cultural. Naturally enough for a youth movement, the protesters counted their parents amongst the ranks of their enemies. And perhaps the best way to challenge the authority of their supposedly so respectable, supposedly so moral parents, this generation soon learned, was to ask uncomfortable questions about their actions during the Third Reich.

As Daniel Cohn-Bendit, a German Jew and himself a famous leader of the student protests in both Germany and France, told me in an interview:

> The 1968 movement in Germany challenged a closed society. It was an anti-authoritarian movement, and it was a movement against the handling of Germany's history by their parents. This was one of the most difficult things. It wasn't merely abstract: for most people, it was about their own parents, their own grandparents. What does it mean to ask your own mother, your own father, what they did? It sounds easy, but if you're at the dinner table, and you start this debate . . .

Most of these confrontations about the past took place in the privacy of the nuclear family's home—behind closed doors. But every now and again these clashes found public expression.

As most of the 68ers were students, and many eventually wound up in academia, the struggle to deal honestly with the past was most pronounced at universities. The best-remembered student slogan of those years brilliantly captured this goal: *"Unter den Talaren / Der Muff von tausend Jahren"* (Under their gowns / the stink of a thousand years). On the one hand, it was directed against the long centuries of tradition that continued to shape the steep hierarchies and arcane rituals that were still prevalent in German universities. On the other hand, referencing the Third Reich's ambition to last one thousand years, it pilloried the continuing influence of Nazi-era ideology and personnel in higher education.

The most memorable act of public contestation, however, did not take place on a university campus. Rather, it was directed against Kurt Georg Kiesinger. As early as March 1933, Kiesinger had become a member of the Nazi Party. During the war, he ascended to a leading position in the Foreign Office. In the early 1960s, accusations surfaced—though in part because Eichmann refused to testify about them at his trial in Jerusalem, they have never been either confirmed or disproven—that Kiesinger was partly responsible for the deaths of 10,000 Greek Jews. No matter. In 1966, Kiesinger became the third chancellor of the Federal Republic.

On November 7, 1968, Chancellor Kiesinger attended the annual conference of the Christian Democratic Party in Berlin. Kiesinger, a tall man popular for his worldly charm, was surrounded by fans keen for his autograph. Suddenly, chaos descended on the festivities. A young woman shouted: "Nazi Kiesinger, resign!" Then, as everybody stood by in shock, she smacked him in the face.

Events become emblematic of a particular historical moment by the force of images. The blurred image of a young German woman physically distancing herself from her country's past with a blow to the chancellor's head was particularly striking. As Beate Klarsfeld, the political activist who that day achieved instant notoriety, explains: "My gesture was symbolic: I am the same age as all those children of Nazis who subconsciously would like to inflict the same punishment upon their fathers." The image, in other words, vividly captured both the 68ers' rebellion against the generation of their parents and their indignation about the past.

Most Germans were horrified by Klarsfeld's attack. But in a sign of the times, a vocal minority supported her. To express his gratitude, Heinrich Böll, the novelist who was later awarded a Nobel Prize for Literature, even sent Klarsfeld a bouquet of red roses.

•

At the height of the student protests, the political establishment was still invested in the old regime. Kiesinger, an ex-Nazi, was chancellor of the Federal Republic (that is, Germany's head of government). Though he himself had never been a Nazi, Heinrich Lübke, the Federal Republic's president (that is, Germany's largely ceremonial head of state), seemed similarly out of place in a modern democracy. After a state visit to Madagascar, for example, he expressed his hope that the island's people "will one day learn how to clean themselves." Allegedly, he even began one of his speeches in South Africa with the line: "Esteemed ladies and gentlemen; dear Negroes . . ."

Then, over the course of 1969, fresh faces ascended to the leadership of the Federal Republic. The German establishment itself now underwent a stunning transformation.

On March 6, 1969, Gustav Heinemann, a devout Lutheran whose prominent role in his church had repeatedly brought him into conflict with the Third Reich, was narrowly elected to succeed Lübke as president. Not only did Heinemann hold a less authoritarian vision of political leadership than his predecessors, but, as he made clear in his inaugural speech, he was also keenly aware of the need to face up to the past:

Some are still invested in the authoritarian state. It has been our misfortune for long enough. In the end, it has led us into the doom of the Third Reich . . . Even now, we stand only at the beginning of the first truly liberal period in our history. Liberal democracy must finally become the lived reality of our society . . . Everywhere, authority and tradition have to accept that their legitimacy will be questioned . . . Not less but rather more democracy—that is the demand, that is the grand goal to which all of us, especially the young, have committed ourselves.

The election of Heinemann, a Social Democrat, already signaled the end of an era. Then, following national elections held on September 28, 1969, the government changed hands as well. In mid-October, the Bundestag elected Willy Brandt, another Social Democrat, as the fourth chancellor of the Federal Republic. For the first time in the history of postwar Germany, the Christian Democratic government had been defeated at the polls.

The contrast between Brandt and his predecessor, Kiesinger, could hardly have been starker. Brandt was born Herbert Frahm in the northern port city of Lübeck on December 18, 1913. While Kiesinger came from a respectable bourgeois family, little Herbert Frahm's mother was working-class. Worse, she wasn't married. Frahm was a "bastard"—a fact that was used as ammunition by his political opponents well into the 1960s.

But that wasn't the only dissimilarity between Kiesinger and Frahm. While Kiesinger joined the NSDAP in March 1933, Frahm, a member of the Socialist Workers' Party, started to work for the resistance movement. He eventually fled to Norway, from where, throughout the war, he actively continued to fight against Hitler, often at immense personal risk. It was during his time in exile that Frahm chose a cover name to protect himself. Henceforth, he was to be known as Willy Brandt.

Now, in 1969, Brandt, whose very name stemmed from his courageous struggle against the Third Reich, succeeded Kiesinger, a former member of the Nazi Party. The significance of this political transition was self-evident.

A marked change in government policy quickly followed. As a candidate for high office, Brandt had invited Germans to "dare more democracy." As chancellor, he liberalized the legal system. Employees gained more rights. Public education became less hierarchical. Across many areas of law, the illiberal rules that had helped to make the postwar era so repressive were abolished. It was no longer illegal for unmarried couples to cohabit. Laws against homosexuality were finally repealed.

Brandt also reshaped Germany's foreign policy. Adenauer had anchored the Federal Republic in a firm alliance with the West. At the beginning of Adenauer's rule, the United States, Great Britain, and France had been Germany's occupying powers. At the end of his rule, Germany was well on its way to becoming their trusted ally. So, by the time Brandt took power, Germany's position in the Western alliance was irrevocable; his government unwaveringly fulfilled the country's obligations to NATO.

But while Brandt's foreign policy stood for continuity in its relations with the Allies, he also advocated for a marked change in his country's relationship to its eastern neighbors. To the dismay of the Christian Democrats, Brandt argued that the Federal Republic needed to perform a rapprochement with the East to complement the country's alliance with the West.

Brandt's reasons for this move were double. On one level, it was strategic. The East of Germany remained under the hegemony of the Soviets. If real progress toward reunification should ever be made, a peaceful relationship between West Germany and the Soviet Union would undoubtedly be a precondition.

On another level, the need for a new foreign policy toward

the East was moral. As Brandt knew, the countries that had suffered most under the Third Reich lay to the east of Germany: Poland was the first country that had been attacked by Germany. Russia had suffered extreme losses after 1941. And the places where the most Jews had met their deaths, from Auschwitz to the many nameless ditches where the Nazis had carried out murderous mass shootings, were located in Central and Eastern Europe.

Brandt's attempt to improve the Federal Republic's relationship with its eastern neighbors was a resounding success. Within four years of assuming office, he had managed to sign treaties with the Soviet Union, Poland, Czechoslovakia, and even East Germany. As a result, the last obstacles to West Germany's membership in the United Nations were eliminated. In hindsight, it is even clear that West Germany's improved relationship with its eastern neighbors did, as Brandt had originally hoped, make it easier for those countries to accept Germany's reunification after the Berlin Wall came down.

The symbolic dimension of Brandt's foreign policy was just as consequential—and even more important to the relations between Jews and Gentiles. On December 7, 1970, Brandt traveled to Warsaw to sign a peace treaty with Poland. It officially renounced Germany's expansionist ambitions by accepting the "Oder-Neisse line," Germany's postwar border with Poland. But his visit was memorable more for one emotional, unplanned gesture than for the resulting political documents.

While in Warsaw, Brandt was scheduled to lay down a wreath at the monument to the victims of the Warsaw Ghetto Uprising. Adenauer and Kiesinger would have regarded this as a rather routine gesture. Like virtually all German politicians of the postwar era, they would have tried to dispense with such a token expression of regret with maximal haste and minimal fuss. Brandt, by contrast, once again proved just how different he was.

Film footage shows Brandt's limousine as it arrives on the

large, barren square where the ghetto had stood before it was brutally liquidated by the SS in April and May of 1943. In the fore-
ground stand the officials, men in heavy black coats, their breath
visible in the biting cold. Far off in the background, a seemingly
never-ending wall of gray apartment blocks lines the horizon. A
cold, Socialist-Realist monument to the victims of the uprising
dominates the square itself. It features a group of heroes in clichéd
gestures: suffering women and children; defiant men; the whole
ensemble enclosed by a massive block of concrete. Overall, the
space, which had once been so full of life, looks devastatingly
empty—a ghost city plucked out of a dystopian thriller.

Two aides now approach the monument. They walk in step,
rather stiffly, carrying a giant wreath adorned with white roses.
Sashes in the colors of the German flag span across its center.
One of them reads: "The Chancellor of the Federal Republic of
Germany." The aides deposit the wreath. They step aside.

Brandt now comes into view. With measured steps, he walks
toward the wreath. He leans down, straightens the sashes with
careful, heavy movements. He steps back. His face is immobile,
stoic, as always when Brandt is agitated. He looks down at the
wreath. He looks up at the monument. Then, in one slow, seam-
less, stunning movement, Brandt sinks to his knees.

For one long moment there is no movement. Faces freeze.
Nobody breathes. After an eternity, Brandt's breath becomes visible: he exhales, perhaps surprised by his own gesture, undoubtedly relieved to have done justice to the occasion. He, who has no
personal guilt, has issued a moving plea for forgiveness. He, who
need not apologize to anybody, has kneeled on behalf of those
who dared not or cared not to. It was a gesture that did as much
for Germany's reconciliation with the victims of the Third Reich
as thirty years of democratic rule.

Ala and Leon had only been in Germany a few months when
Brandt sank to his knees in Warsaw. They were still growing

accustomed to being Jewish in Germany, still learning how to navigate the many complications, from the frequent awkwardnesses to the occasional expression of hostility. Brandt's gesture instantly became a symbol of hope for them: the hope that Germany would truly change for the better; the hope, too, that it had not been a terrible mistake to move from Poland to Germany.

Marcel Reich-Ranicki, a Polish Jew who survived the Warsaw Ghetto and went on to become a leading German literary critic, described this moment in just such terms:

> Brandt on the territory of the Warsaw Ghetto. Precisely on the square where my fate—and that of my wife—was decided. We were led out there, and we did not know yet. To the left, that meant to the *Umschlagplatz* and to the gas chambers? Or to the right, then we would be allowed to live a little longer?
>
> I will never forget that Brandt did this. It's played a big role in my life. Perhaps it was only at this very moment that I fully knew it had been right, when I left Poland in 1958, to decide to live in Germany.

But while Brandt's gesture reassured some Jews that they might have a future in Germany, many Germans were furious. Mass protests called for "resistance" against Brandt. Graffiti on the streets rhymed "Brandt an die Wand!" ("Up against the wall, Brandt!"). Banners called for "traitors" like Brandt to be hung. Though most were not that extreme, in a representative poll, 48 percent of Germans did call Brandt's gesture "exaggerated"; only 41 percent thought it was "appropriate."

How deeply divided Germany was in those years is apparent from footage of the October 20, 1971, session of the Bundestag. In the middle of a debate about the budget, Kai-Uwe von Hassel, the Bundestag's speaker, rang his bell. "Ladies and Gentlemen, I interrupt our session for one moment," he said in a matter-of-fact tone. "A moment ago I have received word that the Nobel Prize commission of the Norwegian parliament has today awarded the Nobel Peace Prize to the chancellor of the Federal Republic."

Brandt's face became immobile once more. Around him, the left side of the house erupted in standing ovations. The right side of the house remained in its seats. Their faces strained, the deputies of the Christian Democrats stared ahead in impotent fury.

•

This same unwillingness to face the past was still in evidence on the German right when ARD, the Federal Republic's most important public television station, planned to air the NBC miniseries *Holocaust* in 1979. *Holocaust* tells the story of two sets of fictional characters—on one side, senior SS man Erik Dorf, who helps orchestrate the extermination of the Jews; on the other side, the Jewish family Weiss, nearly all of whom are murdered by the Nazis.

To air such a show would have been a new departure for ARD: while the taboo against talk of the Holocaust was much less strong by the late 1970s than it had been in the first two postwar decades, public television still kept its coverage of the Third Reich to a minimum.

There were widespread protests against this unprecedented broadcast. Some who objected were honest enough to name the reasons for their anger. They argued that to show the film on public television would be to needlessly drag Germany's name through the mud. It was "*Nestbeschmutzerei*," a pathological urge to foul one's own nest, akin to Brandt's demeaning genuflection in Warsaw.

Other opponents employed more disingenuous arguments. Politicians who were usually strongly at odds with the country's left-leaning cultural establishment suddenly discovered the importance of high art. *Holocaust*, typical of trite American media products, they contended, just wasn't of a sufficiently high artistic level to be shown on German television. Franz Josef Strauss, Bavaria's far-right prime minister, objected that NBC's motives for producing the show had been purely financial ("*Geschäfte-macherei*"). The network's executives, the implication ran, were trying to make a quick buck by pinning guilt on Germany.

The political right's calls to prevent the show from airing were heeded by violent extremists. An anonymous caller threatened to murder Heinz Galinski unless the broadcast was canceled. Then, on January 18, 1979, just as a documentary about the "final solution" was being shown on public television as a prelude to *Holocaust*, a pipe bomb exploded near Koblenz, interrupting transmission for hundreds of thousands of viewers. Less than half an hour later, another such bomb damaged transmission cables near the city of Münster. In the end, this widespread opposition resulted in *Holocaust* being removed from ARD's main schedule: it would now air on a less popular set of regional television channels instead.

Even so, the show's impact proved overwhelming. On its first day, 32 percent of all German television sets were showing *Holocaust*. By the next day, the number of viewers had increased to 36 percent. By the end of the run, the viewership stood at 39 percent. All in all, around 20 million Germans watched in horror as the fictional family Weiss approached its tragic end.

The German public had come a long way since the days when psychologists Alexander and Margarete Mitscherlich spoke of its utter "inability to mourn." Even as the show aired, over thirty thousand viewers called the networks—most to express their shock at the extent of German crimes during the Third Reich. Thousands of university seminars, school classes, and church groups took time out of their usual schedules to talk about *Holocaust*. According to polls taken after the broadcast, 81 percent of viewers had discussions after the film's end, 65 percent were shocked, and 45 percent reported feeling shame upon seeing it.

Before the miniseries was broadcast in West Germany, critics had feared that its minor historical inaccuracies might give Holocaust deniers ammunition. As it turned out, the opposite was true. Much ignorance was dispelled in those four days. As thirteen-year-old Jürgen Knipprath told *Der Spiegel*, a leading newsmagazine, at the time: "Earlier, I thought that the Jews must have committed some kind of a crime. But they hadn't even done anything."

Holocaust had no new insights to offer. Yet historians now believe that the collective catharsis instigated by its broadcast was perhaps the single most consequential event for Germany's changing relationship toward its past. Even before, center-left Germans had started to talk critically about the Nazi era. Even afterward, far-right Germans, including some prominent politicians, continued to ignore or trivialize the past. But it was in these few days in January 1979 that an understanding of the gruesome nature of the Holocaust really hit home in "Middle Germany."

•

Germany was set to commemorate the fortieth anniversary of the end of World War II on May 8, 1985. Much had changed in the previous decades. Debates about how Germans should relate to their past were by no means resolved. The prevailing view, though, was very different. In the 1950s, most Germans had thought of the Third Reich's surrender as a tragic date. Whatever their view of Hitler's "pros and cons," it had seemed obvious to them that a patriot could never desire for his country to be defeated in war.

By the mid-1980s this was no longer the case. Awareness of the crimes of the Third Reich against Germany's neighbors and minorities was starting to become virtually ubiquitous. At the same time, the spread of democratic attitudes made even those whose lives would not have been at risk in the darkest period of Germany's history deeply grateful that they didn't have to live under Hitler. Especially the young, who had grown up as free citizens of a stable and affluent country, now realized that Germany's defeat had been a blessing in disguise.

Richard von Weizsäcker, Germany's president for most of the 1980s, articulated this new view in a moving speech commemorating the fortieth anniversary of Germany's unconditional surrender. During World War II, Weizsäcker said,

> Most Germans had thought that they were fighting and suffering for the good of their own country. And now it was to become clear: All that was not only futile and senseless, but it had also served the inhumane goals of a criminal leadership. Exhaustion, perplexity and new worries characterized the feelings of the majority. Might some missing relatives still be found? Was there even any point in building something new amidst these ruins? Their view was directed backward into the dark abyss of the past and forward towards an uncertain, dark future.
>
> And yet, what today is incumbent for all of us to say, became clearer from day to day: the 8th of May was a day of liberation. It liberated us all from the dehumanizing system of National Socialism's violent rule.

Weizsäcker's felicitous turn of phrase crystallized the changes that had taken root over the preceding twenty years. Germany was no longer bemoaning lost victories. Most people in the country had learned to see the Third Reich's unconditional surrender as the starting point of a better future.

FIVE

The Silent Jew

Most Germans have never met a Jew—let alone shared a meal or been friends with one. So how they treat Jews is determined not by any personal experiences, but rather by the abstract ideas they have about us. And their abstract ideas, in turn, are inevitably mediated by their perception of Germany's past.

As a result, those Germans who have not faced up to the reality of the Third Reich are likely to hold prejudices against Jews, and perhaps even to be hostile when they do meet a Jew. That's what made life so difficult for Leon and Ala when they first arrived in Germany.

Conversely, those Germans who are sincerely horrified by Germany's past are likely to be deeply embarrassed on the rare occasions when they are faced with a Jew in real life. So it's no surprise that, when Germany's attitudes toward the past were radically transformed in the late 1960s, the '70s, and the early '80s, so, too, were interactions between Jews and Gentiles.

Moved by sudden shame about the past, more and more Germans felt a sudden love for the Jews. All the better to demonstrate just how sorry they were about the crimes of the Third Reich, many elite Germans now lavished any Jew they had the good luck of meeting with immoderate attentions and demonstrative kindnesses. Like other German Jews, my assigned role was, all too often, to serve as the flesh-and-blood object for this demonstrative goodwill.

After college, for example, I briefly returned to Germany to work at a theater in Munich. One day during that time, Franz, an old high school friend, threw a party. When I arrived, he was in the middle of a heated discussion with a pretty, soft-spoken blonde I'd never met. I walked over, handed Franz a bottle of wine, and he introduced me.

"So what were you guys talking about?" I asked.

"Woody Allen," the girl, Marie, reported indignantly. "Franz here thinks that Woody is creepy and that his movies are mediocre. Can you believe it?"

"No, no," Franz said, turning bright red. "I never said he was creepy or mediocre."

"You literally said that five seconds ago. You said he was creepy because he married his stepdaughter. And that he's not as serious as—"

"Well," Franz hedged, glancing at me, "I didn't mean it quite like that. Sure, it's a little weird that he married his stepdaughter. But, you know, they were both adults and . . . it's not illegal, so . . ."

"Why are you being so strange?" Marie asked.

"I'm not being strange at all. It's just . . . important to see both sides of the argument. You make it sound as though I had something against Woody Allen. I don't. He's a likeable guy. As you said, his Jew humor is admirable."

Now Marie was upset. "A moment ago you were hating on Woody Allen. Then Yascha here walks in and suddenly you're his biggest fan." She turned to me, a mocking smile curling up on her lips. "You must be the reason for Franz's sudden transformation. What's the deal? Are you writing a dissertation on Woody Allen? Or are you related to him?"

I laughed. "Rest assured that I have no particular horse in this race."

But Franz, shooting Marie an imploring look, mumbled, "Well, actually, yes, in a way, Yascha is re—" Helplessly, he petered out.

"What?" Marie asked doubtfully. "You really *are* related to Woody Allen?"

Franz stared at Marie, Marie stared at me, and I scanned the room for a desperately needed drink.

"No, not at all," I finally replied. "I guess what Franz meant to say is that I'm Jewish."

Marie gasped. "Oh, how exciting. A real Jew!"

Franz, in the meanwhile, set about telling me in painstaking detail how great a work of art *Deconstructing Harry* is.

Marie and Franz are extreme cases. Most Germans were better at hiding their embarrassment. Their displays of enthusiasm were more subtly conspicuous. Even so, in the many years I've spent in Germany, experiences that resembled the one I had with Marie and Franz were depressingly common.

Considering the circumstances, the awkwardness between Jews and Gentiles should not be surprising. It was probably inevitable that Germany's sudden love for the Jews would be too abstract, too cerebral, too ideological.

Until 1990 there were fewer than thirty thousand Jews in the Federal Republic. By comparison, the population as a whole stood near 60 million. Each Jew had to be shared out among two thousand Gentiles. From the very start, the German crush on Jews lacked for a real-life object.

A growing number of Germans, in search of an outlet for their newfound love, responded by frequenting one of the small Jewish communities, seeking to convert to Judaism. Others searched high and low until they proudly procured a Jewish spouse, or friend, or at least an acquaintance. Numbers being what they were, even this solution remained restricted to a small minority. On the whole, the love affair between Germans and Jews remained unconsummated, leaving all parties with a keen feeling of frustration.

In lieu of a real love affair, all things Jewish suddenly became fashionable. Some would-be philo-Semites turned to political activism against right-wing extremists, or to the support of Israel. Others partook in a guilt-ridden renaissance of every last aspect of Jewish culture. Community colleges started offering Hebrew classes. Literary events included the recitation of a few choice poems in Yiddish. Gallery openings featured a small ensemble of blond and blue-eyed Germans playing klezmer music.

Some turned to history. Spurred by their painful rediscovery of the Third Reich, they roamed into the more distant past to reconstruct a happier age of Jewish life in Germany. Many writers and artists—some because of their opposition to National Socialism, others merely because of their Jewish roots—had been relegated to oblivion for well-nigh four decades. Now they became hyperfashionable. Finally, there were large exhibitions of painters like Marc Chagall, George Grosz, Otto Dix, Wassily Kandinsky, and Ernst Ludwig Kirchner, all of whose work the Nazis had banned as "degenerate art." Jewish writers like Heinrich Heine, Else Lasker-Schüler, Stefan Zweig, and Lion Feuchtwanger were read more widely than ever before.

For many Germans, the renewed interest in these long neglected cultural treasures seemed to add a further bitterness to the tragedy of the gas chambers. Not only had they incurred terrible guilt toward the Jews by acting so barbarously, philo-Semites now argued. Worse, Germans themselves turned out to rank among the losers. Hadn't there once been a golden era of German cultural life, an era to which the contributions of Jews had been absolutely central? And wasn't the possibility of this cross-fertilization now irretrievably lost?

In the new mood—certain aspects of which persist until today—lamentations for the dead of the Holocaust were routinely accompanied by lamentations for the violent end of the "German-Jewish symbiosis."

—

A lot of this was easy talk, of course. It's not just that the idea of a golden age of German-Jewish relations obscures the fact that anti-Semitism had existed long before the Third Reich; it's also that, both at the individual and at the collective level, Germany's fashionable philo-Semitism often ranges from self-congratulatory to self-interested.

And yet, at least at times, Germans did follow up words with real action.

Perhaps the most important instance of a willingness to go the extra mile to help Jews came in the waning days of the Eastern bloc. Many Russian Jews had mixed feelings about the radical changes that were happening in the Soviet Union. Most of them had grown to hate the Soviet Union and the many forms of discrimination and humiliation the regime had long visited upon the country's Jews. But as the regime collapsed, they also looked on with fear as nationalists exploited the general crumbling of order to engage in increasingly virulent anti-Semitic attacks.

When the Berlin Wall fell, a small number of Soviet Jews began to look to East Germany as a temporary safe haven and an eventual stepping-stone to the West. This suited the East German government very well. Elected in March of 1990, in the only free elections the disingenuously named German Democratic Republic ever witnessed, they were in an odd position: popularly elected, but now leading an imploding dictatorship for the sole purpose of subsuming it into the Federal Republic of Germany as swiftly as possible. The government of Prime Minister Lothar de Maizière did not have many opportunities to distinguish itself; one of the few was to invite any Soviet Jews who feared for their safety to come to Germany.

With German unity officially achieved on October 3, 1990, the interior ministers of the sixteen German *Bundesländer*, or federal states, had the awkward task of deciding whether to rescind this invitation so generously issued in the dying days of the GDR. Since they recognized that doing so would hardly have made for an auspicious beginning to the immigration policy of a newly united Germany, on January 9, 1991, they found a permanent solution: Jews from the crumbling Eastern bloc would be allowed to come to Germany as so-called *Kontingentflüchtlinge*, a special legal category designed to facilitate the immigration of specific groups during times of humanitarian crisis. (Previously, it had, for example, been used to allow Vietnamese boat people to come to Germany.)

This category gave Soviet Jews some important privileges that ordinary asylum seekers, like my grandfather Leon, had never enjoyed: when they first arrived in Germany, they were granted housing subsidies, a somewhat larger monthly welfare check, and a free language course. But they were also excluded from the significantly more generous benefits, such as the very quick path to citizenship, which were offered to those immigrants from the former Soviet Union who claimed to be ethnically German.

Over the next fifteen years, as Russia descended into economic and political chaos, a large number of Jews decided to come to Germany: including their spouses and children, 219,604 of them arrived as *Kontingentflüchtlinge*. (Over the same time period, 2 million *Volksdeutsche*, or ethnic Germans, arrived in the Federal Republic.)

As a result, there are now many more Jews in Germany than there had been for most of the postwar era. Between 1989 and today, membership in Jewish communities grew from around 30,000 to just over 100,000. Since some Jews remain unaffiliated with any of the official Jewish organizations in the country, the real number of ethnic Jews living in Germany today is probably higher still.

So, while it is tempting to mock the more absurd manifestations of the fad for philo-Semitism, Germany's changed view of the past did have some very real effects. It helped persuade the country to open its doors to Jews from the Soviet Union—and it even convinced tens of thousands of Jews from around the world that reunified Germany might be the right place to settle for the future.

(Whether it actually allowed the growing number of German Jews to feel at home in their new country, or even to succeed there, is, of course, another question. Though they are highly educated—and though their children are doing rather well—most Soviet Jews have found it surprisingly difficult to integrate into mainstream German society. An estimated 70 to 75 percent of them were university graduates. But German bureaucrats rarely accepted their qualifications. German employers expected them to speak the language without an accent. The old-boy networks and family connections that help many Germans find their jobs remained closed to them. As a result, a recent study found that about 40 percent of highly qualified Jewish immigrants in Germany are stuck in long-term unemployment; in the United States, the equivalent figure stands at only 3 percent.)

•

For the first part of my childhood, Germany's newfound love for the Jews barely affected me.

In Laupheim, where I first started to think about what it might mean to be Jewish, an older set of attitudes was still more prevalent. Like my classmates at the former Carl-Laemmle-Gymnasium, or those shopkeepers who blithely celebrated the sixtieth anniversaries of their establishments, most people either were, or pretended to be, ignorant about the Jews. A few others, like that drunk singer at the Ulm opera house, were unabashedly anti-Semitic.

Faced with a relatively hostile environment, I became increasingly defiant. I'm not sure that I liked being Jewish. But neither did I want to act as though I were ashamed of the fact.

Since having Jewish ancestors marked me out as alien, or even inferior, I was all the more determined to call myself a Jew.

Feeling increasingly out of place in Laupheim, I longed for us to move to a bigger city where I might be able to pursue my Jewish interests. So I was ecstatic when, in the spring of 1994, Ala told me that we would soon move back to Munich.

Once we'd moved, I joined a Jewish youth club. A little later, I opted to travel halfway across town every Thursday afternoon to take classes in Judaism that were given at another high school. I still wasn't religious; when I turned thirteen, I decided not to have a bar mitzvah. But if my experiences in Laupheim had turned me into a Jew, at least I would now start to learn a little more about what being Jewish actually entailed.

I also had another hope for my move from Laupheim to Munich. In Munich, a city that, to my twelve-year-old self, seemed vast and cosmopolitan, I would no longer stand out as I'd done in provincial Laupheim. Finally, I assumed, I would get to be both a Jew and a German.

Turns out I was mistaken. The obstacles that confronted me in Munich were rather different from the ones to which I'd grown accustomed in Laupheim: not ignorance, but an all too painful awareness of the past; not hostility, but an exaggerated eagerness to please; not anti-Semitism, but rather an insistent form of philo-Semitism. Better obstacles, I suppose, but real obstacles nonetheless.

Sometimes, when I mentioned that I was a Jew, I still looked into blank faces or stared out at clenched teeth. Much more often, I now saw that being Jewish turned me into a kind of celebrity—a fascinating, exotic specimen to be treated with kid gloves.

Gradually, without me even noticing it at first, this led to a funny change within me. While the general ignorance about all things Jewish that still reigned in Laupheim had made me think of myself as a Jew, the awkwardness that now surrounded me made me more cautious about revealing my identity. The kind of stilted relationship I ended up having with most people who found out that I was Jewish was not what I wanted—neither for my friends nor for myself. Better, I decided, to avoid mentioning that I was a Jew at all.

Going out of my way to make sure that the people I knew wouldn't find out I was Jewish was a solution of sorts. If I wished to, I could easily pass as a Gentile. But even as this self-imposed silence made me fit in externally, in my own mind it alienated me further from what should have felt like my own country.

Back in Laupheim, when my problem had been general ignorance and occasional hostility, I could at least be defiant about the whole thing. There was something vaguely noble in mentioning that I was a Jew and dealing with the consequences, knowing full well that they were likely to be negative. To go out of my way to avoid mentioning that I'm a Jew just because I wanted to avoid embarrassed silences and stilted compliments, by contrast, didn't feel noble in the least. I began to feel like a cheat or a fake: somebody who changes who they are in order to try and fit in.

Up until I moved to Munich, I had never laid particular store in being German. But neither had I doubted that, at some level, I in fact was. Once I'd be old enough to surround myself with a more "enlightened" set, I assumed, all of the things that had made me an outsider would disappear.

Now my encounters with the most enlightened of philo-Semites—encounters that were much like my later experience with Franz and Marie—changed that. It slowly dawned on me that, despite (or perhaps *because of*) their obsessive political correctness, these philo-Semites saw me as a Jew first and a German second. With every passing day, I now became more aware of being a Jew—albeit one who preferred to keep his true identity a secret. At the same time, I also grew more and more doubtful that I could ever be a German.

•

My growing sense that being "Jewish" and being "German" were somehow incompatible was hardly unique. Like me, for example, Ala never quite came to feel at home in Germany.

Outwardly, Germany has, for the past forty years, been the center of Ala's life. In all these years, Ala has had many German colleagues, acquaintances, and friends. While Ala still has a tiny trace of an accent when she speaks German, she now undoubtedly knows Germany's culture and literature better than that of Poland, her original home country.

Even so, Ala has never felt that she belonged. Through all these years, she—at least in her own mind—was never quite part of the club: not quite a fully paid-up member of the circles she moved in, and certainly not a part of the German nation, either. While outwardly she has prospered in Germany, somehow that wasn't enough to make her feel that the country whose passport she carries is indeed "hers."

For a long time, I simply put Ala's inability to feel at home in Germany down to her character. Though she is warm and exuberant toward her family and close friends, she refuses to play nice with those she dislikes. At times, her intransigence runs the danger of making her overly mistrustful of strangers. But the more I read about other German Jews who have been successful in Germany, the more Ala's predicament seems to me to be emblematic of the unbridgeable gulf that, despite the country's evident good intentions, still divides Jews from Gentiles.

Peter Zadek, for example, was perhaps the best-known theater director of Germany's postwar period. Born in Berlin in May 1926, he fled with his family to Britain in the summer of 1933. Zadek first returned to Germany in 1958 and soon made a mark as one of the most innovative and experimental directors there.

In the 1960s, Zadek first provoked a scandal with a production of *The Merchant of Venice* in which Shylock, the Jew, was portrayed as unabashedly evil. (This was at the same theater in Ulm where, some three decades later, my mother would become chief conductor.) Though he himself is Jewish, Zadek was immediately accused of anti-Semitism. In response, he claimed that "so long as Germans refuse to say anything negative about Jews they have not begun to engage with their own anti-Semitism."

Toward the end of his stellar career, Zadek's assessment of German-Jewish relations had hardly improved. In one of the last interviews before his death, carried out in May 2009, he was still uncomfortable about philo-Semitism—going so far as to question the real reasons for his own success:

> Philo-Semites are really something very German. They only see you as a victim. And I never felt as though I was a victim. In fact, this philo-Semitism was so extreme that I was never sure why theater directors gave me work. Did they just want me because I was a Jew?

Another good example for the internal contradictions felt even by the most successful and assimilated of German Jews was Marcel Reich-Ranicki, the recently deceased literary critic who survived the Warsaw Ghetto and moved to Germany in 1958.

In his autobiography, Reich-Ranicki wrote that when he first arrived there, he did not think that his being a Jew made him an outsider. He simply assumed, for instance, that he was a full member of the influential literary circle Gruppe 47, to whose annual conventions he was always invited. And though he found it strange that none of the newspapers or magazines for which he regularly wrote offered him a staff position, he just assumed that this, too, had some innocuous explanation.

But in his last years, Reich-Ranicki grew much more pessimistic about his life as a German Jew.

Hans Werner Richter, the head of Gruppe 47, confirmed decades later that the critic "somehow always remained an outsider," one who "said 'we,' as a matter of course, as though he already belonged to us, even though nobody had given him a right to that." In retrospect, Reich-Ranicki, though he insisted that Richter was by no means an anti-Semite, found an explanation for his exclusion in the fact that he was Jewish: "Even forty years after the end of World War II, Richter's attitude toward Jews remained self-conscious and inhibited."

Similarly, in 1996, *Die Zeit*, Germany's most important weekly, published a large tome to celebrate its fiftieth anniversary. In the 1960s, Reich-Ranicki had been a regular contributor; only now did he learn, to his surprise, that editors had had extensive discussions about whether to offer him a staff position at the time. But in the end, he read, they had decided against it because they thought they might not be able to tolerate as their colleague a person who was so *"rabulistisch."*

Rabulistisch, as Reich-Ranicki pointed out, is a strange word. Referring to an overly argumentative or opinionated person, it is virtually extinct in today's German. "But it could frequently be found in the rabble-rousing press of the National Socialists, especially in articles by Joseph Goebbels. Virtually always, he used this term as a noun, accompanying it with an adjective—for example, he would say 'Jewish *Rabulistik*' or 'Jewish-Marxist *Rabulistik*.'" In light of this news, Reich-Ranicki now conceded, he was no longer so sure as to the true reasons for his exclusion from a staff position at *Die Zeit*.

Is all of this true? Was Zadek really given work in German theaters because he was a Jew, while Reich-Ranicki was excluded from Gruppe 47 and *Die Zeit* for the very same reason?

I don't know. Nor is it important to me. The tragic fact is not what did or did not go on in the head of some newspaper executive or theater manager when he was making decisions about whom to hire. The tragic fact is that, toward the end of their lives, Zadek and Reich-Ranicki, two of the most distinguished Jews who had made their lives in postwar Germany, were still tormented by such questions.

Neither Zadek nor Reich-Ranicki lacked for success, ego, or

self-confidence. Yet, like Ala, they were unable to overcome two seemingly opposite fears. On the one hand, they worried that they were never fully included in the German establishment because they were Jewish. On the other hand, they feared that their successes might partially have been owed to their being Jewish.

An air of paradox hovers over this double anxiety. But, in point of fact, it is not nearly as paradoxical as it may appear. In a certain manner, both fears are caused by the same phenomenon: the philo-Semitism of good intentions. It is this misguided philo-Semitism that explains why even successful Jews are deeply self-conscious about the role they play in German society, just as it is this misguided philo-Semitism that helps to explain why they won't ever fully feel at home there.

SIX

Failed Friendships

"Yascha? That's a Jewish name, isn't it?" Markus asked me as soon as I met him, back in the fall of 2003. Though I never answered his question, and though Markus never dared to ask me again, he seemed strangely keen to befriend me—so much so that, over time, I increasingly had a hunch that something about him was a little off.

"I hate being German," Markus once said to me, out of the blue. Another time he produced a theatrical sigh, and then exclaimed: "We carry such a historical burden. I think of it every day!"

Even so, I didn't realize the extent to which Markus was obsessed with my being Jewish until, one morning, he greeted me with "*Chag sameach!*" in perfect Hebrew pronunciation.

"Happy holiday to you, too," I replied. "But, honestly, I don't even know what festival we have today."

"The most important one. *Yom Kippur.* The Day of Atonement."

"How do you know that?"

"I learned about all the holidays for my bar mitzvah."

"Your bar mitzvah? I didn't realize you're Jewish!"

"Well, I'm not really. Or rather, not anymore. I was for a few years, though. You see, when I was thirteen, I saw a documentary about the Holocaust. It devastated me. I felt so ashamed. I didn't know what I could do. So I converted to Judaism."

"But now you're not religious anymore?"

"I guess I just realized that it had all been a mistake."

"Because you never believed in God?"

"No, because I still feel guilty."

I suppose I could have chalked up my encounter with Markus as yet another in a long litany of personal experiences with philo-Semitism. After all, at some level at least, the awkwardness between us had the same roots (his good intentions) and the same timbre (our mutual neuroses) as that between me, Franz, and Marie.

And yet I found that there was something even more disturbing about my encounter with Markus. For all of the silliness between Franz, Marie, and me, I could still imagine the three of us being friends. But Markus, somehow, was a step too far. If he was so obsessed with my being a Jew, was there any sense at all in which he actually found me good company? Worse still, if his philo-Semitism was so extreme, might he not have continued to be friends with me even if I'd started to behave badly toward him, or others?

As my mind raced from question to question, I instinctively knew that I couldn't bring myself to continue being friends with Markus. I politely took my leave and never saw him again.

Until today, I often think back on our short, failed friendship. The reason, I think, is that ever since my encounter with Markus another hunch took hold in me: Could an obsession with the past mislead somebody like Markus into committing terrible acts for the best of reasons?

•

When I met Markus, I had just graduated from Trinity College, Cambridge, and was back in Munich working as an assistant director at the city's Kammerspiele theater. When I'd accepted the position, about half a year earlier, I was sure that I wanted to become a theater director; within a few months, I realized that I hated my job. Increasingly miserable, I started to cast about for an exit plan.

One day during that time, I picked up *History as Making Sense of the Senseless*, a book written by Theodor Lessing during the darkest hours of the First World War. It was a very strange book, full of overblown rhetoric. But it was intriguing. Its main message, so far as I could make out, was that history is written by the victors. Human life, Lessing argued, consists of senseless slaughter—and it is the slaughterers who get to say what happened, retroactively justifying their cruel exploits. The stories of the vanquished, meanwhile, are generally forgotten.

In my pessimistic mood, that struck me as an interesting thought. I decided to read a little more of Lessing.

It quickly turned out that Lessing was all the rage in Germany. New editions of his works were flooding the book market. Historians and literary scholars were publishing new works about Lessing in droves. Unanimously, they hailed him as an important, unjustly neglected voice.

Hannover, his native city, had just renamed a public square, a big foundation, and a community college in Lessing's name. The student union of Hannover's university was campaigning to rename their institution Theodor Lessing Universität. *Unsere Besten*, a popular television show that was looking for "the greatest German who had ever lived," even listed Theodor Lessing as one of the candidates—along with philosophers like Immanuel Kant and Friedrich Nietzsche.

Lessing's biography, I quickly realized, was just as interesting as his recent revival. He had been born into an assimilated, upper-middle-class Jewish household in the central German city of Hannover on February 8, 1872. Though Lessing had grand philosophical ambitions, he never managed to establish himself as a respected academic. Rather, it was thanks to a short opinion piece he published in a local newspaper in 1925 that he found a place in the history of the Weimar Republic.

At the time, General Paul von Hindenburg—who, as the head of the army, had exercised quasi-dictatorial power over Germany during World War I—was campaigning to become president of the Weimar Republic. In his article, Lessing fiercely criticized Hindenburg. Hindenburg, he claimed, seemed like a harmless "zero" in his old age. But, Lessing continued, he was especially dangerous to democracy because his political incompetence might open the way for a future "Nero." (Lessing's somber prediction was to prove right. Hindenburg was elected, and indeed it was this senile nobody who, on January 30, 1933, sealed the fate of the first German democracy when he appointed Hitler as *Reichskanzler.*)

In the combustible political atmosphere of the Weimar Republic, Lessing's irreverent treatment of a war hero like Hindenburg provoked violent protests. Lessing received graphic threats and was dismissed from his teaching job. The ensuing scandal instilled such intense enmity against Lessing among Germany's extreme right that, once in power, the Nazis marked him for death.

On August 30, 1933, two assassins duly murdered Lessing in the Czech town of Marienbad. A few days later, at the Nuremberg Party Conference, Joseph Goebbels, Hitler's propaganda minister, triumphantly announced that he had "cast off that yoke."

I found all of this gripping. When some cursory research confirmed that very little had been written about Lessing in English so far, I came to a decision. At the end of the theater season, I would quit my job and go back to the university, where I'd write a master's thesis on Lessing.

As soon as I returned to Cambridge to try to make sense of Lessing's work and intellectual development, the problems started. When I read all of Lessing's books, I quickly realized that they contained pages upon pages of peculiar—even sinister—rants. The following example, taken from the 1927 edition of *Europe and Asia*, is just one of many distasteful sets of policy prescriptions I forced myself to wade through (read it at your own peril):

> *Conscious control of all births on earth.* Breeding of all that has been born to achieve the highest fulfillment of all its inherent possibilities. A conscious ideal, which should be realized in the fabric and the body of human beings. Breaking with history; breaking with nature— as realms of the alogical, merely coincidental.—Much rather: socialization to closer and closest commune in the interest of both practicality and life. Women's freedom. *Support of all sectarian aristocracies* as a counterbalance to Europe's future conscious socialization. Support of all particularism and self-government. Finally: *conscious annihilation of all irremediably diseased, rotten, criminal, parasitical existences; be it by means of killing them, be it by means of castrating them. Laws governing marriages.* Breeding of ever higher intellectual needs and ever deeper refinement of the soul. *Struggle against capital and the worshipping of Mammon in every, yes really every practically realizable form.*

Weeks passed, and still I failed to make sense of Lessing's politics. That was worrying enough. But when I turned to Lessing's philosophical musings, I became utterly helpless: they seemed even more incoherent to me than his political writings. All of this led me into a deep crisis. Clearly, I thought, I wasn't clever or well-read enough to understand the method behind the madness.

I was just about to give up on my master's thesis when a strange thought hit me. What if I had been right all along? What if all those scholars and politicians who had sung Lessing's praises were so desperate to atone for the sins of their country's past that they didn't realize to what extent Lessing, who had been murdered because of the Nazis' racism, was himself a racist?

In a rush of excitement, I reread some key passages. Lo and behold, I realized that his works, once you cut through their opacity and their brazen self-contradictions, had precious little substance. Lessing's philosophy, I now realized, was just an arbitrary hodge-podge of early-twentieth-century philosophical fads, from vitalist philosophy to social Darwinism. His politics, meanwhile, were deeply troubling. Lessing may have disliked the Nazis, but he did not seem to like democracy any better. And, yes, it was suddenly blindingly obvious that he flirted with eugenicist, racist, and even anti-Semitic positions throughout his writings.

Even as late as 1933, I discovered, Lessing wrote that the National Socialists were right to "announce to the world the well-known teachings about the improvement of peoples and the breeding of a nobler race. These are my own teachings. I have laid them down again and again in many works." As Thomas Mann noted in his diaries, "by and large, Lessing shared his ideology with his murderers."

My master's thesis thus morphed from an appreciation into a takedown of Lessing. But if my primary concern on the page was with rectifying the strange scholarly literature on someone I now considered a second-rate philosophical hack, off the page I was grappling with a set of questions I thought much more interesting. How could so many careful, intelligent scholars have gone so wrong in their assessment of Lessing? Why, if they were so concerned with anti-Semitism, did they end up glossing over—come to think of it, "hushing up" might be the more appropriate term—Lessing's own anti-Semitism?

Luckily, once I started to look for evidence of what motivated these German scholars, it was staring me right in the face. Regarding the negative assessments of Lessing by his contemporaries, for example, Rainer Marwedel, the best-respected modern German authority on Lessing, wrote that "the history of his public reputation is, above all else, to be understood as the history of his

persecution, which has continued throughout the secondary literature virtually without fail." Marwedel considered it his task to
right these wrongs. As he frankly states, his goal was "to reconstruct the life of a Jewish philosopher and to remind us of recent
German history."

I can't blame Marwedel and his comrades-in-arms. It is no
surprise that a seemingly prophetic Jewish philosopher, one
whose assassination Goebbels himself had loudly bragged about,
should have come to the attention of scholars intent on atoning
for the sins of their nation's past. Even so, it is striking just how
uncritical the resulting praise of Lessing turned out to be. In the
changed intellectual climate, anti-Semitic passages in Lessing's
work were ignored or deemed inoffensive simply because he was
of Jewish descent himself. As a result, a whole coterie of philo-
Semitic scholars turned themselves into cheerleaders for a body
of work that could hardly have been more at odds with their own
earnest ideals.

Germany's sudden love of Lessing has its funny side, of course.
But the misunderstandings that made the ascent of a Jewish racist
to a German cultural hero possible also indicate that something
more serious is amiss. The case of Lessing shows how transfixed
philo-Semites can become by their noble political goals. In the
end, they literally risk being so busy with self-congratulatory activism that they erect monuments to racists and anti-Semites.

Lessing's hagiographers thus made me even more wary of the
Markuses of the world. Why should I indulge people who want to
be my friends for purely notional reasons—but who, if only it
helped them feel better about their country, would just as happily
hang out with a Jewish racist?

•

As I read more about recent history, I came to realize that, outside
academia, a rather similar impulse to draw lessons from Auschwitz

at whatever price can have much more pernicious consequences. The slow descent of the leading members of Germany's 1968 student movement into violence and terrorism is perhaps the most extreme example.

The leaders of 1968 were obsessed by the thought that their parents had been Nazis. In a sense, this might have been liberating: What better excuse to rebel against authority and make their country anew? But, as Hans Kundnani convincingly argues in *Utopia or Auschwitz: Germany's 1968 Generation and the Holocaust*, by and large the leaders of the student movement were unnerved by this knowledge.

They were their parents' flesh and blood. If their parents, apparently normal people, had committed such terrible crimes, then how could they themselves be sure that the same genes would not propel them to the same actions? Worse, if the seemingly civilized Weimar Republic had given way to the barbarism of the Third Reich, who was to guarantee that the Federal Republic—which, after all, had its own share of obvious shortcomings—would not degenerate into similar violence?

A misguided application of the views of the so-called Frankfurt School further exacerbated this worry. Even before World War II, Max Horkheimer and Theodor Adorno had argued that fascism was a necessary consequence of capitalism's internal laws of motion. Fascist regimes, including the Third Reich, should be understood as examples of what they termed "state capitalism." Following this view, any capitalist system suffers from internal contradictions that would ordinarily lead it toward economic collapse. The only way for it to avoid such a collapse is to employ ever-escalating forms of state coercion.

Far-left students in Frankfurt and Berlin now appropriated this theory to highlight similarities between the Third Reich and the Federal Republic. In their eyes, both were instances of "state capitalism": both were repressive regimes that relied on the manipulation of a conformist population molded by the mass media and "the culture industry." These similarities didn't just show how far the Federal Republic was from being a genuine democracy; worse still, they seemed to augur a disastrous future. What little freedom was left in the Federal Republic, activists grew convinced, would soon fall prey to the dictates of economic necessity.

For the 68ers, in short, the Federal Republic was merely a fascist state adorned by a democratic fig leaf. This idea, which soon started to obsess the most radical leaders of the student movement, was a potent justification for rebellion against the state. Activists could dispense with democratic scruples, such as worries about whether it was legitimate to impose their views on the rest of the population. After all, in challenging the present order they were resisting a slide back to full-scale Hitlerism.

The parallel to the Third Reich also implied that passive resistance wouldn't be enough. Their parents had meekly claimed that, far from being convinced Nazis, they had merely been following orders. Now, if they themselves failed to act decisively, wouldn't the leaders of the student movement become just as guilty as their parents had been?

Together, they took these responses to Germany's past to justify revolutionary violence—and, ultimately, terrorism.

From 1969 onward, most student rebels saw Brandt's far-reaching social reforms and conciliatory foreign policy as an indication that the Federal Republic was not irremediably fascist after all. They continued to emphasize the real and persisting continuities with the Third Reich, but grew convinced that these could be done away with through social activism and democratic reform. A peaceful left-wing youth movement helped reelect Brandt with a record share of the vote in 1973.

But a minority of the 68ers, including many of the movement's original leaders, remained unconvinced. They insisted on seeing the Federal Republic as just one more instantiation of state capitalism—perhaps not quite as ferocious as the Third Reich, but the same kind of beast nevertheless.

The hard core of the protest movement quickly became isolated from the mainstream of left-wing opinion. And as it grew increasingly isolated, it also grew increasingly radical.

Take the case of Ulrike Meinhof. A well-known journalist in the 1960s, Meinhof wrote eloquent tracts against the Vietnam War and against the many old Nazis who had made new careers for themselves in postwar Germany. During the first mass protests, she supported the students, but from afar. When Germany's tabloids waged an inflammatory war of words against the 68ers— a media campaign that contributed to the shooting of student leader Rudi Dutschke—Meinhof became increasingly vocal as the movement's public defender. But then the revolutionary fervor of 1968 began to fade, and with it the violent opposition it had engendered. Even so, Meinhof remained convinced that the Federal Republic was about to degenerate into fascism. Increasingly paranoid, she joined like-minded veterans of the student movement who, feeling similarly besieged, had founded what they took to be an antifascist urban guerilla movement: the Red Army Faction (RAF).

Meinhof's turn to violence, then, took place not despite the 1968 movement's obsession with Germany's past but because of it. As the RAF unleashed a brutal campaign of far-left terrorism on the Federal Republic, it continued to justify its actions with a simple slogan: "Never Again Auschwitz!"

The 68ers' habit of invoking the fascist past for their immediate purposes had been visible even in the first days of the student movement, when protesters in Berlin compared Shah Pahlavi to the SS. But it gathered momentum in the following months, as the form of the "continuity thesis" advocated by the RAF became more and more divorced from reality.

The student leaders had started from the correct observation that there were some deeply troubling continuities between the Third Reich and the Federal Republic. In the next step, some had jumped to the altogether erroneous conclusion that this rendered the two systems morally equivalent. Now the conclusions they were willing to draw grew even more abstruse.

Ulrike Meinhof, for example, had initially been genuinely shocked by the Holocaust. According to Reich-Ranicki, whom she interviewed in the mid-1960s, when she was still a little-known journalist, Meinhof was the first person he met in West Germany who really wanted to know what he had experienced in the Warsaw Ghetto. But in the 1970s, Meinhof started to see the whole world through the monochrome filter of fascism. She now spoke of Auschwitz and the Allied bombings of German cities like Hamburg and Dresden in one breath—both were fascist and, by implication, morally equivalent. Paradoxically, Meinhof's obsessions with the Third Reich quickly led her to trivialize the Holocaust.

Eventually, the violent fringes of the 1968 movement would go so far as to invoke the name of Auschwitz to justify lethal attacks on Jews. Identifying fascism with capitalism, capitalism with the Federal Republic, the Federal Republic with the United States, the United States with Israel, and Israel with all Jews, they soon came to think of Jews as the true fascists.

On November 10, 1969, one day after a commemoration of the Kristallnacht pogroms, a ticking bomb was discovered in the Jewish community center in Berlin. As Wolfgang Kraushaar, a German historian, has argued in a painstaking reconstruction of the events, it is virtually certain that 68ers had planned the attack. But, far from self-identifying as Nazis, the bombers saw their intended victims as the true fascists. As they announced in a leaflet titled "Shalom + Napalm":

On the 31st anniversary of the fascist Kristallnacht a number of Jewish monuments were besmeared . . . A firebomb was placed in the Jewish community center. Neither action should be defamed as an instance of right-wing excess. Rather, both are crucial links for international socialist solidarity. The previous intransigence and theoretical paralysis of the left when dealing with the Middle East conflict is a product of its consciousness of German guilt . . . But the true form of antifascism is clear and simple solidarity with the militant Palestinian resistance fighters . . . Every official commemoration in West Berlin and West Germany reminds us that the Kristallnacht of 1938 is daily repeated in occupied territories, in refugee camps and in Israeli prisons. The Jews, driven out by fascism, have themselves become fascists. In collaboration with American capital, they seek to rub out the Palestinian people.

This perverse logic remained unchanged even as the attacks it justified grew increasingly bloody. A month later, a bomb placed in the vicinity of the Berlin offices of the Israeli airline El Al was discovered just in time. An attack on a Jewish kindergarten never progressed beyond the planning stage.

Then, on February 13, 1970, at about 9:00 p.m., unknown perpetrators set fire to a Jewish old peoples' home in Munich. For over two hours, firefighters failed to get it under control. When they finally managed to enter the heavily damaged building, seven inhabitants were found dead. Each and every single one of them had survived the Holocaust in concentration camps. Their murderers were never caught. But circumstantial evidence suggests that these survivors of Dachau or Buchenwald or Auschwitz found their death at the hands of German "antifascists."

(The old people's home where they died had been located at Reichenbachstraße 27, in the heart of Munich. When my mother accepted a position as a conductor in the nearby Gärtnerplatz-theater a few years before I was born, she found an apartment on the very same street, at 25 Reichenbachstraße, just one house down. It was here, only a few steps away from one of the worst anti-Semitic attacks to have taken place in Germany since 1945, that I was to spend the first years of my life.)

As left-wing terrorists cast Jews as their capitalist enemies, they started to see Palestinians, their enemy's enemies, as their allies. At the 1972 Olympic Games, in Munich, Palestinian terrorists captured eleven members of the Israeli team. The German police botched an attempt to liberate them. All were killed. As the RAF made clear, it supported the attack: "Israel is shedding crocodile tears. It sent its sportsmen to their slaughter just as the Nazis did with the Jews—as fuel for an Imperialist policy of extermination."

The radical left's hostility to Israel finally found its macabre culmination on an airfield in Africa. Acting in concert with a Palestinian terrorist group, on June 27, 1976, a group calling itself the "Revolutionary Cells" hijacked an Air France plane on its way from Tel Aviv to Athens and Paris. The plane, carrying 260 passengers and crew, was rerouted to Entebbe, Uganda. Once there, Gentile passengers were allowed to leave; only the eighty-five Jews onboard had to stay. It was Wilfried Böse, a member of another far-left German terrorist group, who volunteered to separate the Jewish passengers from the Aryan ones.

As Böse went about his despicable task of spotting Jews, one hostage, a concentration-camp survivor, indignantly bared the registration number tattooed on his arm. Wasn't Böse taking on the same role as the SS camp guards who separated those who would be allowed to live from those destined for the gas chambers?

Böse denied any parallel. "I am no Nazi," he declared. "I am an idealist!"

To be sure, far-left anti-Semites were a minority within the student movement. Even pro-Palestinian leftists like Joschka Fischer, who would later become Germany's foreign secretary, eventually overcame all sympathy for the RAF and similar organizations—in part as a result of their horror at Böse's 1976 sorting of Jews and non-Jews.

Nonetheless, the bitter truth still holds: since 1945, the Germans who have committed the most radical attacks on Jews were not right-wing radicals; they were self-described left-wing idealists who understood themselves to be enacting the lessons of Auschwitz.

The 1968 generation was genuinely haunted by Auschwitz. It forced at least some discussion of the Third Reich onto an unwilling public. And yet, to a surprising extent, it was precisely this generation's obsession with Germany's past that led its erstwhile leaders astray.

This implies a troubling conclusion: perhaps it wasn't a coincidence that it was people like Meinhof, who had at first looked on the past more honestly than others, who ended up seeing Auschwitz everywhere. Perhaps it was the very horror they felt at their parents' deeds, coupled with their paranoia that they themselves might secretly be just like them, that made it so tempting for them to blame the Jews.

On this view, the RAF's inversion of the roles of victim and perpetrator was not just the logical consequence of a dubious ideological starting point; it was a kind of psychological coping mechanism. Henryk Broder, a controversial (and, especially in his views on Muslim immigrants, at times loathsome) German-Jewish journalist, explained the underlying logic lucidly:

> And so you alleviate your anguish by transposing the dispute that you never dared have with your parents onto your parents' victims. It works. The Jews are the Nazis, the Palestinians are the victims of the Jews, and your parents have nothing to do with any of it . . . You can look them in the face once more, for now you know where to

find those Nazis that, after all, have never existed here in Germany.

Before I'd ever heard of 1776, 1789, or 1989, I already knew all about 1968. That was natural enough, for the 1968 revolution in Germany had democratized the country, given rights to the oppressed, and dispelled the long shadow of a terrible dictatorship. This, at any rate, is how things looked to me when I was growing up—so much so that, as a teenager, I even had the vague feeling that I'd been born in the wrong decade.

My overly positive view of 1968 was naïve. But if I was naïve, then so were the people—many of them intelligent and admirable—who had instilled these views in me: my mother's artist friends; some of my high school teachers; many a newspaper columnist.

The reasons why an overly positive view of 1968 was so dear to all of us are intertwined with our view of German history. Anyone who wants to see contemporary Germany as safe from the contamination of the Third Reich is tempted to look for a clear moment of rupture. For German conservatives, that moment came at "zero hour," the collapse of the Third Reich in 1945. But, given the obvious imperfections of postwar Germany, this had always been unacceptable to the German left, and even more so to German Jews. The idyllic version of 1968 thus came to fill this gap. It became a more radical version of zero hour—a cathartic moment of national renewal that dealt with the past so well as to make possible a pristine future.

That's why, even today, the story about the redemptive heroism of a whole generation of "good Germans" remains so seductive. But if the 1968 generation's obsession with the past led many of its protagonists into dangerous delusions, then our idealization of 1968 is mostly wrong. Far from making the country anew in its own image, these "good Germans" who were desperate to atone for the sins of their country's past were themselves shaped by all the contradictions of postwar Germany. 1968 was no more the hour of national rebirth than 1945.

•

On the whole, Germany's transformation during the 1960s, '70s, and '80s was an impressive accomplishment.

In public life, the prevailing atmosphere changed from silence about the past to an ideologically self-conscious desire to face up to the Nazi era. A thorough reevaluation of the Third Reich helped change Germans' political attitudes toward the present as well as the past. By gaining a better understanding of the evils of fascism, Germans became more determined to overcome what Gustav Heinemann had called the "authoritarian state"; they also became more convinced of the benefits of a society based on human rights and the rule of law. This educative process has been crucial in making Germany the consolidated democracy it is today.

As Germans' conception of their own past changed, so did their attitude toward Jews. A well-nigh callous lack of sympathy for Jews was replaced by widespread philo-Semitism. This, too, was in some ways a positive development: Jews now felt more welcome in Germany; in the wake of the Soviet Union's collapse, tens of thousands of them even decided that Germany could be a good place to settle.

Nonetheless, these changes have also created their own problems. Good intentions toward Jews abounded in 1968, and to some degree they still abound today. All of the good intentions in the world, however, will never be enough to create a clean break between the present and the past.

That is in part because, as my interaction with Markus once again reminded me, it is hard to feel at home among people who treat you with demonstrative, overbearing friendliness. Kid gloves, no less than hostile remarks, render a genuine rapport unattainable. Philo-Semitism, not just anti-Semitism, can erect an invisible wall between Jews and Gentiles—with good intentions for brick and mortar.

PART III

Ding Dong, the Jews Are Gone

He never did anything to me, it's true, but I once played a most shameless, nasty trick on him, and the moment I did it, I immediately hated him for it.

—Fyodor Dostoyevsky, *The Brothers Karamazov*

And it is the Jew who is guilty because he makes us guilty, for he is here. Had he stayed where he came from, or had they gassed him, I could sleep better today. They forgot to gas him. This is no joke, that's what I think, deep inside of me.

—Rainer Werner Fassbinder, *Garbage, the City, and Death*

SEVEN

The Closed Season Ends

I'd been planning my exit for three-quarters of an hour. I was prepared. As soon as the bell rang, I stormed out of the classroom.

A friend waved hello in the hallway, but I flew past her, down four long flights of stairs. The younger kids, whose classrooms were on the ground floor, thronged the exit. I'd expected that. I pushed, shoved, and elbowed my way through the crowd of smaller bodies until, finally, I was clear of them all, free to run the half-mile or so that separated me from the tram stop, and from safety.

Only as I ran through the market, past busty saleswomen pushing their wares in broad Bavarian accents, did I realize that I didn't know just why I was in such a panic. Sure, Daniel, a good year older and a large head taller than me, was a scary guy. But when he'd tried to beat me up just a month before, I'd remained much calmer.

And, yes, sure, I hated the idea of losing my long hair. But wasn't it better to lose my hair than to be beaten up?

Yet, somehow, stubbornly—for reasons that seemed at once momentous and incomprehensible—what he was threatening to do this time seemed far worse.

"Here you are," Daniel said when I reached the tram stop, proudly displaying the forced nonchalance of an aspiring tough guy who's watched one too many mafia movies. "We were just starting to get impatient."

Of course. Naïve as I was, I thought that I could get a head start on them by running away as soon as school was out. But Daniel's crew had skipped class, probably sneaked a few beers in the park, and now here they were, all leisurely, waiting for me to rush into their arms.

Daniel gestured for Adrian and Philip to pin me down. I tried to run a few steps, more to save face than because I thought I could actually get away. The two of them quickly subdued me. Then Daniel got out an electric razor, switching it to the highest setting as though he were revving a motorcycle engine.

"You've been lording it over us for too long," Daniel told me.

This came as a genuine surprise.

"I . . . what?"

He smiled. "You know what I'm talking about. Jews are always telling us what to do. Ever since Auschwitz. Even my dad"—his face turned momentarily sour—"is in love with you people. But that's all over now. We'll show you who's in charge all right."

At long last I understood what had put me in such a panic. I was only thirteen years old, and didn't yet know all that much about Auschwitz. But I did know that the Nazis had shaved the heads of everyone they'd deported. Judging from Daniel's face, he knew, too.

This made me incredibly angry, perhaps the angriest I'd ever been. I flailed and punched and kicked. Somehow, miraculously, I managed to hit Adrian in the balls. He shrunk together in pain, Philip looked up in surprise, and I took off.

When, still running as fast as my short legs would carry me, I finally looked around, Adrian was lying on the ground. Daniel and Philip were laughing hysterically. I couldn't tell whether they were savoring Adrian's pain, or my humiliation, or both.

There is never an end to history. Even as many ordinary Germans accepted the need for an earnest and ongoing engagement with the past, others were chipping away at the new consensus. The more their compatriots talked about the darkest chapters of Germany's history, or engaged in the philo-Semitic fads that had been so prevalent in the 1980s, the more a new generation of Germans came to resent the idea that they should be ashamed of the country's past.

Their resentment rarely manifests itself as violently as Daniel's determination to reenact the history of the camps at a Munich tram stop. Nor is it always as crude as the joke that Stephanie was to tell me at the Oktoberfest a few years later.

And yet, in a way, Daniel and Stephanie did take their cues from those refined intellectuals who argue that it is time to change Germany's relationship to its past. Like them, they are convinced that Jews have been given special treatment for too long. Like them, too, they have concluded that it is high time to draw a "finish line" underneath the country's preoccupation with the Third Reich.

•

In January 1984, Chancellor Helmut Kohl traveled to Israel for what, to any German politician, remained the most difficult of state visits. After Willy Brandt, Kohl was only the second German head of government to visit the "Promised Land" while in office. But unlike Brandt, that master at communicating a powerful moral message through simple gestures, Kohl seemed utterly inept at representing his country in these difficult circumstances.

On a visit to Yad Vashem, Israel's main memorial to the Holocaust, Kohl was shown a book containing the names of the then 3 million identified victims of the Nazi extermination machine. By way of a response, he inquired whether the names were arranged in alphabetical order. His wife, Hannelore, meanwhile, was curious whether computers had been used in assembling the list.

Explicit references to Germany's past seemed to make Kohl particularly ill at ease. When Yad Vashem's deputy director gave his party a tour of the museum, Kohl interrupted him with visible impatience: "I know German history very well. That was another era, another Germany."

Later, when Kohl addressed the Knesset, Israel's Parliament, he opened his speech by emphasizing that his being born in 1930 set him apart from earlier generations of German leaders: "I am speaking to you as somebody who could not come to guilt during the Nazi era due to the grace of late birth."

Relations between Germany and Israel, Kohl argued in his speech, could now be perfectly "normal."

At first, Kohl's visit to Israel was received with disappointment, but not hostility. The provincial Kohl, many observers assumed, had just fallen prey to understandable awkwardness.

In hindsight, though, it is clear that Kohl's apparent missteps were an early indication of his conscious goals. When Kohl had ascended to the chancellorship through a no-confidence vote against Helmut Schmidt, his Social Democratic predecessor, he'd promised a "geistig-moralische Wende," a spiritual and moral turning point. Ostensibly, this slogan was directed against what German conservatives perceived as the excesses and moral corruption of the 68ers; it was a promise to return Germany to the staid respectability of the postwar era. Over the years, however, it became clear that it also hinted at something further: a desire to alter Germany's relationship to its past.

Kohl, in other words, was not incompetent at symbolic politics after all. On the contrary, on his visit to Israel he had deliberately been standoffish to signal that Germans were determined to put their past behind them.

Kohl's next move in this campaign for a "spiritual and moral turning point" came when he visited the United States later that year. At the White House, he persuaded President Ronald Reagan to honor the new friendship between the United States and Germany by visiting a military cemetery in Bitburg during his upcoming trip to Europe. Initially, Reagan appeared to have been under the impression that U.S. military personnel as well as regular German soldiers were buried at Bitburg. But in April of 1985, when the trip was imminent, it became clear that the cemetery contained no American graves at all. It did, however, honor forty-nine SS men.

As soon as news of this broke in the United States, intense opposition to Reagan's proposed visit formed. A majority of congressmen signed a letter of protest. In an unprecedented move, eighty-two U.S. senators voted for a resolution asking the president not to go to Bitburg. But Reagan, feeling that he owed Kohl a favor for his pro-American military policy, decided to stick with his plans.

Reagan visited the Bitburg cemetery on May 5, 1985. For Kohl, it was a big PR coup. Coming just a year after his remarks in Israel, the proceedings at Bitburg were but another step in the chancellor's subtle campaign to trivialize the past in order to emancipate Germany from any special responsibility in the present. By willingly making himself a pawn in Kohl's game, Reagan seemed, to most German observers, to be giving Kohl's project a very public blessing.

In the aftermath of the Bitburg affair, an editorial in *Die Zeit* neatly summed up the backlash that earlier attempts at facing up to the past had clearly brought about: "The demand that is gaining more and more support in West Germany is: Forty years are enough. Nobody wants to be blackmailed with Auschwitz anymore."

•

What better way to stop being blackmailed by Auschwitz than to deny its unique status? Or, better still, to insist that the Nazis' aggression was no more than a response to the threat posed by the Communists—an exaggerated response, to be sure, but one that followed the sporting logic that a good offense is the best defense?

In the 1980s, the most vocal advocates of the "finish line" increasingly adopted this logic. Erich Nolte, then professor of modern history at the Free University in Berlin, published their unofficial manifesto in June of 1986. Camouflaged as an essay about recent trends in German historiography, it amounted to no less than a call for the wholesale revision of the Third Reich's role in Germany's self-understanding.

According to Nolte, a "conspicuous shortcoming" of contemporary scholarship on the Third Reich was that it neglected to what extent the Nazis had copied Bolshevik methods. "With the sole exception of the technical mechanisms used to kill people in the gas chambers," he argued, "everything the National Socialists later did had already been described in copious writings in the early 1920s."

Once historians began to think about the possibility that Nazi violence might have been inspired by fears of comparable acts of Bolshevik brutality, a number of much larger questions about the Third Reich supposedly came to seem "permissible, even unavoidable":

> Did the National Socialists, and did Hitler, perhaps commit an "Asiatic" deed because they regarded themselves as potential or actual victims of an "Asiatic" deed? Was not the "Gulag Archipelago" more foundational than Auschwitz? Did the "class murder" of the Bolsheviks not constitute the logical and factual prior to the "race murder" of the National Socialists?

Such a "causal nexus" between Bolshevik aggression and the National Socialist response, Nolte concluded, is indeed "likely."

—

The degree to which Nolte's questionable interpretation of the past implicitly exculpated the Nazis was striking. But what was perhaps even more striking was the extent to which Nolte was openly guided by contemporary concerns.

Titled "The Past That Won't Go Away," his article's first paragraphs lamented that, unlike the ages of Napoleon or of Augustine, the Holocaust was not "becoming less oppressive" as time went on. In Nolte's mind, a good part of the blame for this lay with those public intellectuals who insisted that Germany should face up to the past; after all, they refused to ask themselves whether the reasons why the past won't go away might not have to do with "the interests of the persecuted and their descendants in safeguarding a permanent status of specialness and privilege."

As a result, Nolte complained, Germans did not adequately stand up for their own interests. The debate about Reagan's visit to the Bitburg cemetery, for example, had not allowed "for the simple question about what it might have meant if, in 1953, the chancellor of the Federal Republic would have refused to visit Arlington National Cemetery on the grounds that it contained the graves of men who had participated in terroristic attacks on German civilians."

To counter such injustices, Nolte concluded, Germany should finally draw a "finish line" underneath generalized criticisms of "'the' Jews," "'the' Russians," or indeed "'the' Germans."

Nolte's article triggered what has come to be known as the *Historikerstreit*: a massive, year-long debate between historians and public intellectuals.

Jürgen Habermas fired the opening salvo with a lengthy critique of what he regarded as an "exculpating trend" in German historiography in general, and Nolte's essay in particular. Left-leaning historians and journalists like Hans Mommsen and Rudolf Augstein built on Habermas's essay to mount a strong case against the growing desire to minimize both the importance and the relevance of the Third Reich.

But if Nolte had many critics, he boasted just as many influential defenders. Klaus Hildebrandt and Joachim Fest were particularly staunch supporters. They claimed that it was Habermas, not Nolte, who was trying to rewrite the past for the purposes of the present.

In retrospect, it is difficult to say what impact this debate might have had on Germans' changing attitudes toward the Holocaust. Most German historians ultimately rejected Nolte's "causal nexus." Despite his intervention, the study of the Third Reich retains a central place in German historiography.

But in some ways it was Nolte who won. The debate he triggered had a real effect on popular views of the Holocaust. His rhetorical strategy has since been replicated thousands of times. Nolte's insistence that the Holocaust wasn't unique has become a standard trope for Germans who resent "being made to feel guilty." They point at anything from war crimes committed by the Red Army to Israel's settlement policies to reach the conclusion that, in the end, Germany's past is no more sinister than that of any other country.

In this sense, they understood Nolte's implicit message perfectly. For, in the end, the *Historikerstreit* wasn't about the complicated question of what, if anything, makes the Holocaust unique; it was about whether it was legitimate for Germans to make facile comparisons between the Holocaust and other crimes to justify their desire to move on from the past.

•

The change of attitudes about the Third Reich embodied by Kohl and Nolte had an immediate impact on relations between Jews and Gentiles. The increasing militancy with which part of the population insisted that "enough is enough" pertained to the treatment of Jews as well as to the role the past should play in the present. If Auschwitz was so long ago that it was simply irrelevant for contemporary Germany, then the nervous taboo against all forms of anti-Semitism could finally be lifted, too. Forty years after Auschwitz, Germans should be allowed to criticize Jews again.

This debate came to a head in the least likely of ways. In 1974, Rainer Werner Fassbinder, the German author and filmmaker, had written a play titled *Garbage, the City, and Death*, an extremely polemical portrayal of a Frankfurt real estate magnate. As the plot unfolds, this one-dimensional character justifies the devastation he wreaks by his lust for "revenge on the little people," celebrates the fact that no German can resist him because he's a Jew, and strangles a prostitute. What shocked critics even more was how candidly Fassbinder's play depicts German anti-Semitism stewing behind an outward veneer of philo-Semitism. In a particularly shocking diatribe, one of the Aryan characters says:

> And it is the Jew who is guilty because he makes us guilty, for he is here. Had he stayed where he came from, or had they gassed him, I could sleep better today. They forgot to gas him. This is no joke, that's what I think, deep inside of me.

Supporters of Fassbinder tried to defend such rants as descriptive, the playwright's attempt to hold up a mirror to society. This is true, up to a point: Fassbinder was describing a mood he considered widespread in society (and largely hidden from public view). But it is not the whole truth. For, unfortunately, anti-Semitic stereotypes are too integral a part of the text for it to be credible that Fassbinder's characters don't, to some extent, speak the feelings of their creator.

The main character, for example, doesn't merely happen to be Jewish; his being Jewish is so central to what he stands for that Fassbinder doesn't even bother giving him a name. He identifies him merely as "The Rich Jew." To make things worse, the real estate magnate portrayed in Fassbinder's play seemed to many readers to represent Ignatz Bubis, a representative of Frankfurt's Jewish community who had become very unpopular with leaders of the 1968 movement when he sought to evict leftist squatters from houses he owned.

All in all, it seems that Fassbinder did not just mean to portray anti-Semitism; his authorial intent was anti-Semitic as well. In the 1970s, commentators in the major national papers were quick to come to the same conclusion. Fassbinder's publisher ceased selling copies of the play. Theaters that had planned to stage *Garbage, the City, and Death* abandoned their plans.

A decade later, in the changed atmosphere of the 1980s, Günther Rühle, the manager of Frankfurt's publicly funded theater, decided that the time was ripe to perform Fassbinder's controversial play. Echoing Kohl's remarks in Israel, he claimed that to allow criticisms of Jews to take the stage would be a step toward "positive normality."

Frankfurt's Jewish community, at the time the largest in the country, saw things differently. On the day of the planned premiere, in October 1985, a thousand Jewish citizens, including my grandfather Leon, picketed the performance—the first Jewish protest of this kind or magnitude in the history of the Federal Republic. Inside the theater, two dozen representatives of Frankfurt's Jewish community went so far as to occupy the stage, unfolding a banner that accused the theater of "state-funded anti-Semitism." The performance had to be canceled.

The clash over Fassbinder's play signaled a much wider change of mood. On the Jewish side, it demonstrated a new willingness to stick out one's neck. Jews in Germany, as I know from my own experience, are always tempted to hide themselves, or at least to hide the fact of their being Jewish. To a small extent, the reason for this might still be an instinctive fear that the German anti-Semitism of old might suddenly bolt back to life.

But, to a much greater extent, the reason why German Jews prefer to remain invisible lies in the myriad complications of today's German-Jewish relationship. We fear that Fassbinder's description, according to which the mere presence of a Jew makes some Germans feel guilty and resentful, might be right. And if that is the case, we conclude, then perhaps it really would be for the best to pretend not to exist.

With the Frankfurt protests, German Jews overcame this self-censorship for one liberating moment. Unfortunate though the whole altercation was, at least it seemed to instill in them the temporary courage to stand up for themselves.

But if the Fassbinder controversy was revelatory about the state of mind of Jews, it was doubly revelatory about the changing attitudes of Germans. Some strikingly open anti-Semitism came to the fore on the opening night—onstage, but also in slurs directed at the Jewish protesters from the auditorium. Then, in the following days, well-known theater critics went so far as to echo Fassbinder's anti-Semitic clichés in print. Peter Iden, for example, wrote in the *Frankfurter Rundschau*, a well-respected national paper, that criticism of Jews should once again be possible in order to expose the "membership of several representatives of Jewish capital in a right-wing power cartel."

Even when they were not quite so infelicitous in their choice of words, many Germans reacted to the scandal with a passive-aggressive insistence that enough is enough. The prevailing sentiment was neatly summarized in a phrase that Rühle, according to multiple witnesses, proclaimed in a public discussion about the play: "The closed season is over!"

This strange expression, which soon came into wide usage, demonstrates how easy it is, in trying to jump out of the frying pan of philo-Semitism, to land in an all-consuming fire. Rühle, a little like Kohl and others, wanted to overcome embarrassment and awkwardness by simply willing it away. His ambition was not necessarily malign: if a sheer act of will could normalize relations between Jews and Gentiles, it would indeed be desirable. But as it turns out, sheer acts of will are often expressions of poor judgment. In the end, the likes of Rühle risk becoming so obsessed with forgetting the past that they think it normal to reopen the hunting season—as if Jews were animals and normality consisted in hunting them.

Such semantic slippage is probably not conscious. But neither can it be a complete coincidence that, in German public discourse about Jews, the metaphors that win out in the end are virtually always all wrong. In the case of the debate about *Garbage, the City, and Death,* it is clear that pent-up frustration about philo-Semitic political correctness had morphed into aggression against Jews, just as Fassbinder's play predicted. The hunting metaphor, conscious or not, indicates just how nasty the desire to draw a finish line can turn.

•

On October 11, 1998, government ministers, party leaders, publishers, journalists, and writers—as well as a few representatives of Germany's growing Jewish community—assembled at the Paulskirche in Frankfurt. A century and a half earlier, during the short-lived liberal revolution of 1848, Germany's first democratically elected parliament had found a temporary home there. Now, the beautiful church in the middle of Frankfurt's old town was to serve as the backdrop for the ceremony to award the prestigious Peace Prize of the German Book Trade to Martin Walser, one of Germany's most respected novelists and public intellectuals.

It was Walser who, after witnessing the Auschwitz trials in the early 1960s, had penned "Our Auschwitz," that important early call for a more serious engagement with the Nazi past. The acceptance speech he now gave concerned a similar topic. The content, however, contrasted sharply with Walser's earlier views:

> A routine of accusation has arisen in the media. At least twenty times have I averted my eyes from the worst footage of concentration camps. No serious person denies Auschwitz; no person of sound mind quibbles about the horror of Auschwitz; but when this past is held up to me every day in the media, I notice that something in me rebels against this perennial presentation of our disgrace. Instead of being grateful for this never-ending presentation of our disgrace, I begin to look away. When I notice something in me rebelling, I try to seek out the motives of those holding up our disgrace, and I am almost happy when I believe I can discover that often the motive is no longer to keep alive the memory or the impermissibility of forgetting, but rather to exploit our disgrace for present purposes . . .
>
> I tremble with my own audacity when I say: Auschwitz is not suited to become a routine threat—a means of intimidation to be deployed at any time—or a moral cudgel, or even a compulsory exercise. All that comes into being through ritualization has the quality of lip service. But what suspicion does one invite when one says that the Germans today are a perfectly normal people, a perfectly ordinary society?

The audience in the Paulskirche listened to Walser in earnest silence. Tension was visibly building in the auditorium. Many agreed with Walser. But could they publicly show their support for such opinions? Finally, upon hearing Walser call Auschwitz a *Moralkeule*, a moral cudgel with which anybody who dares resist the cult of Auschwitz will likely be beaten up, Germany's elite no longer held back. The Gentiles in the audience broke out into enthusiastic applause.

Auschwitz, eine Moralkeule. Auschwitz, a moral baseball bat. It is a strange image: one that conceals as much as it reveals.

What Germany did Walser want to defend against the bat-wielding hordes who supposedly exploit the memory of the Holocaust? Who, in Walser's opinion, is threatening to use this mighty weapon? And against whom?

I don't know. But perhaps a hint can be found in an earlier part of the speech. There, Walser objected to journalists who vividly describe—and condemn—events like those that took place in Rostock in 1992, when thousands of ordinary Germans cheered on neo-Nazis as they set fire to the homes of asylum seekers:

> Inside me an unprovable hunch begins to take hold: those who take the stage with such statements want to hurt us, because they think we deserve it. Probably they want to hurt themselves as well. But us, too. All of us. With one restriction: all Germans. For this much is clear: in no other language could one speak in such a way about an entire people, an entire population, an entire society over the last quarter of the twentieth century. You can only say that about Germans.

For all the studied ambiguity of Walser's speech, then, he made one thing abundantly clear. Ultimately, he considered himself—not the asylum seekers who had feared for their lives in Rostock—a victim. As a German, Walser was being harmed by "those who take the stage with such statements." And, as a victim, he felt entitled to be resentful against those who hold up the past to him every day to serve their own purposes.

Walser was not alone in feeling this way. In the aftermath of his speech, opinion polls revealed that 63 percent of Germans were in favor of "drawing a finish line under discussions about the persecution of Jews." And the wish of many was not restricted to putting an end to Germany's engagement with the past. Like Walser, they also wanted to rebel against the threateningly impersonal force of "those"—Jew, foreigner, or philo-Semitic German—who had held them in subjection for so long.

I have my own, deeply personal memory of the moment when Walser spoke of moral cudgels, lastingly changing Germany's view of itself. Sixteen years old at the time, I was watching the speech live on TV. Sitting next to me in my family's Munich living room was my grandfather Leon.

Leon Gottlieb is a German name—his surname, literally, means "the love of God." When Leon was born in Kolomea, he was a subject of the German-speaking Austro-Hungarian Empire. Even now, in his old age, he still retained an elaborate, slightly antiquated manner of speaking German, and a deep love of German literature.

The few German poems I still know by heart I owe to my grandfather, not to my German schooling. (At about the time of Walser's speech, my literature teacher told Ala at a PTA meeting that studying poetry with children as young as fifteen or sixteen was a waste of time; better for us to learn how to write instruction manuals.)

Leon particularly loved Heinrich Heine. So when, as a seven-year-old, I visited him in Frankfurt for a week, Leon cajoled me, with a lot of love and a few slices of ham, to memorize Heine's touching description of his homecoming to Germany after years of exile in Paris:

> The wind left the trees naked,
> the days leaden and cloudy.

November, mournful month—that's when
I came back to Germany.

And as I reached the border
my heart leapt and leapt
within my breast, harder and harder.
I almost wept.

It was the strangest thing—
and make no mistake—
I thought my heart was bleeding
(and with such pleasure) when I heard them speak.

Heine, an assimilated Jew, was hardly uncritical of Germany. Among other themes, his poem gives a detailed account of the reactionary political mood of the pre-1848 period, when even the short-lived parliament that was soon to assemble in the Pauls-kirche would have seemed unimaginable. And yet, what a touch-ingly melancholic expression of Jewish-German patriotism Heine's lines are, lines that my grandfather—despite the loss of his parents, siblings, and eldest child at the hands of Germans—still held so dear toward the end of his life that he had his grandson commit them to memory.

But as I discreetly studied my beloved Zaza Leon now, sitting in front of the television, I beheld a more bitter variety of melancholy. Stone-faced, he wiped the corner of his eye, even though he hadn't allowed any tears to form.

Reich-Ranicki, in 1970, had looked upon Willy Brandt's gen-uflection in Warsaw as a sign that coming to Germany had been the right decision—a sentiment that my grandfather, by and large, had seemed to share. But now, as I gleaned from Leon's gestures, Walser's resentful, aggressive language, applauded by Germany's assembled establishment, was forcing him to reconsider.

•

Emboldened by Walser, even well-known politicians were soon exploiting the popular clamor for a finish line. In 2002, for example, Jürgen Möllemann—a former vice chancellor of the Federal Republic and a senior player in the FDP, an influential pro-business party—justified Palestinian suicide bombings against Israeli civilians: "What would you do if Germany were occupied? I would also resist, and resist by force. It would then be my mission to defend myself. And I would do it not only in my own land, but also in the country of the aggressor."

Many Germans, Jews and non-Jews alike, criticized Möllemann for his simplistic remarks. In responding to them, Möllemann implied that all criticism of his views were simply attempts to use the past as an instrument against today's Germans. Instead of defending his analogy on its questionable merits, Möllemann shrewdly decided to don the cloak of the renegade hero who would willingly martyr himself for the German nation.

He further assumed this role by singling out, from among the many people who had criticized him, one prominent Jew: Michel Friedman, who was then the vice president of the Central Council of Jews in Germany. Neither his many opaque statements on Jews and Israel, nor even his refusal to clarify them, Möllemann insisted, were anti-Semitic. On the contrary, if anyone was fanning the flames of anti-Semitism, it was German Jews like Friedman: "I fear that hardly anybody feeds the anti-Semitism, which unfortunately exists in Germany and which we must fight against, more than Mr. Sharon [then the Israeli prime minister] and, in Germany, Mr. Friedman with his intolerant, hateful and arrogant manner."

While Möllemann played upon the perversions of the relationship between Germans and Jews for electoral gain, Guido Westerwelle—then the head of the FDP, and later Germany's foreign secretary—tried to convince voters that his was the party of "fun." Westerwelle's conception of fun included, among other embarrassing stunts, a stint on the German version of the "reality" TV show *Big Brother*. But apparently it did not—at least not before the 2002 federal elections—include such un-fun activities as decisively distancing himself from Möllemann's statements.

After the elections, when it was revealed that Möllemann had used illegal donations to mail anti-Semitic fliers to would-be voters, the FDP finally moved to exclude him from their parliamentary grouping; on June 5, 2003, just as the Bundestag was voting to lift his immunity from criminal prosecution, Möllemann, a skydiving enthusiast, allegedly committed suicide by jumping from a plane with a faulty parachute.

The FDP's electoral bid was brilliantly lampooned in a practical joke played on the party by *Titanic*, Germany's foremost satirical magazine. In June 2002, *Titanic's* editorial team painted a van in the FDP's style, donned outfits in the party's nauseating yellow-and-blue color scheme, and took to the main squares of East German towns with preposterous campaign materials in tow. A questionnaire, playing on the widespread assumption that Jews aren't really Germans, read: "Should Friedman be sent back to his home country?" A poster, echoing a Nazi slogan used during the 1933 SA boycott against Jewish businesses, implored: "Germans, Defend Yourselves! Vote FDP!"

An even less subtle poster satirized both Westerwelle's insistence on "fun" and Möllemann's off-color remarks. Accompanied by a picture of a gagged Michel Friedman, the poster echoed the Nazis' term for declaring a town to have been cleansed of Jews: "*FDP—Judenfrei und Spass dabei!*" (FDP—Rid of Jews and Having Fun!).

A few passersby vehemently protested these anti-Semitic posters. Many others, however, seemed pleased that the FDP's electoral pitch was so frank. An elderly woman, for example, happily exclaimed: "That Friedman has to apologize to Mr. Möllemann. The man is one hundred percent in the right. I was alive during that time, I have lived through all of that!"

Another exchange nicely illustrates how attuned average people have become to what I'd like to call "anti-Semitism by insinuation": code words that retain an outward veneer of political correctness, but are understood by everybody who is accustomed to the fine tones of populist resistance as a covert expression of anti-Semitism. Says one woman, in words that subtly invert the role of victim and perpetrator:

> I feel ambivalent about Möllemann. But is he an anti-Semite? I don't think so. Especially if we think about what we've done to the Jews, it is our duty to be critical toward Israel. The Israeli settlements, after all, are like "*Volk ohne Raum*" [the Nazi doctrine according to which the German nation needed to expand its territory]. Möllemann said just that. But Friedman is a really, really evil character. Inhuman!

Adds her sister, picking up on the cue: "No country pays for Hitler like us!"

•

Since the 1980s, the idea that Germans should finally put their past behind them has spread from being the obsession of a small insurrectionary minority to becoming ever more respectable among Germany's establishment. But perhaps the most striking development has been the extent to which even the last bastion of contrite respectability—the German intellectual class that had, just a couple of decades earlier, championed the need for Germans to address their past head on—has now been conquered by the advocates of a finish line.

This is clearly true of a new generation of German academics, writers, and filmmakers who are trying to make a name for themselves by refocusing the national debate on German victimhood.

In the late 1940s, '50s, and early '60s, most Germans thought that the legacy of the war consisted primarily in the suffering it had brought upon their own nation. There were the dead or missing husbands and fathers. There was the immense physical destruction that Allied bombings had wreaked upon German cities, factories, and bridges in the last years of the war. There were, too, the millions of refugees from the lost eastern territories of the Reich who had endured terrible trials and now had to make a new life for themselves far from their ancestral homes. In short, insofar as it revolved around the legacy of World War II at all, the cultural and intellectual life of the early Federal Republic was largely concerned with German victims.

But once Germans started to acknowledge to what extent the war had been the creation of the Third Reich—once they began to grasp at least the basic facts about the enormity of the Holocaust—this started to change. During the era when Germans were keen to atone for the past, German intellectuals were, by and large, less interested in German victims than in Germany's victims.

Now, in the new millennium, the pendulum has swung back again. Perhaps the first great success in this vein, an instant bestseller by the name of *The Fire: The Bombing of Germany, 1940–1945*, came in 2002. In it, author Jörg Friedrich gives a detailed account of the Allied bombing raids during World War II, which claimed half a million victims. Parts of the book are meticulously researched. In principle, it brings an important topic to the attention of a nonspecialist German public for the first time in decades.

The book's flaws, however, are more considerable. Friedrich

says next to nothing about the context of the bombings. That these bombing campaigns occurred at the conclusion of a war that Germany had instigated, for example, is rarely mentioned. Worse, when Friedrich does discuss the larger context, his purpose seems to be to heap extra blame on the Allies. By downplaying or omitting earlier Nazi bombing campaigns like the Blitz, for example, he gives the impression that Nazi planes had never targeted civilians.

Friedrich's language is more problematic still. As many reviewers noted at the time, it isn't just emotional; it seems to be appropriating the language of the Holocaust for itself. Friedrich relabels the Royal Air Force's Bomber Group Number 5 as the "group of mass extermination Nr. 5." The Allies as a whole are said to have pursued a "politics of extermination." The cellars of German buildings are described as "crematoria."

The Fire's huge success set the tone for an increasingly popular genre that, under the rhetoric of finally breaking with oppressive taboos, eschewed analysis and context for emotion and an exclusive focus on German victims. In 2006, ZDF, one of Germany's two public broadcasting corporations, aired a miniseries about the Allied bombing of Dresden. A year later, in 2007, ARD, Germany's other public broadcasting corporation, produced its own miniseries about German suffering. Called *The Escape*, it chronicles the heroic leadership of a noblewoman who helps her charges flee the onslaught of the Red Army, finally leading them to safety in Bavaria. In the years since then, many more books, documentaries, and films on related topics have become popular.

A younger generation of intellectuals, in short, has become willing to talk about the German victims of World War II without feeling the need to put their ancestors' suffering into context. But that isn't all. Many among the old guard—members of the fabled generation that had always been most adamant about the need for a forthright engagement with the country's past—have, toward the end of their careers, appropriated this new mood for themselves.

Martin Walser, who has gone from being one of the first public voices to take seriously the implications of Auschwitz to being the foremost intellectual leader of a movement that wants Germans to forget all about it, is perhaps the most infamous example. The contrast between his early essays on the Holocaust and the callow speech he gave at the Frankfurt award ceremony is stark enough. To add insult to injury, Walser followed that speech up with a roman à clef in which he graphically fantasizes about killing a book critic who bears an obvious resemblance to Marcel Reich-Ranicki; as Frank Schirrmacher, a publisher of the *Frankfurter Allgemeine Zeitung*, put it, the whole point of the novel seems to have been to allow Walser to take pleasure in the thought of killing a Jew.

But even Günter Grass, for decades considered one of the highest moral authorities in the country, has clearly kept step with the transformation of his younger brethren. Like Walser, Grass was born in 1927, making him just old enough for active service in the last years of World War II. Again like Walser, Grass, after the war, became one of the most prominent intellectual supporters of the need for a thorough engagement with Germany's past.

His novels, like the widely acclaimed *Tin Drum*, contributed to this undertaking in important ways: set in the multicultural city of Danzig, it explores the disintegration of the relationship between Germans, Poles, and Jews amid the horrors of World War II. But it was Grass's public voice as much as his literary work that set him up as something of an unofficial national conscience.

Grass spoke out early and eloquently about the horrors of the Third Reich. He supported Willy Brandt's election campaign, defending the proposed reconciliation with Germany's eastern neighbors as morally imperative. In the 1970s, when Hans

Filbinger, then the prime minister of Baden-Württemberg, was discovered to have sentenced deserters to death in the last months of World War II, Grass publicly called on him to resign. Later still, he fiercely criticized Kohl and Reagan's 1985 visit to the graves of forty-nine SS men at Bitburg.

So it is deeply ironic that, as late as 2006—possibly motivated less by an urge to admit the truth than by the fear that a researcher was about to expose him—Grass disclosed that he himself had been a youthful member of the SS.

The news that Grass, Germany's national conscience, had become a member of the SS in November 1944, at age seventeen, shocked the nation. Immediately, an emotional debate broke out about whether or not such a young man could be blamed for being a part of the SS. (The issue was further complicated by an inconclusive historical debate about whether Grass volunteered for the SS or, rather, as he claims, volunteered for active military duty in an ordinary Wehrmacht division and was attached to the SS without his initial knowledge.)

Grass's defenders pointed to the fact that he had been indoctrinated with the murderous ideology of National Socialism for virtually all of his conscious life; in their view, this mitigated, or even eliminated, any moral censure we might otherwise feel entitled to. Grass's opponents, meanwhile, argued that it would be absurd to say that an intelligent seventeen-year-old could claim complete moral exoneration for being a part of the SS, whatever the circumstances.

In light of Grass's genuine achievements and the ardent sincerity of his contributions to a reconciliation with Germany's victims after 1945, most people, including many German Jews, would probably have felt inclined to forgive Grass. They considered his serious moral failings as a teenager a sad reflection on the fallibility of even the most intelligent and empathetic men, not a lasting condemnation of his work or character.

What many found more difficult to forgive, however, was the

fact that Grass had waited over sixty years to acknowledge his youthful misdeeds. Especially considering his public statements about the need for an honest confrontation with Germany's past—reiterated countless times over the span of decades—it was difficult not to be shocked by the fact that, in all these years, Grass had seen fit to keep silent about his own.

Far from making Grass more reluctant to set himself up as a moral authority, the controversy about his long-concealed past only made him more self-righteous. That his past should have come back to haunt him after a lifetime spent fighting the good fight seemed to embitter him beyond measure.

The full extent to which, in his own eyes, Grass remained a morally pure intellectual whose calling it was to sit in judgment of others became evident in the spring of 2012, when he published a highly controversial attack on Israel. Though billed as a poem, in tone and purpose "What Has to Be Said" was much closer to an op-ed. And though it supposedly dealt with the looming conflict between Israel and Iran, its real subjects were the need to leave the past behind and the moral purity of the German nation.

In nine brief, rhymeless, meterless verses, Grass identified an easy culprit for the spiraling tensions in the Middle East. His poem painted Israel as the aggressor. The Jewish state, because it "suspects that it might be within Iran's power to build an atomic bomb," was, according to Grass, threatening to "annihilate the Iranian people." Iran, by contrast, was depicted as the potential victim, a valiant nation suppressed by a mere "loudmouth" (Mahmoud Ahmadinejad).

Many observers would have agreed with Grass's criticism of Israeli foreign policy if he had limited himself to pointing out that the country's hardline government is in danger of overreacting to the Iranian threat. Instead, Grass depicted the conflict in such

Manichean terms, and reversed the presumptive roles of goodie and baddie so completely, that even many of his would-be sympathizers felt repelled. They pointed out that it was by no means so uncertain that Iran will soon be able to build the bomb; that it was Iranian, not Israeli, leaders who routinely talk about "wiping their enemy off the map"; and that an Israeli attack on Iranian nuclear facilities, however morally and politically disastrous it might prove, would hardly "annihilate" the Iranian people.

In the German context, the extent to which Grass seemed to ally himself with those conservatives who want irksome talk of the past to cease once and for all was even more striking than these misrepresentations. In the poem's first line, Grass asks himself: "Why do I remain silent, why have I remained silent for too long?" His answer echoes the widespread populist trope that Germans aren't allowed to speak freely about Jewish topics:

> *The general silence about this fact,*
> *to which I've subordinated my own silence,*
> *is a burdensome lie,*
> *a form of coercion upheld by the threat of punishment,*
> *meted out as soon as it's disobeyed;*
> *the verdict of 'anti-Semitism' is well-known.*

Most striking of all, however, was Grass's insistence on the grave threat that Israel supposedly posed to Germany's moral purity. If Germany should sell another submarine to Israel, Grass worried, it would truly inflict upon the German nation a guilt so extreme that it "could not be extinguished by the usual excuses."

It's difficult to avoid the conclusion that the very same psychological imperative that tempted the most extremist 68ers to paint Jews as the "true Nazis" is at play here. Desperate to leave behind his time in the SS, Grass cleverly manipulates the present until it looks like a neat inversion of the past. Jews are the annihilators;

Germans are the innocents; and it is Grass who rides to the rescue of civilization.

Grass's desire to cast himself as the victim of Nazi-like forces remained evident even after the poem's publication. Most German writers and politicians, including many of those who are generally sympathetic to the idea of a finish line, criticized the poem for being quite so crude. But instead of taking their criticisms to heart, Grass likened the German press to the Third Reich's propaganda machine.

When Hitler took power in January of 1933, he quickly moved to accomplish the so-called *Gleichschaltung*, or "bringing into line," of the public sphere. Similarly, Grass now said, hostility to his poem was owed to a "*Gleichschaltung* of opinion" in contemporary Germany.

It would be difficult to conceive of a more ironic end to the career of an intellectual who had, for so long, personified his generation's rebellion against postwar Germany's trivialization of the past.

EIGHT

Poisoning the Well

In the minds of most Germans, their country finally managed to overcome its complex about the past in the summer of 2006, when it hosted the World Cup for the very first time. All over the country, black, red, and gold, the three colors of the German flag, were everywhere—from house windows to painted faces. Germans, until recently reluctant to display their patriotism in public, had lost many of their longstanding inhibitions.

For the duration of the tournament, the papers talked about little else. German nationalism had returned, and in a much more friendly and cosmopolitan form than most had dared to hope. Germany, everyone was saying, had become a "normal nation." The "finish line," for which Germans had long been so impatient, had finally been drawn.

The trope of a country that has finally become just another normal nation is very appealing. From the Jewish perspective, it promises to overcome the invisible wall that philo-Semitism has erected between Jews and Gentiles. From the German perspective, it finally makes it possible to treat Jews as individuals, rather than as complex-inducing representations of eternal historical guilt. Jews, just as much as Gentiles, would love it if we could establish a normal, complex-free relationship toward each other.

Unfortunately, though, the reality on the ground remains rather more complicated.

To some degree, Germany really has shed its complexes: in itself, the newfound readiness to fly the German flag, for example, is perfectly innocuous. But in most "normal" countries, newspapers don't compete to emphasize just how normal the nation is. Indeed, just as a country's attitude toward itself cannot be normal if its newspapers consider it necessary to proclaim, dissect, champion, and defend that normality in self-conscious editorials, so, too, a sheer act of will does not suffice to free the relationship of Jews and Gentiles from the neuroses that have long plagued it.

All of us, Jews and non-Jews alike, are ready to get behind a banner that demands: NO MORE MARKUS! But this seemingly attractive demand neglects to answer a simple set of questions: Who will stand in his place? Would it really be an improvement to move from Markus's deeply flawed obsession with guilt to Stephanie's ruthless, self-satisfied attack on what she considers the oppressive strictures of political correctness?

However much they, too, might long for normality in their daily lives, most German Jews find it impossible to ignore these questions. In their eyes, Germany remains a deeply ambivalent home. Far from ringing in a new era of normality, the recent agitation for a finish line has served only to make things distinctly less normal for them.

I was reminded of these hard lessons far from "home" when, a few years ago, I joined a private discussion group at an Ivy League university. The group consisted of prominent philosophers and political scientists; a few graduate students had also been invited to attend. Each week, someone would present an informal talk on a topic of particular interest to them. On my first visit, an expert was talking about "black nationalism" and the historical feeling of alienation from mainstream culture among African-Americans in the United States. It was, I imagine, a touchy subject for some of the professors in the predominantly white group, but the discussion, though impassioned, was very congenial.

Late in the evening, when those who knew far more about the topic than I do had already said their bit, I cautiously spoke up. I admitted to knowing little about being black in the United States, especially in the poorer neighborhoods. But, I suggested guardedly, in certain respects my experience as a Jew in Germany might resemble the situation of middle-class African-Americans in predominantly white, self-consciously politically correct circles.

The host of our little group seemed intrigued by my opening, and started asking me questions about my experiences. So I told him about my brief encounter with the German military, as well as about my failed friendship with Markus. Then I recounted a conversation I'd had at Harvard in February of 2008, at the height of the primary battle between Hillary Clinton and Barack Obama.

Cathy, a fellow student in my Ph.D. program, was a passionate Hillary supporter. "Obama just isn't ready," she told a group of us over lunch. "He's only been in the Senate for a few years. He may be a great orator, but does he have Hillary's command of the actual policy issues? Of course he doesn't."

At that point, Mike walked in. When Cathy spotted Mike, who is black, she immediately changed her tune. To be sure, she still insisted that Hillary was the better candidate. But her tone was conspicuously different. Until a minute ago, she, like any political partisan, had thrown punches at her opponent. But now she made sure to laud Obama as much as she could—clearly because she was worried that Mike might somehow get the idea that she disliked Obama for racist reasons.

"You've got to understand," Cathy said, suddenly sounding nervous. "I honestly do think that Barack is an amazing guy. He's so, so smart. Special. Really, he is. I'm definitely in favor of him getting the nomination in 2016. But for now, you see . . ."

Liberal guilt among some white Americans, I told the audience at the discussion group, might not be entirely unlike historical guilt among educated Germans. Despite the innumerable dissimilarities between the situation of Jews and blacks, interactions between liberal whites and African-Americans may at times be rather similar to the interactions between philo-Semitic Germans and Jews.

Even as I was explaining my ideas, I could see, out of the corner of my eye, that Professor Schmidt, a senior professor of philosophy at this prestigious institution, was getting quite upset. Professor Schmidt is German. Unlike most other Germans, Professor Schmidt must have had ample contacts with Jews in his life—after all, he has been living in the United States and teaching philosophy at universities here for well over a decade. Yet now that the conversation had turned to the topic of German Jews, Professor Schmidt seemed visibly uncomfortable. He sweated profusely. His face turned an angry shade of red.

Finally, just as I was about to stop talking, Professor Schmidt cut me off. "The real problem isn't the Germans. The real problem is that German Jews are so thin-skinned. Let me give you an example . . ."

I don't remember the whole of Professor Schmidt's intervention—which might, I suppose, have aired on Fox News, if only he had been talking about the NAACP instead of representatives of German Jews. But the last couple of sentences are etched into my memory:

> Instead of letting debates play out on their own, the Jews always have to make a statement about everything. They may think that they're just defending the interests of Jews. But they only manage to ruin the relationship between Jews and Germans. By being so insolent, it is the Central Council of Jews in Germany that keeps poisoning the well.

Keeps poisoning the well?

For centuries, this sinister phrase had been the instigator of anti-Semitic pogroms. When the Black Death, medically inexplicable until the nineteenth century, ravaged up to a third of the population of Europe, the battle cry went out: "The Jews must have poisoned the well!" and so, to the tragic deaths caused by a virus, a further set of tragic deaths, caused by violence, was added. Why on earth, then, would Professor Schmidt—who surely must have known about the history of the term—invoke this macabre image? Is he, a tenured professor of philosophy at an Ivy League university, deep down an anti-Semite?

I don't think that Professor Schmidt is anti-Semitic. Rather, I think that he was desperately afraid of sounding politically incorrect even as he was arguing against political correctness. God forbid, he must have been thinking, that one of his assembled colleagues, many of whom were Jewish, should mistake him for an anti-Semite . . . So while Professor Schmidt's real indignation about the role that Jews play in German discourse explained his visible anger, his sweat was owed, I imagine, to his fear of the very political correctness he was attacking.

This also helps to explain his last, shocking turn of phrase. As Sigmund Freud argued in *The Psychopathology of Everyday Life*, when people are very worried about breaching a taboo, they take great care to repress any wording that might give them away. But once this immense tension eases—such as at the end of a little lecture or monologue, when they are already congratulating themselves on having avoided all the treacherous pitfalls—the phrases they had consciously been suppressing slip out after all.

Schmidt's Freudian slip doesn't necessarily betray anti-Semitism, then. Rather, it demonstrates the strain that even the most highly educated and cosmopolitan Germans seem to be under when talking about Jews. It only underscores, once again, the fact that normality in conversations between Jews and Gentiles will never come about by a passive-aggressive insistence that "enough is enough."

Professor Schmidt's choice of words didn't do him any favors. But that is no reason to dismiss what he was trying to get at. Perhaps he—and advocates of the finish line more generally—have a point in claiming that it is German Jews who are responsible for making conversations about these kinds of topics so awkward. Might the aggressive backlash against political correctness not, to some degree, be our own fault?

To a limited degree, perhaps, yes. Emboldened by the spread of philo-Semitism, in the 1980s Jews began to play a more assertive role in Germany. The Frankfurt protest against Fassbinder's play was the most visible manifestation of this new confidence. But if ordinary Jews were now less cowed into a nervous silence than they had been in the postwar era, the role of the leadership of German Jews was changing even more drastically.

Earlier chairmen of the Central Council of Jews in Germany, like Heinz Galinski, had seen their role as making nice with the leaders of the Federal Republic even as they tried to put their small communities on a solid financial footing. But with funding more secure and German Jews less isolated internationally, new leaders like Ignatz Bubis grew more confident in their dealings with German politicians. Whereas Werner Nachmann, as late as 1978, had gone so far as to defend Hans Filbinger, Bubis now regularly criticized anti-Semitic and xenophobic statements by well-known public figures.

Given that the leadership of the Central Council of Jews in Germany has become increasingly outspoken over the years, it is little wonder that they have, on occasion, committed errors of judgment. In July 2009, for example, an artist, Ottmar Hörl, decided to combine two quintessentially German things: an obsession with the Nazis and . . . garden gnomes. So he sculpted a golden garden gnome raising his right arm in the Hitler salute. On sale at a private Nuremberg gallery for a mere fifty euros, the work of art was meant to be funny as well as somehow, vaguely, subversive. "Portraying the German 'master race' as garden gnomes," Hörl explained, "was an ironic gesture."

But Arno Hamburger, the head of Nuremberg's small Jewish community, was not amused. "The joke stops here. It is offensive," he told the press, explaining that the gnome betrayed "a complete lack of taste."

It's difficult to see why all this fuss should have been necessary. While the Hitler-saluting garden gnome may not exactly qualify as an important work of art, it is hardly the stuff to inspire far-right violence. Perhaps, then, Professor Schmidt and Martin Walser are right that representatives of German Jews would do well to let debates such as this one play out without insisting, in identity politics' favorite and most vacuous turn of phrase, how "offended" they are by an arguably tasteless, yet ultimately inconsequential, work of art.

Even so, it would be a mistake to conclude that German Jews are usually, or even frequently, hysterical over anything they consider an attack on their special status as victims. In fact, mainstream representatives of Jews in Germany play a moderating role just as often.

In the summer of 2008, for example, Faruk Sen, the director of the Center for Turkish Studies, in Essen, called attention to increasing xenophobia and anti-Turkish discrimination. To make his point more vivid, he called Turks "the new Jews of Europe." Outraged at this purported trivialization of the Holocaust, Armin Laschet—both the responsible government minister and the head of the center's board of overseers—had Sen dismissed.

But, far from attacking Sen in his own right, Stefan Kramer, the secretary general of the Central Council of Jews in Germany, came to his defense. Kramer agreed with Laschet that the comparison was unfortunate. Even so, he suggested that "it is true that ethnically Turkish Muslims in Germany, and indeed all over Europe, daily experience discrimination and exclusion . . . Instead of shooting the messenger, we should all take the fears and feelings of Turkish-origin Muslims and other minorities in our country more seriously." This does not sound to me like the maneuverings of a group self-servingly guarding its own special victim status to monopolize potential benefits for itself.

Pointing to the more active role played by the Central Council of Jews in Germany, Germans now frequently complain that Jews function as a kind of thought police. In point of fact, however, it is very difficult for German Jews to shape what they are perceived as saying, in part because the German media select whose comments they broadcast.

In an earlier era, when the media were mostly interested in exculpating Germans, any Jew willing to laud postwar Germany would quickly be made a media spokesman for all Jews. Today, when the media have realized that Jewish outrage makes for good stories, it is enough for one out of 100,000 Jews to find an event or statement offensive for papers and television stations to run a breathless story about it—never mind the fact that the large majority of German Jews knows perfectly well that nothing scandalous has occurred.

What all this talk about the self-righteousness of Jews thus overlooks is that it is the Germans themselves who obsessively look toward Jews—or foreigners—to play the role of censors. When a racist or anti-Semitic crime takes place in Germany, the mantra-like condemnations by leading politicians are as often about its "adverse effect on international public opinion" as they are about the suffering of the victims themselves. Similarly, when a prominent public figure makes anti-Semitic remarks, the story isn't about the outrageousness of what he said; instead, it ends up being about Jews labeling the remarks outrageous.

A few years ago, for instance, Bernie Ecclestone, head of the racing circuit known as Formula One, gave a bizarre and rambling interview in which he denied that Hitler planned the Holocaust, and expressed his admiration for dictatorships of all kinds. The headlines in the European press simply summarized his

rambling remarks. As *The Times* (London) had it: HITLER? HE
GOT THINGS DONE, SAYS FORMULA ONE CHIEF BERNIE ECCLE-
STONE. The headline in *El País*: ECCLESTONE HOLDS A EULOGY
ON HITLER. Finally, a blog on a leading British paper punned,
simply: FORMULA DUMB.

The headlines of the German papers, by contrast, looked rather
different. Spiegel Online, the biggest German news website, ran
with: JEWISH WORLD CONGRESS CALLS FOR ECCLESTONE TO
RESIGN. *Bild*, a tabloid and Germany's largest-circulation daily,
screamed: CENTRAL COUNCIL OF JEWS ASKS FOR BOYCOTT OF
FORMULA ONE (an exaggeration of their actual position). *Stern*, a
popular newsmagazine, headlined, even more sweepingly: JEWS
ASK FORMULA ONE TEAMS TO BOYCOTT ECCLESTONE. You get the
picture.

In Germany, Jews sell. So does the Holocaust. Magazines love to
run cover stories about Nazis—with striking pictures of Hitler and
other leading members of the regime splashed across the front
page. German television stations frequently air documentaries
about the Third Reich. Bookshops prominently display titles
about the Second World War.

According to Martin Walser and like-minded advocates of the
finish line, Germany's obsession with its own past is inflicted
upon the country from the outside. But if magazines sell particularly well when they put Hitler on the cover, it can hardly be because of the 0.2 percent of the German population that is Jewish.
Who, then, buys all the magazines adorned with Hitler's thrill-
ingly evil visage? And who watches all the documentaries about
the Third Reich's war machine?

The answer is clear enough. For every German Jew who
watches a documentary about the Nazis, there must be, if only for
sheer numbers, two right-wing extremists watching the same program for their own, rather different, purposes. For every guilt-
ridden German who reads *Der Spiegel*'s cover story out of genuine

historical interest, there are probably five who—like millions of people around the world who have made the History Channel such a commercial success—simply enjoy the easy thrill of evil. And for every philo-Semitic intellectual who schedules a serious documentary about the Third Reich out of shame for his nation's past, there are ten ratings-obsessed executives happy to put on a cheaply made, headline-grabbing Nazi extravaganza sure to sell ad space.

Martin Walser, in one respect, is not wrong. The memory of the Holocaust really can be too omnipresent in a society, especially so if most of its manifestations are designed to appeal to the basest and most voyeuristic of human instincts. Walser may even be right that, at this point, in Germany—and probably in many other countries, too—the presence of a *certain kind* of Holocaust-remembrance really is too perennial. But Walser and his followers are, nonetheless, wrong—deeply and dangerously wrong—in their insinuations that the fault for this lies with outsiders who wish to foist a sense of collective guilt on Germans.

A similar point holds true for Germans' broader obsession with modern-day Jews. My experience with Professor Schmidt was, in that regard, typical enough. I wasn't primarily addressing him, let alone setting out to cow him into some kind of submission by mention of my special weapon. All I was doing, some four thousand miles to the west of Germany, was trying to add to the interesting discussion we all were having by drawing on my own experiences. But from Professor Schmidt's perspective, what I was saying sounded like an attack. Fed up with what he perceived as perpetual accusations against the German nation, he wasted no time in mounting his defense—a defense that, as is so often the case, just led to further conflict and acrimony.

It's impossible to predict the future. Perhaps Germany really is on the way toward becoming unreflectively, unself-consciously normal. That would be wonderful.

But, for now, the country's normality is overly demonstrative.

It remains poised to prove itself, in potentially passive-aggressive ways, to anybody who calls it into doubt.

As a result, the new mood of "enough is enough" has, for the time being, only succeeded in adding an extra layer of awkwardness to interactions between Jews and Gentiles. The intentions of advocates of a finish line may have been good; but the consequences of their movement have, so far, proven disappointing.

One of the more counterintuitive effects of the failure of the finish line movement has been to downplay Germany's postwar successes. The impressive process of introspection, atonement, and liberalization that many Germans fought so hard to bring about in the 1970s and '80s is said to have been foisted on the German nation from the outside. Following Walser's lead, most Germans now think that the imperative forever to remember the Holocaust casts Germany in an overly harsh light. After all these years of consolidated democracy and heartfelt torment, they complain, can we never hope for a time when Auschwitz is safely relegated to history books and public memorials?

If we put the question like that, it hardly seems surprising that Walser is asking for a finish line to cordon off the past from the present—and that he has largely succeeded in shaping the self-understanding of a younger generation of Germans. But a realistic view of Germany's postwar history need not lead to so pessimistic a conclusion.

The 68ers who insist that they made Germany anew and the young Germans who clamor for an arbitrary finish line have more in common than they think. Aspiring to purity, both groups are in search of an elusive moment of redemption. They therefore fail to see that Germans might have reason to be proud of the Federal Republic even though it has been shaped—and, yes, to some degree also contaminated—by the legacy of the Third Reich.

The gas chambers are not the only reason why the legacy of the Third Reich might long remain central to Germany's self-conception. Another reason is that the history of the Federal

Republic has, to a considerable degree, been the history of Germany's protracted, often admirable, yet inevitably imperfect, attempt to come to terms with its own past. If Germans were to stop engaging with the Third Reich, they would no longer understand much of Germany's postwar history: not even episodes like 1968, Germany's gradual liberalization, and the national catharsis experienced over the broadcast of *Holocaust*—which, for all their own flaws and limitations, rank among the Federal Republic's most impressive achievements.

But advocates of a "finish line" shy away from a view of history that deals in shades of gray. They want their nation to be resplendent in unblemished white. In thinking that they can be proud of their country only if they block out its failings in a decisive act of self-amnesty, they also forget one of the celebrated insights of Immanuel Kant, Germany's greatest philosopher: "Out of the crooked timber of humanity no straight thing was ever made."

History has certainly not made anything straight out of the crooked timber of the German nation. But that need not be a reason to despair. If the current generation of Germans, instead of seeking to draw an arbitrary finish line, would only learn to be honest about the shades of gray that still mark the German landscape, they would be better able to appreciate their own achievements of the past sixty years.

•

Germany's overattention to—and simultaneous resentment of—Jews puts us in an awkward position.

Even as a kid, I frequently had the sense that I was somehow on show. If the people I met didn't know any other Jews, wouldn't they think that all Jews were like me? And didn't that mean that I had to behave especially well, lest they somehow conclude that all Jews have the same faults as I do?

These fears were of course exaggerated. Yet, even today, I am extremely aware that anything I say will be read as a statement on behalf of the whole group. Before speaking up, I ask myself whether what I say will be read as *my* good or bad opinion, *my* insightful or wrongheaded perspective, *my* self-interested or altruistic political demand—or as an expression of *the* Jewish opinion, or *the* Jewish perspective, or even, simply, *Jewish* self-interest?

Like many German Jews, I was, for a long time, paralyzed by the fear of being cast in any one of these roles. I was loath to criticize any Jew for fear that anti-Semites might quote me approvingly. But I was also loath to criticize Germans for fear that I would be accused of using Auschwitz as a "moral baseball bat." In the end, it often seemed easiest just to shut up.

In Dostoyevsky's *The Brothers Karamazov*, Fyodor Pavlovich has a striking explanation for why he hates one of his neighbors: "He never did anything to me, it's true, but I once played a most shameless, nasty trick on him, and the moment I did it, I immediately hated him for it."

Pavlovich is the more interesting literary character, but, in light of my own experiences, I am just as interested in his neighbor. What should this poor guy, forced to live next door to his erstwhile tormentor, and still treated badly by him for the mere reason that he is an irksome reminder of that ignoble past, do to ease the tension? His very presence makes Pavlovich uncomfortable. But so, presumably, would his demonstrative absence. Mentioning Pavlovich's nasty trick would certainly make things worse. But wouldn't it be just as conspicuous nervously, deliberately to omit it from conversation?

I sometimes feel that German Jews face a similar quandary.

One solution that's open to us is to try to oblige Gentiles as best we can—to promise never again to hark back to the past, and to let bygones be bygones. This strategy is, for example, chosen by Oliver Polak in *Ich darf das, ich bin Jude* (I'm Jewish So I'm Allowed to Do This), a satirical account of his childhood in Germany. Referring to a controversial former leader of the Jewish community attacked by Jürgen Möllemann (the same one whom Möllemann, the one-time vice chancellor of the Federal Republic who jumped to his death after being politically disgraced, had blamed for any anti-Semitism still lingering in Germany), Polak offers his readers a deal at the outset of the book: "I won't mention that Holocaust and you won't mention Michel Friedman."

It's a funny line. But as a prescription for German Jews, it's disastrous. The problem isn't just that Polak jokingly posits an equivalence between the Holocaust and the suffering inflicted on the German nation by one "uppity" Jew. Nor is it that the kind of relationship Polak proposes—one based on willful blindness and anticipatory self-abnegation—is likely to be pretty unsatisfying. The problem, rather, is that the strategy of anticipatory self-abnegation won't work in the first place.

Zvi Rex, an Israeli psychoanalyst, once observed that the Germans will never forgive the Jews for the Holocaust. Though I always found this witticism a little too pat, I fear that it does hint at one important point: to the extent that we Jews are reminders of Germany's national blemishes, we inadvertently—even inevitably— call into question Germany's new self-image as a normal nation. Like Pavlovich's neighbor, we are, by our very presence, perceived as spoilsports.

Realizing that even the promise never to say anything to disturb Germany's precious normality isn't enough to make us fit in, some prominent German Jews are now tempted to make the opposite choice. Since their very presence makes them uncomfortable reminders of the past, they have decided to turn themselves into professional spoilsports.

For figures like Michel Friedman, Henryk Broder, and Maxim Biller, this rebellion was motivated, in good part, by the reticent and somewhat pathetic role Jews had been content to play for much of the Federal Republic's history. As Biller observes in his memoir:

> At the beginning of the eighties, there were only two kinds of Jews in Germany. The Jews who weren't alive anymore, who had fled to Palestine or America, who were written up in encyclopedias. And Jews who were still here, a few invisible businessmen, doctors, and their children, who, every year on the 9th of November [the anniversary of the Kristallnacht], briefly appeared on TV. Huddled together in a small, dark group, they stood in front of a huge menorah or underneath a dramatic slate inscribed with barely legible Hebrew letters. It rained, and it was windy, and then they were blown away, only to reappear in the news for thirty seconds on the next 9th of November.

Like Friedman and Broder, Biller was no longer willing to play this submissive role. Like them, he resolved that he would no longer hold back on talking about all those things that his neighbors would hate to hear about. And so a small, but highly visible, set of German Jews have embarked on careers based on pointing out all the country's failings: embracing the role of spoilsport, they now offer the "Jewish" perspective on scandals big and small.

It would be easy to underestimate how much courage it takes to play the role of public nuisance for a living: in the end, nobody likes to be hated by much of the population of the country in which they live. But, courageous though it might be, this choice, too, ultimately seems like a defeat to me.

Biller's objection to being one of the small, dark, huddled mass of Jews briefly flitting across television screens on the ninth of November had been that he had never chosen the role of victim for himself. But his new role is no more self-determined: in the end, Friedman, Broder, Biller, and friends still play to an audience that is looking to them for "*the* Jewish perspective" on any one issue.

I can see why, given the unhappy choice between playing the invisible Jew and the imperious Jew, they chose the latter option— but, for all that, their primary characteristic remains, quite simply, that of being a Jew.

From my perspective, neither of the two options that are readily available to German Jews seems particularly appealing. I certainly don't want to make a career out of being a nuisance. But neither am I willing to choose Polak's solution and internalize a list of topics about which I had better keep *stumm*.

This has turned out to be the last, and perhaps the most decisive, in a long series of realizations that have made me feel that I am destined to remain an outsider in Germany.

Back in Laupheim, I had considered it my task to be vocal about the fact that I was Jewish, bravely soldiering on when I encountered ignorance or hostility. That did set me apart from other German children. But I still retained the hope that I would, one day, when I could surround myself with more "enlightened" friends, be seen as fully German.

Living in Munich as a teenager, I found the philo-Semitism I encountered just as difficult to deal with. I never asked to be treated differently from anybody else; even so, whenever it emerged that I was a Jew, this simple fact seemed to mark me out for special treatment. I now realized that I would never quite be German. But for all my disappointment, I could still imagine living in Germany: after all, the reasons for which I was made to feel like an outsider seemed merely coincidental, unfortunate, tragicomic.

Only now, encountering people like Daniel and Stephanie, did I start to think that my being Jewish didn't just happen to make me an outsider; it was also a reason to leave Germany.

Nervous philo-Semitism, even ignorant anti-Semitism, was

something I was willing to put up with. But if my very presence made people think that I wanted them to feel guilty—and if they then took that as their cue to rebel against this guilt by lashing out against me—this was not the sort of situation I wanted to put myself in again and again.

I don't want to overstate the effect that the finish line had on my life. There were a lot of factors that went into my decision to study in England, and then in the United States. I was keen to see more of the world. I was lucky enough to be offered admission at some wonderful universities. I might, in short, have left Germany even if I weren't Jewish. Nevertheless, as I decided to leave Germany, thoughts about what it would mean to live there as a Jew were at the front of my mind.

Today, they remain a good part of the reason why I can't really imagine moving back.

PART IV

The Past and Germany's Future

It is true: we have set out on our path, on our German path . . .
This Germany, our Germany, is a self-confident country.

—Gerhard Schröder

To say "Let's have some multiculturalism in our country, and live
our days next to each other, and take pleasure in each other"—that
basic approach has failed, absolutely failed.   —Angela Merkel

NINE

The New German Question

Germany's debate about the past is ultimately about much more than memory politics, or even relations between Jews and Gentiles—it is about the policies Germany should pursue in the present.

Over the last two decades, many Germans have grown hostile to what they consider an unhealthy obsession with the dark chapters of German history. They object when teachers talk too much about the Third Reich, or when TV stations show too many documentaries about the Holocaust. It is time, they say, to draw a finish line underneath the past.

But the real ire of proponents of a finish line derives from the idea that outsiders are using Germany's past to cow contemporary Germany into submission. In their view, Germany has long been so ashamed of its own past that it has failed to assert its national identity and self-interest as strongly as it could—and should—have done.

Germany's foreign policy is said to be especially captive to this misdirected sense of shame about the past. Since the inception of the Federal Republic, many Germans claim, their leaders have been so afraid to be perceived as the "ugly Germans" of yore that they have been far too deferential, both toward their European partners and toward the United States. Now, they conclude, it is high time for Berlin to push its own interest more confidently—even when this comes at the expense of Germany's allies.

Just as other aspects of the finish line movement were propelled by the best of intentions, the motivation for a more assertive foreign policy is also largely benign. It has grown strong not out of some pernicious ultranationalism, but rather out of a sensible desire to overcome what many Germans perceive as the pathologies of the country's long-standing foreign policy tradition. Some (though not all) of these pathologies are real enough. To name but one example, German leaders have long reserved a special place for demonstrative celebrations of *Völkerverständigung*, or an "understanding between peoples." At one point in history, these had a real purpose. In the postwar era, the fact that the German chancellor and the French president could enjoy cordial relations was a breathtaking symbol of Europe's unexpected progress toward peace; during these years, public shows of friendship, like those between Konrad Adenauer and Charles de Gaulle, could still be genuinely inspiring.

But as a younger generation of Germans has become used to vacationing, studying, and even working abroad, these same old rituals have increasingly taken on an artificial, rote quality. Attempts by leaders like Helmut Kohl and Gerhard Schröder to prove that they were even better buddies with their international counterparts than their predecessors had been came to seem hollow at best, and self-indulgent at worst.

The desire to move beyond the artificial niceties of the postwar era is just as understandable in the field of foreign policy, then, as it is in relations between Jews and Gentiles. But, just like that other attempt to draw a finish line, it, too, is now in danger of inspiring strange missteps. In particular, the widespread assumption that Germany has long been too submissive, and should now assert itself without hesitation, is misleading in two crucial respects.

First, it overstates to what degree the policies pursued by the Federal Republic have been shaped by a sense of shame about the past.

Yes, German politicians have long gone out of their way to

demonstrate how friendly they are with other world leaders. And, yes, the Federal Republic has long been a very reliable partner to the United States and its European neighbors. But this is not to say that German foreign-policy elites have, all along, been sacrificing their national self-interest. Demonstrative shows of friendship are, after all, largely costless. Similarly, the notion that the Federal Republic has, since its founding, been overly generous toward its European and American partners misunderstands the actual reasons why the country's foreign policy has long been so cooperative.

At times, German foreign-policy makers really were willing to help out the United States even if this wasn't in their immediate self-interest: their willingness to allow midrange atomic missiles to be stationed in Germany despite widespread domestic opposition is one such example. But the current backlash overlooks the fact that those short-term concessions were made with the knowledge that their allies' help would prove very valuable in the long run. Compared to China or Russia, Germany is a small country with an even smaller military. As became scarily evident during the Berlin Airlift, West Germany desperately needed the help of its American and European partners to have a reliable defense against the expansionist ambitions of the Soviet Union. The perception of being a reliable partner was thus crucial to postwar Germany's security—and, in turn, to its economic success.

It is thus too easy to conclude from the Federal Republic's eagerness to please its allies that its foreign policy has been one of self-inflicted weakness. In truth, its willingness to make short-term sacrifices has, to a considerable degree, been owed to the cold facts of geopolitics; lofty talk of contrition was, as often as not, a convenient way to ornament policies that were necessitated by the realities of the Cold War.

Second, in the same way that many Germans overestimate to what degree their leaders "sold out" the national interest in the past, so are they mistaken as to how best to serve that interest in the present.

Over the last years, German diplomats and politicians, keen to demonstrate that they are no longer so intent on accommodation, have become reluctant to help their international partners. Under Angela Merkel's leadership, for example, the country has refused to participate in the international mission that helped topple Libya's Colonel Muhammar Qaddafi; it has also been rather reluctant to bail out its partners in the euro zone.

Both of these policies are, on the face of them, reasonable approaches. It would be strange to suggest—as did a few misguided German commentators—that the country's past gave it a special obligation to support the Libya mission, or to bail out Greece. But though Germany's past has little to do with whether or not these policies were legitimate, this is not to say that they were sensible. On the contrary: in the end, I fear that they will harm the interests both of Berlin's allies and of Germany itself.

Over the long run, an unwillingness to support its allies will leave Germany less, not more, able to defend its interests on the international stage. Similarly, the fact that many ordinary Germans are adamantly opposed to bailing out their neighbors—even though the costs of the evolving crisis will ultimately be borne by German, as well as Greek and Spanish, businesses—is one of the reasons why a definitive solution to the euro crisis is still not in sight.

In other words, their desire for a definitive finish line isn't just making Germans more insistent on their national interest; it may also be pushing them to a mistaken conception of where that interest actually lies.

(In chapter 10, I argue that a similar dynamic is hardening German attitudes toward immigration. More and more Germans now believe that the country's attitude toward Turkish immigrants has long been too lenient. Convinced that foreigners have not done enough to "integrate" into German society, they are increasingly gung-ho about demanding total assimilation as the price of membership. Sticking to a traditionally ethnic conception of what

makes a true German, they are also increasingly opposed to opening the border for additional immigration.

As I see it, both of these attitudes are likely to harm Germany
over the long run. A refusal to accept that immigrants will retain
somewhat different customs makes civil strife between immigrants and natives more, not less, likely. Similarly, in light of the
fact that Germany's native-born population is rapidly shrinking,
an unwillingness to welcome more immigrants to the country
will harm, not serve, Germany's economic interests.)

•

For half a century, the foreign policy of the Federal Republic has
been characterized by two basic commitments: an aversion to using force, and unwavering support for the country's allies.

At the time of reunification, Margaret Thatcher and François
Mitterrand feared that a strengthened Germany might waver on
these commitments, revert to its former self, and once again pose
a threat to its neighbors. In its most pessimistic rendering, these
fears soon proved to be utterly misplaced: Germany has remained
a largely benign power, with no desire to expand its territory or
take revenge for its defeat in World War II. With the benefit of
hindsight, Thatcher's predictions can safely be called alarmist.

But though the foreign policy of the new Germany has not
changed in the manner feared by the most pessimistic opponents
of German reunification, change it did. In fact, the two key commitments that have oriented the Federal Republic's foreign policy
since its inception have, over the last two decades, both been
thrown overboard.

After World War II, the Federal Republic was constituted as a de-
militarized state. Even when the country raised a standing army
and joined NATO in 1955, its constitution prohibited the country's
armed forces from performing anything other than defensive

operations or assisting allies who had been attacked. Until the fall of the Berlin Wall, the Bundeswehr was never deployed outside the area constituted by EU or NATO countries—neither for wars of choice nor even for peacekeeping missions.

But in the 1990s, a host of factors put pressure on this traditional reluctance to use the Bundeswehr for missions in hostile territory. The most immediate cause was the bloody civil war in Yugoslavia. Looking on helplessly as genocidal massacres like the terrible tragedy at Srebrenica unfolded a few hundred miles from German soil, many politicians began to ask themselves what lessons their country's past held out to them. Was it an intransigent commitment to pacifism? Or was it a willingness to use force to protect the victims of ethnic hatred?

This debate came to a head in the spring of 1999. U.S. president Bill Clinton and U.K. prime minister Tony Blair were calling on NATO countries, including Germany, to use military force to protect Kosovar Albanians against Serbia.

For the German government, the timing could hardly have been worse. Just a few months earlier, federal elections had thrown out long-time chancellor Helmut Kohl and installed in power Gerhard Schröder and Joschka Fischer, two veterans of the 1968 student movement. The governing coalition of Social Democrats and Greens, with its deep roots in the peace movement, now needed to decide whether to break ranks with its NATO allies or to lead the Bundeswehr on its very first military mission in hostile territory.

The decision was particularly difficult for Joschka Fischer, the foreign secretary. Fischer had made his name in the German left as a street fighter, defending leftists who occupied buildings owned by Ignatz Bubis against the police in the Frankfurt of the 1970s. Embracing an ideal of urban guerrilla warfare that bears at least a family resemblance to the tactics of the Red Army Faction, Fischer participated in numerous acts of violence. (To his embarrassment, photographs of him throwing stones at policemen were discovered and published during his tenure as foreign secretary.) He even knew Böse, the "antifascist" who separated Jews from non-Jews at Entebbe.

But for Fischer, whose own support of the Palestinian cause had led him to participate at a PLO conference in 1969, the news of Böse's deplorable actions provoked a remarkable political watershed. He now realized, as he later put it, that "those who emphatically set themselves apart from National Socialism and its crimes had almost compulsively repeated the crimes of the Nazis."

Even after his political transformation, Fischer never dropped his preoccupation with Auschwitz. But he now understood that it was all too easy to draw the wrong lessons from Germany's past. For Fischer, this shift in worldview manifested itself in a reinterpretation of contemporary Germany. Instead of seeing the Federal Republic as standing in direct continuity with the Third Reich, as so many 68ers had done, he increasingly hailed its constitution as an anti-Nazi bulwark.

In the early 1980s, no longer an enemy of the current order, Fischer decided to enter electoral politics. He joined the Green Party, which had only recently emerged from a heterogeneous peace movement, tenuously uniting nationalist anti-Americans, conservative opponents of nuclear energy, and anticapitalist 68ers under the slogan "Never again war!" Within a few years, he was the party's star.

For most rank-and-file members of the Green Party, Germany's history mandated pacifism. Fischer, by contrast, derived from his own understanding of German history an imperative to stop genocide by whatever means necessary. He found it unconscionable to look on from the sidelines as ethnic cleansing was going on in nearby Kosovo. He didn't just learn "Never again war," Fischer told activists at a tense party conference in Bielefeld that had to green-light Germany's participation in the NATO mission. He also learned "Never again Auschwitz."

Yielding to Fischer's rhetoric, an initially hostile Green Party voted for the Kosovo mission. Under his leadership, and in the name of Auschwitz, German planes assisted in bombing Serbia. It was the German army's first offensive mission since World War II. For better or worse, the once absolute taboo against the use of force outside its borders—and, with it, one of the two basic commitments that had shaped German foreign policy throughout the postwar era—had become obsolete.

Fischer's determination to apply the lessons from Auschwitz is only half the story behind Germany's first true military mission since World War II. Gerhard Schröder, Germany's chancellor, was, if anything, an even more adamant champion of the Kosovo bombing campaign. But whereas Fischer championed the Kosovo mission because he thought Auschwitz had continuing relevance for Germany's left, Schröder advocated a more muscular German foreign policy because he wanted to move beyond the left's preoccupation with the past. From his perspective, Kosovo, perhaps even more than a chance to prevent genocide, was an opportunity to show that a reunified Germany would no longer be hampered by neurotic hang-ups about the Third Reich. The Kosovo mission, he hoped, would be a way, "if not to forget, then to fade out" Germany's guilt.

Fischer's focus on the lessons of Auschwitz was one reason why Germany's government decided to intervene in Kosovo. But Schröder's determination that Germany should finally move on from Auschwitz was another, just as important, reason. In the years since 1999, it has been Schröder's, not Fischer's, attitude that has imprinted itself on German foreign policy.

Schröder expressed his determination to free Germany from the remaining postwar strictures regarding its foreign policy even more forcefully in the run-up to the Iraq War. Most Germans sincerely shared the solidarity with the United States expressed by the governing coalition of Social Democrats and Greens in the aftermath of 9/11. Nevertheless, George W. Bush remained, as he always had been throughout Western Europe, deeply unpopular. As for the much-discussed prospect of a U.S. invasion of Iraq, a clear majority of the German population was adamantly opposed to it. Fighting for his political survival at national elections in September 2002, Schröder, a brilliant campaign strategist, decided to make his opposition to any U.S. intervention in Iraq a prime theme of his bid for reelection. His refusal to cooperate with the United States—and, even more so, his promise to vote against a legal authorization for the Iraq mission at the UN—was a clear departure from the previous half century of German foreign policy.

But it was the way Schröder seemed to revel in breaking ranks with the United States, not his sensible opposition to the Iraq War itself, that indicated the true novelty of his stance. On one occasion, Schröder went so far as to call for Germany's "emancipation" from the United States—a statement as striking for the view of recent history it implied as for the future it promised. On another occasion, declaring his outright opposition to the looming war in a fiery campaign speech, Schröder roundly criticized the "American way." In future, he announced, his government would pursue the "German way."

Schröder's ploy worked like a charm. Though most political commentators had already given him up for dead, he narrowly won reelection. And it was clear that his victory had been helped, not hampered, by the aggressive tone he took in dealings with the United States. Evidently, a lot of voters were delighted that Germany was "emancipating" itself from its transatlantic big brother.

The willingness to use force in extreme circumstances hasn't been the only respect in which the Federal Republic's foreign policy has changed over the past two decades, then. An equally important—but less widely noted—transformation has set the Federal Republic free from its second long-standing commitment: its once unwavering partnership with both the United States and its European neighbors.

—

At the time of Schröder's anti-American statements, leaders of Germany's center right, like Angela Merkel and Guido Wester-welle, roundly criticized him for endangering Germany's alliance with the United States. They insisted that, for both historical and strategic reasons, Germany's ability to act in concert with its allies was much more important than electoral considerations. But in the years since they themselves have come to power, it's become evident that they share much with Schröder's approach to foreign policy: like Schröder, they ended up privileging electoral consid-erations over principles; and, again like Schröder, they, too, have been keen to demonstrate that Germany no longer feels the need to support its allies when this would undermine its own short-term interests.

This paradigm shift became apparent in the run-up to the military operation in Libya, in the spring of 2011. Like Schröder before the Iraq War, Merkel and Westerwelle were just weeks away from a tough election when they had to decide whether or not to help stop Colonel Muhammar Qaddafi from massacring rebels—and countless civilians—in the insurgent city of Benghazi.

Visibly running out of ideas, the government of Chancellor Angela Merkel was increasingly fragmented. When a host of un-expected events—from a botched renovation of Stuttgart's main train station to the nuclear accident in Fukushima, Japan—added to the government's general malaise, the Green Party looked set to poach a lot of center-right and independent voters at upcoming elections in Baden-Württemberg. For the very first time, Chris-tian Democrats and the FDP were in danger of losing control of a state they had dominated without interruption for half a century.

That was the last straw. Merkel and Westerwelle realized that, should they make the unpopular decision to send German sol-diers to Libya, they would be even more likely to lose control of Baden-Württemberg. So they refused. In fact, they even went so far as to abstain at the UN when the United States, Britain, and France sought an international mandate for the mission. (As it happened, they lost the election anyway.)

There is an air of paradox here. Both Schröder and Merkel, I argue, no longer wanted to be hamstrung by Germany's past. But while this led Schröder to order German planes to bomb Belgrade, Merkel, supposedly to make the same point, *refused* to order those very planes to Benghazi.

What seems paradoxical at first sight, however, makes perfect sense in light of the twin commitments of Germany's postwar foreign-policy tradition. In participating in the Kosovo campaign, German decision makers broke with the stricture against the Federal Republic's use of force. But since Clinton and Blair had asked Schröder for military backup, the Kosovo mission could also be interpreted as upholding the Federal Republic's other major commitment: a willingness to take painful steps, if necessary, to keep its allies happy.

By the time of the Libya mission, the stricture against the use of force was moot: over the preceding decade, the Bundeswehr had engaged in military or peacekeeping operations in Afghanistan, Bosnia, and Lebanon, among others. But real questions lingered about whether Schröder's distancing from his Western allies would turn out to be a mere aberration. In the wake of his chancellorship, to what degree would German leaders be willing to ignore the wishes of their ostensible allies?

Merkel's refusal to do so much as support France, Britain, and the United States in the UN when they sought authorization for the Libya mission offered a decisive enough answer to that question: it now became clear that, at least at times, she would be just as willing to sacrifice the health of the transatlantic alliance to Germany's short-term interests—or, indeed, to her own electoral advantage. By refusing to say yes to the Libya mission, Merkel effectively buried the last remaining stricture of Germany's postwar foreign policy.

—

This same set of changes may also help to shed light on Merkel's reluctance to do what it takes to resolve the sovereign debt crisis that, even as I write these lines, is still threatening to sink the euro and tear asunder the EU.

Germany is the biggest and economically most successful country of the euro zone. From the start, it was obvious that any long-term solution to the debt crisis would have to be supported by Germany, and draw substantially on German funds. Even so, Merkel—especially in the first years of the crisis—preferred to dither and dodge.

As Greece and then Ireland, Portugal, Spain, and, finally, Italy were pushed to the brink of bankruptcy, Merkel never categorically ruled out emergency funds to stop these countries from defaulting on their debts. But she also refused to push for the decisive steps—like so-called eurobonds, or even a coordinated fiscal policy—that would have been necessary to restore the confidence of the international markets and safeguard the stability of the euro. As a result, since its beginnings in 2008, Merkel has simply been sitting out the spiraling debt crisis—doing just enough at every moment to avert imminent financial Armageddon, while seemingly hoping that the crisis will eventually go away of its own accord.

But that is a dangerous game to play: the patience of the markets might run out at any moment, and once they decide that Spanish or Italian or French sovereign debt is worthless, there may be nothing left for Merkel to do.

Most economists outside Germany have long realized that Germany's reluctance to help its allies solve the euro crisis might, at any moment, turn into a massive own goal. To them, it is obvious that even Germans who have never liked the euro should be able to appreciate how costly its chaotic collapse would inevitably turn out to be. The world economy would slide back into recession. German exports would fall precipitously. German banks, which have large holdings of Greek and Italian assets, would require vast sums from taxpayers to survive. Unemployment and the national deficit would skyrocket.

All of this has made Merkel's lack of action very puzzling to outside observers: if a rescue of the euro is in Germany's overwhelming self-interest, why has the government been so hesitant in taking the necessary steps to bring it about?

By and large, people have answered this important question in one of two ways.

Those who credit Merkel with great foresight argue that she is simply very adept at playing chicken. Since countries like Greece, Portugal, and Italy would prefer not to make painful spending cuts or implement ill-loved structural reforms, any step that takes pressure off their governments is liable to be counterproductive. If Germany promised to keep giving these countries emergency funds no matter what, they would stop making necessary economic reforms. In the long run, the debt crisis would only get worse.

This so-called moral-hazard argument certainly has some truth to it. There are good reasons why Germany should be reluctant to write a blank check. (Ideally, the conditions that Merkel would attach to the payment of emergency funds would require real structural reforms rather than the kinds of spending cuts that, according to economists like Paul Krugman, have only served to deepen Europe's economic crisis.)

The problem with this interpretation, however, is that it explains too little. Germany's refusal to write blank checks may be driven by worries about moral hazard. But if Germany were truly concerned about the fate of its neighbors—or of the euro in general—it could champion any one of a number of institutional reforms or economic policies that do not pose the same risks. To give but one example, countries at the euro zone's periphery would be greatly helped if Germany raised its wages in line with productivity gains; but, intent on safeguarding their competitive advantage, German policymakers refuse to encourage big wage increases.

Since worries about moral hazard can't fully account for Germany's failure to act decisively, some observers have invoked economic history to explain Merkel's course of action. In this view, the shock of hyperinflation in 1923, which destroyed the savings of millions of Germans within a few painful months, has made Germans particularly worried about how stable their currency is. That, it is said, is why the German public is so vehemently opposed to any measures that might increase the money supply and lead to a slight devaluation of their currency.

This explanation has some plausibility, as far as it goes. It is true, for example, that Germans have always been extremely proud of the success of their currency. In part because they don't trust the euro as much as their beloved deutschmark, many ordinary Germans remain much more worried about inflation than voters in neighboring states. Even Ala, who rarely takes the remotest interest in economic policy, has repeatedly asked me whether, like her friends, she, too, should take steps to protect herself against the dangers of hyperinflation.

Like the moral-hazard argument, however, this explanation for Germany's inaction ultimately remains incomplete. It doesn't explain why German economists don't ascribe greater importance to the fact that a cheaper euro would lead to lower production prices, boosting Germany's large export sector. It ignores the fact that, even if a stable currency were the only goal of German economists, they should, at this point, be falling over themselves to prevent a collapse of the euro and the concomitant devaluation of euro assets. Finally, even insofar as it can explain the intransigence of a few leading economists, Germany's historic opposition to inflation can hardly explain how widespread and emotional the animus against any German contribution to the bailout funds has been.

Since the two standard narratives about moral hazard and Germany's long-standing aversion to hyperinflation remain incomplete, we need to add a third explanation. The most plausible candidate, I believe, is the fact that Germany's public discussion about bailouts and eurobonds has to a large extent become yet another way of debating whether the country should draw a finish line underneath the past.

Europe Doesn't Need the Euro, a 2012 bestseller by Thilo Sarrazin, a former member of the board of the Bundesbank, captures—and in turn entrenches—the parameters of this debate very well. (I'll have more to say about Sarrazin in chapter 10.) In his book, Sarrazin argues that Germany was forced to give up the deutschmark as a form of contrition for the past, even though the single European currency has never been in the country's economic interest.

Sarrazin's claims are dubious, to say the least. It is far too simplistic to call the introduction of the euro a form of contrition for the past. France did look toward a common currency to allay fears about how an emboldened Germany might change after reunification. But this doesn't mean that the euro was foisted upon an unwilling Germany. On the contrary, throughout the 1990s, much of the country's political class enthusiastically welcomed the single currency as a step toward a joint European future.

Similarly, while all euro zone countries are suffering from the current instability, many economists believe that Germany has profited substantially from the single currency in the first years of its existence. Blessed with a dynamic export economy that does most of its trade within the euro zone, the country has gained more than any of its neighbors from the greater ease of doing business with them. What's more, it was only because of the introduction of the euro that, over the last decade, production prices in Germany could be kept artificially low even as the easy supply of money on the periphery of the euro zone increased demand for German products.

But these inaccuracies aren't the real problem with Sarrazin's argument. The real problem is that he encourages readers to ask all the wrong questions. His book gives a tendentious answer to a counterfactual question about whether Germany might have been better off if the euro had never been introduced in the first place. But it hardly mentions how disastrous a collapse of the single currency would now be for everybody on the Continent. In this way, Sarrazin actively discourages readers from pondering the much more important question of what course of action is now in Germany's interest.

By adopting this convenient avoidance tactic, Sarrazin and others have transformed the tough and complicated economic choices facing Germany into a simplistic morality play: What do we owe our profligate neighbors in light of our history? Once the question is put like that, it's little wonder that most Germans are happy to answer with a resounding: Nothing! As Otmar Issing, a former member of the board of both the Bundesbank and the European Central Bank (ECB), said in an interview with the German edition of *The Wall Street Journal*: "half a century after the end of World War II, it can't be a matter of blackmailing Germany with its past."

So, if we are looking to explain why Germany has done less to rescue the euro than, according to most economists, is in the country's own interest, the desire to emancipate itself from both its recent and its more distant past has to be a part of the explanation. Yes, the moral-hazard argument and a longstanding aversion to inflation play an important role. But so does the determination of many Germans to stand on their head the supposedly submissive policies that the Federal Republic has pursued for most of the postwar era.

In light of overwhelming evidence about the disasters that would await Germany's economy if the euro collapsed, Merkel eventually became receptive to somewhat more radical solutions to the crisis. Over the course of the last year or two, she has finally given up resistance to such sensible measures as the ECB's program to buy debt from troubled states in the euro zone. At long last, she has also started to push for the kinds of institutional reforms, like a European banking union, that might make the euro sustainable in the long run.

But a lot of damage has already been done. Domestic opinions about the euro crisis have probably hardened beyond reprieve. Once questions about what Germany should do were allowed to turn into a kind of morality play, most Germans became adamantly opposed to helping their supposedly profligate neighbors.

Now, whenever a few Greek protesters suggest that, in light of Germany's history, the country has a special moral obligation to bail them out, the tabloids giddily rile up the public. As *Bild*, Germany's largest daily, put it at one point: "In 1960, Adenauer's government doled out 115 million deutschmarks to indemnify Greek victims of the Nazis and their descendants. 'Once and for all,' as the contract stated."

It is little wonder, then, that a poll taken at the height of discussions about the Greek bailout showed 69 percent of Germans favoring a Greek exit from the euro zone—even though the fallout from a chaotic "Grexit" would have been disastrous for the German economy.

The long-term effects of this hostile attitude toward the "profligate" nations of Europe's South may still be playing themselves out: having unleashed the public's resentment against Germany's supposedly self-abnegating stance, policy makers may, over the next years, find it increasingly difficult to secure public support for necessary steps like further bailouts or large-scale institutional reforms.

Worse still, Merkel's years of dithering have already cost Europe dearly. With every month of German reluctance, hopes for a quick recovery on the Continent receded, and the troubled economies of Southern Europe fell into deeper gloom. The consequences of the Continent's malaise are now coming home to roost: after years of healthy growth, Germany's economic growth slowed to a snail's pace in 2012 and 2013.

•

Some people might think that Germany's new foreign policy should be encouraged. After all, it is, within certain legal and moral limits, entirely legitimate for German national interest to guide German foreign policy. Similarly, it's perfectly understandable that German voters feel bitter that their money will end up paying for the failings of Greek politicians, or indeed that they already share a disproportionate burden for the financing of the EU.

But if public outrage against the imagined tyranny of the past will stop Germany from doing what is in its own, as well as its neighbors', interests, then it is simply self-defeating. It may be unfair that Germans are now forced to spend their hard-earned money to help out Italy and Greece. But that doesn't make it rational for Germany to let the European economy go up in flames.

Similarly, Germany may no longer be under immediate threat from a nearby superpower. Even so, much of what was true throughout the postwar era remains true now: for all its regional dominance, Germany needs the help of its allies to protect its own interests on the world stage. In policy areas ranging from the War on Terror to the rules of international trade, Germany's ability to defend its interests is predicated on its ability to enlist European and American support.

Given the long history of cooperation within NATO, a few instances in which Germany refuses to help out its allies may not have an immediate effect on the alliance's willingness to stand up for Germany in an hour of need. But over the long run, Germany would find itself uncomfortably isolated if Berlin came to be perceived as a free rider who takes the support of its allies for granted and is not willing to give back.

Over the last years, American perceptions of Germany have already started to shift in that direction. John Kornblum, a long-time U.S. ambassador to Germany, for example, has recently written that, over the last decade, Berlin "followed its own instincts with little apparent concern for European, let alone Atlantic, unity." The story of Berlin's recent foreign policy has, he argues, been one "of increasing egoism whenever its national interests are concerned."

At a time when American politicians are assigning less and less importance to the transatlantic partnership, this kind of judgment should set off real alarm bells in Berlin. Earlier generations of U.S. foreign-policy makers had come into their own at a time when America's first line of defense against the Soviet Union ran right through the heart of Berlin. For Henry Kissinger, and even Madeleine Albright, the importance of cooperation with Western Europe was as much a question of geopolitical necessity as of personal biography or fellow feeling.

The orthodoxy that Europe mattered enjoyed a nice afterglow in Washington even in the wake of 1989. Today, in the age of the "Pacific pivot," this afterglow is fast dimming. Increasingly focused on security challenges in the Middle East and the need to manage China's rise, a new generation of U.S. foreign-policy makers will be willing to help Europe with its problems only if Europeans are reliably willing and capable of helping the United States in turn.

Paradoxically, then, Germany's determination to overcome its supposedly submissive past now poses a serious danger for the future success not only of Germany's allies, but of Germany itself. Everyone agrees that it is legitimate for Merkel to stand up for her country's interests. But right now many Germans are so caught up in an emotional overreaction to the past that they are in serious danger of failing to recognize where their own interests lie in the long run.

TEN

The Rebellion Against Pluralism

"You're in luck. As it happens, I do still have two movers available for tomorrow," a friendly voice who identified herself as Frau Schuster told me when I called the Federal Agency for Work, in Karlsruhe. "They're students, you know. Very nice students."

Delighted to have found somebody to help me move on such short notice, I couldn't have cared less about their day job. "Sure, whatever . . ."

"There is just one, um, problem," the woman at the other end of the line said. "These students, they are . . . They're awfully nice, really."

"Well, that's good then."

"Yes, but . . . I'd rather ask you now whether you mind that they are black."

"Black?" The connection was good, but I was sure I must have misheard.

"Yes. Africans, as a matter of fact. Here to study, you see."

"And?" I went, not getting her point.

"Well," the woman said, "if you do have a strong preference against Africans, I suppose I could go ahead and check whether some white movers might not be available."

"What? No! I'm just . . . I can't believe you're even asking me this!"

The friendliness of the voice on the other end of the line was imperturbable. "Oh, how nice of you. So you really don't mind about the movers being black?"

"I told you. I don't."

"So we're all set then. When and where?"

"Ten a.m., I guess. Sophienstraße 21. But . . . why on earth do you ask people whether they mind if their movers are black?"

"I see what you mean. I don't like asking about it myself, to tell you the truth. But our black movers have had some bad experiences with previous customers. So we thought, you know, better check in advance whether the black ones are welcome!"

The woman I spoke to on the phone—a state employee, no less—wasn't racist. She seemed mildly displeased when she thought I might object to my movers being black and mildly pleased when she realized that I didn't object to them after all. For all I know, the rationale behind her agency's policy may even have been perfectly well-meaning: it must be horrific to arrive at somebody's house to help them move their stuff for a modest wage, only to realize that your employers are hostile—or assume you would try to steal their things—just because you're black. As long as their economic shortfall from avowed racists wasn't too big, I suppose that, in a way, the arrangement spared these students a fair bit of trauma.

And yet, the policy of the state agency is surely unacceptable. It doesn't just acknowledge the existence of racism; it actively tolerates race-based work discrimination. Worse still, it gives a stamp of official approval to refusing somebody a job for no better reason than the color of their skin.

In the United States, the existence of an equivalent policy by a public agency would delight the producers of twenty-four-hour news channels: quite rightly, they would devote a good deal of airtime to discussing such an outrage. In Germany, by contrast, academic articles proving the persistence of job discrimination against minorities get, at best, a few lines in the back pages of the more serious-minded newspapers; practices like the one employed by the Federal Agency for Work in Karlsruhe don't get any media attention at all.

The discriminatory practices at Karlsruhe, then, are a function of a broader set of attitudes toward people who aren't ethnically German. In fact, while ordinary Germans now have a multifaceted, contradictory attitude toward Jews, many of them express hostility against other kinds of immigrants and foreigners with breathtaking frankness.

In primary school, I remember, our teachers made us play a version of "What's the Time, Mr. Wolf?" that they unapologetically called "Who's Afraid of the Black Man?" When I played soccer as a teenager, my teammates, after matches, would order a thirst-quenching mix of beer and Coke known to them simply as *"der Neger,"* or "the Negro." Most ubiquitous of all were jokes directed at the 3 million German residents of Turkish extraction. "What do you say to a Turk in a suit and tie?" my high school English teacher asked us. "Two Big Macs and a Coke," a bored student, who had clearly heard the joke many times before, replied.

This kind of open hostility helps to explain why so few immigrants fully assimilate into German society. But the difficulty that immigrants experience in becoming German, as well as the reason why so many Germans are hostile to immigrants in the first place, is intertwined with yet another problematic legacy from the past: Germany's thoroughly ethnic conception of who is a German.

Germans don't just think of Jews as foreigners; for many of them, anybody who doesn't look like a German, or doesn't descend from a German, is a foreigner—even if they, their parents, and even their grandparents were born here. My friend Alessandra, for example, has one German and one Brazilian parent. She grew up in Germany and, naturally, speaks without an accent. Even so, strangers often tell her, in evident surprise: "You speak such good German!"

Similarly, many Germans instinctively consider second- and even third-generation Germans of Turkish extraction to be foreigners. If you look Turkish and have a Turkish name, you're a Turk—even if you were born in Berlin, have taken German citizenship, are well-integrated into German society, and don't speak a word of your ancestors' language.

Cem Özdemir, the most famous and successful German politician of foreign extraction, is a particularly striking example of this sort of attitude. Born to Turkish parents in Germany's southwest, he speaks perfect German, colored only by the local accent of his native Swabia. Yet there are, he says, many "who feel that somebody who is called Cem Özdemir cannot be a German." On campaign appearances, Özdemir is frequently told that he should "run for parliament in Ankara."

Thinking back to my own childhood, I am shocked to recall to what extent most Germans thought of Turks, including even the children of the children of immigrants, as foreigners. But what shocks me even more is how little contact I, like many middle-class people of my generation, had with Turkish immigrants and their descendants.

The German educational system divides children into three different streams when they are only ten years old. Officially, the purpose is to prepare the top third (who are presumed to have the greatest intellectual potential) for university, the middle third for skilled white-collar work, and the bottom third for manual and technical jobs.

In reality such an early selection mechanism merely ensures that those children who hail from better-educated households and wealthier backgrounds get a vast head start. Talented children who didn't start out with the same advantages simply don't have enough time to catch up to their more privileged peers. To make things worse, multiple studies have shown that, when making decisions about children with the same level of academic performance, teachers are far more likely to recommend that those from wealthy—or "German"—backgrounds be admitted to the top schools. (In my own experience, I would estimate that my classmates were, with few exceptions, recruited from the top 30 percent of the socioeconomic spectrum and the top 70 percent of the talent pool.)

As the children of the so-called guest workers are among the least privileged segments of society, one result of the system is that, for most of them, any hopes they might have harbored of attending college are all but dashed by age nine or ten. Another effect, of course, is that those who attend the top-tier schools— and go on to replenish the ranks of the country's politicians, journalists, artists, and businessmen—will hardly know any immigrant children.

This was certainly true for me. Over eighteen years of living in a country where 4 percent of the population now has Turkish roots, I encountered many of them when riding the subway or buying a late-night kebab. But after age nine I rarely encountered them as peers. In the five *Gymnasien* (or, upper-tier middle and high schools) I attended, in my social life, even in my numerous extracurricular activities, I met, as best I can remember, a grand total of three Turks. One of them, it soon turned out, wasn't even a descendant of guest workers but rather the son of architects from Istanbul who had recently moved to Munich for a prestigious assignment.

According to an (obviously unrepresentative) straw poll among my German friends, my experience was not atypical. None of the middle-class Germans I asked had Turkish friends in high school. Among those who now live in the United States or the U.K., most have had closer relations with people of Turkish extraction since they've moved abroad than they had in their teenage years.

It may be tempting to assume that these problems are owed, in good part, to the fact that Germany has little experience with immigration. But the opposite is closer to being true. In absolute terms, few countries in the world have experienced as much immigration as Germany in the last half century.

Why, then, do so many Germans still have trouble accepting that people of foreign descent might truly be part of the German nation?

Part of the explanation, I think, lies in the fact that, despite overwhelming evidence to the contrary, German politicians have until very recently pretended that their homeland wasn't a "country of immigration." When the German *Wirtschaftswunder*, or "economic miracle," came into full swing in the late 1950s and early 1960s, German industry found itself in desperate need of cheap, low-skilled labor. To general acclaim, the Federal Republic concluded contracts in the late 1950s that would allow for temporary migration from Italy, Spain, and Yugoslavia; from 1960, workers from Turkey and Portugal could also move to Germany; eventually, the German government even sought to attract workers from as far afield as Tunisia, Morocco, and South Korea. At the height of Germany's economic miracle, the government was so desperate to attract workers to the country that it even put up posters seeking would-be immigrants in areas of high unemployment, including remote corners of Sicily and Anatolia.

When the first of these immigrants set foot in Germany, a "principle of rotation" was meant to ensure that, after a mere two years, they would be sent back to their country of origin, their places to be taken by new arrivals. But soon companies lobbied the government to be allowed to keep their employees for longer than two years, sparing them the disruption of training ever new waves of unskilled substitutes. As a result, immigrants were allowed to stay on indefinitely. Soon they moved their families to Germany. Eventually, they even gained the legal right to stay in the country for the rest of their lives. To anybody who cared to notice, it became clear that most of them were here to stay.

Even so, the idea that these hardworking immigrants were

ultimately supposed to go home—so why even think about how to integrate them into the monocultural fabric of German society?—stuck with most Germans. The term that politicians, media outlets, and ordinary people had initially employed for them never changed: after decades in Germany, they were still known as *Gastarbeiter*, or "guest workers."

Few people are still aware that the origins of this peculiar term are rather sinister. Usages of it are recorded as early as the first decades of the twentieth century. But it did not come into common usage until World War II, when the civilian populations of occupied nations were pressured or forced into migrating to the Third Reich to contribute to the Nazi war machine.

Even without these historical connotations, though, it would be clear that "guest worker" is a troubling euphemism: the term virtually reeks of an Orwellian joy in matching phrases with pleasant associations up with a reality that is anything but. On the surface, it may seem to emphasize how welcome these "guests" are in Germany; but, evidently, its more important function has been to emphasize that, as guests, they should neither come to feel at home in Germany nor plan to stay on beyond their hosts' sufferance.

It is only logical, then, that most of these "guest workers" were also denied the ultimate sign of belonging to the club: German citizenship.

German citizenship had always been based on the principle of jus sanguinis (law of the blood), which provided for the acquisition of German citizenship by being born as the child of a German; the American principle of jus soli (law of the earth), which provided for the acquisition of American citizenship by being born on American territory, has never come to be recognized in Germany.

Thus, even long after 1945, Germany's citizenship laws continued to enshrine an exclusively ethnic understanding of what makes a German. While "true" Germans whose ancestors had left the country centuries ago could return to Germany freely and be naturalized within a few years, legal immigrants, their children, and their children's children had no standard road to citizenship. Throughout the 1960s, '70s, and '80s, with close to 2 million Turks living in Germany, only about 13,000 Turks gained German citizenship—in virtually all cases by marrying a German. Not until the 1990s and 2000s did a series of legal reforms allow the descendants of immigrants to acquire German citizenship more readily.

Today, immigrants who have lived and worked in the country for at least eight years can usually acquire German citizenship; second- or third-generation immigrants are granted citizenship at birth. However, most immigrants still have to give up their original citizenship in order to become German: a proposal that would have allowed naturalized immigrants to keep their old passports was abandoned after a staggering 5 million Germans signed a petition against dual citizenship.

•

Germany's willful blindness about immigration, the resultant lack of long-term planning, and the de facto segregation of the children of Germany's elite and the children of guest workers all help to explain the extent to which the country has failed to integrate newcomers. But if this problem has quietly bubbled underneath the surface for decades, it is now coming to the boiling point.

An intense backlash against immigration is under way. Opinion polls show an increase in the number of Germans who harbor strong resentments against (the descendants of) immigrants in general, and people of Turkish extraction or Muslim faith in particular. The "immigrant problem" is at the center of political debate. The very idea that people of different ethnicities and cultural heritages could coexist peacefully is increasingly coming under attack.

In the same way that many Germans now think the country's foreign policy used to be deeply self-abnegating, so, too, are they convinced that all criticism of foreigners used to be taboo. Their reaction is the same in both cases: liberated from a set of imagined constraints, they are rushing to assert their newfound freedom. Advocates of the finish line don't just demand: "Let's show the Jews that we don't have to treat them with special consideration anymore!" or "Let's stand up for Germany's national interests again!" They also demand: "Let's finally say the truth about Turks and Muslims!"

In 2011, this new form of populism reached unprecedented heights. "Germany Is Abolishing Itself" (*Deutschland schafft sich ab*), an anti-immigrant treatise penned by Thilo Sarrazin, then a director of Germany's central bank, sold a million copies over the course of a few months. It now ranks as one of the bestselling books in Germany since World War II.

Sarrazin's book comprises 464 densely printed pages. The former bureaucrat takes particular pleasure in quoting other bureaucrats who write in devastatingly turgid prose, only to point out that his own prose is marginally less turgid. That may be true, but his book is, to put it mildly, a struggle to read. Sarrazin tries to veil his reprehensible views behind pages of statistics, which invariably turn out to be rather less informative than they at first seem. Worse still, his nine lengthy chapters don't seem to follow any internal logic; to read them in random order would not make the experience any worse. (In one of his many controversial public comments, Sarrazin once said about Josef Goebbels, the Third Reich's minister of propaganda, that he was "very good with words." Despite myself, I couldn't help wishing that Sarrazin might have learned a few more lessons from the man he professes to admire.)

Stylistic criticisms of Sarrazin may seem irrelevant. They aren't. After all, the fact that his book is so boring raises one simple question: Why would more than one and a half million Germans have spent hard-earned money on it?

The answer, I think, lies in the simple fact that a great majority of those who bought the book haven't read it—and, indeed,
never even intended to do so. They bought the book not because
they hoped to be enlightened or even entertained by it, but rather
because placing it on their bookshelf was a handy way for them to
express their support for its central message.

For, despite the obscurity of much of Sarrazin's writing, his
basic point had been hotly debated in the German media in the
weeks leading up to its release: in his tome, Sarrazin claims that
Turkish immigrants are genetically predisposed to be less intelligent than "real" Germans. They also bear more children. Conse-
quently, he predicts, the Turks are in the process of dumbing
Germany down.

Sarrazin's book made him wildly popular. The political establishment was so frightened that, at first, it did not dare close ranks
against him. Even as a few leading politicians called on Sarrazin
to resign from the board of Germany's central bank, they implicitly endorsed his ideas.

In the wake of the book's release, Horst Seehofer, the prime
minister of Bavaria, called for an end to Muslim immigration, and
then presented a very restrictive "Seven Point Plan" painting the
mass of immigrants as threats to German safety, culture, and identity. Far from criticizing Seehofer's brand of populism, Angela
Merkel went him one better. Addressing the youth organization
of her party, the Christian Democrats, she found an overly lenient
attitude toward immigrants responsible for many of Germany's
problems: "To say 'Let's have some multiculturalism in our country, and live our days next to each other, and take pleasure in each
other'—that basic approach has failed, absolutely failed."

According to Merkel, the problem is that Germany's Turks so-
cialize within their own community and speak Turkish at home.
They should, she said, no longer form a recognizably separate
group—something which in the United States might be considered

a harmless immigrant "community." Instead, they must follow Germany's *Leitkultur*, or "lead culture."

In essence, Merkel's speech was an exhortation to Turks to leave behind their own culture and become indistinguishable from Germans. Her vision is not that of a salad bowl in which individuals can retain some aspects of their own identity. Nor even is it that of a melting pot, in which the resulting flavor, though homogeneous, would nonetheless bear the mark of all its ingredients. Rather, it is simply the prescription of a one-way road toward total assimilation, in which Turks and other immigrants would accept to copy the Germans, without ever being invited to make their own contribution to the country's culture.

Both the salad bowl and the melting pot are plausible culinary metaphors. It is telling, then, that no easy culinary metaphor comes to mind for Merkel's unforgiving proposal. Perhaps the closest would be to picture German politicians as fussy chefs, and German natives as a perfectly spiced soup. Because the politicians don't want to change the taste of their chef d'oeuvre, they are rabidly opposed to adding any foreign ingredients. "If you really want in," they tell the unhappy Turks, "just turn yourself into a substance that won't change the taste or texture of our soup. If you're too stubborn to do that, then it's your own damn fault." The problem, of course, is that no such miraculous substance— one that has neither taste nor texture of its own—exists.

Like many of their colleagues across the Continent, some of the leaders of Germany's right have slowly shed their remaining inhibitions: they now openly use criticisms of immigrants to hunt for votes. But Germany's left, which is traditionally more sympathetic to immigrants, has recently been sending deeply mixed signals as well.

It may be a coincidence that Sarrazin has long been a card-carrying member of the Social Democrats, a party that—by German standards—has long been relatively friendly toward immigrants. But it surely is no coincidence that the party's leader-ship, after initiating proceedings to expel Sarrazin from the party when his book was published, ultimately struck an embarrassing deal: in return for his feeble assurance that he did not mean for his discriminatory book to be discriminatory, Sarrazin was allowed to stay.

If even the left is now at a loss as to its own position, part of the reason lies in a confusion about multiculturalism that reaches across the political spectrum. At least since Merkel loudly rejected multiculturalism, the term has become a useful shorthand for ev-erything that right-wing populists don't like: Islam and any kind of immigration from non-Western countries, of course; but also the loss of cultural traditions, the EU's encroachment on national sovereignty, and even certain forms of cultural relativism.

That all of these diverse grievances can conveniently be at-tacked under one label is in the interest of the populists. But Europe's left has only itself to blame for allowing its position on multiculturalism to be caricatured to this extent. After all, its own pronouncements on the topic have long been insufficiently nuanced as well.

In the heyday of left-wing support for multiculturalism, the majority of left-wingers rather sensibly argued that a peaceful co-existence between natives and immigrants was possible. An influx of foreign cultures could enrich Europe. Integration would be a two-way street, in which Europeans would learn to appreciate im-migrant cultures, even as immigrants came to accept Germany's legal system and political values.

At the same time, a small yet vocal minority conceived of multiculturalism as a much more radical project. They didn't just want to make sure that liberal democracy's promise to be neutral among different religions, ethnicities, and value systems would be honored for everybody; in the hope of expiating their country's past sins and reversing the cultural imperialism of the Nazis, they went so far as to affirm that all political positions and belief systems

are equally reasonable. In the minds of its most extreme supporters, this could even provide a ready excuse for crimes committed
by immigrants—or give imams and other authority figures the
right to coerce members of their own communities in the name
of tradition.

From the outset, multiculturalism was thus an ambiguous
concept. In the minds of some it referred to the notion that people of different cultures and ethnicities can be full citizens of
the same polity—a liberal idea that should be uncontroversial in a
modern democracy. But in the minds of others it stood for the idea
that freedom and human rights are cultural preferences on a par
with intolerance, religious fundamentalism, or dictatorship—a
form of cultural relativism that no democracy can accept without
undermining its own legitimacy.

The populist right soon began to exploit this ambiguity.
Latching on to the culturally relativist interpretation of multiculturalism, it cleverly began to attack it for being yet another form
of national self-abnegation. Then it went on to draw the unwar-
ranted conclusion that *everything* associated with multiculturalism is deeply misguided: not just cases of excess deference, where
state authorities have been too reluctant to protect the weakest
members of ethnic minorities against threats or violence from more
powerful members of their own groups, but also the essential liberal ideal that the state should not have preferences in questions
of religion or ethnicity.

The left, meanwhile, has been busy throwing out the baby
with the bathwater. After having tolerated a pernicious form of
cultural relativism under the banner of multiculturalism, it now
balks at defending anything at all that the populist right chooses
to associate with that term. If we want to keep our jobs, hundreds
of scared left-wing parliamentarians seem to be whispering to one
another in beleaguered halls of power all over Europe, we had
better shut up about our commitment to ethnic pluralism and religious tolerance.

The end result of this undignified spectacle is that both the left and the right are going on about the need to defend the West's universalist principles against the threat from Turkish immigrants. But neither the left nor the right seems to remember that a central part of this universalist heritage consists precisely in a citizen's right to worship and think as he pleases—not to mention the seemingly more trivial rights to cook the food he happens to like best or to speak to his children in whatever language he deems fit.

In other words, what is under attack in Germany (and much of Europe) is not some radical concept of multiculturalism. Rather, it is the core of democracy as we conceive of it: the conviction that different people can live together peacefully and that the state should not elevate one religion or ethnicity above all others.

There is one last reason why the fight for pluralism is so important: demographic projections unanimously predict that Germany's population will plummet precipitously over the coming decades. The social and economic effects of such rapid depopulation would be disastrous. The economy would shrink. The welfare state would become unaffordable. Social tensions would multiply. Unless Germany accepts mass immigration—and finds a way to make millions of newcomers feel truly welcome—the country's future looks increasingly bleak.

Just over 80 million people now live in Germany. According to a relatively cautious projection by researchers at Germany's Ministry for Statistics, that number is set to fall to at most 73.8 million by 2040, and 64.7 million by 2060.

Even that none-too-rosy picture is based on one key assumption: that Germany will experience net immigration of 100,000 people per year. That figure may not sound like much. But since well over half a million people leave Germany in a typical year, it's a lot more difficult to achieve annual net immigration of 100,000 people than might immediately be apparent.

In other words, even the Ministry of Statistics's cautious model, which predicts that Germany will lose nearly a quarter of its population over the next half century, assumes that the country manages to absorb well over half a million newcomers a year. If, instead, politicians decide to aim for zero net migration—a goal that would still require integrating hundreds of thousands of immigrants every year—Germany's population would shrink even more quickly.

Politicians have long ignored this looming demographic crisis. Now, as it is becoming too imminent to ignore, they have begun to hope for a convenient solution: they count on being able to persuade German women to have more kids. But while a push for higher birthrates will have to be a part of the solution, it is simply unrealistic to hope that it could ever make enough of a difference to solve Germany's demographic crisis.

To boost birthrates, Germany could introduce policies that make it easier for working mothers to have children. But this approach suffers from in-built limits. While demographers agree that "natalist" policies have some positive effect on birthrates, its magnitude is probably limited. Even countries like France and Sweden, who have long provided extremely generous benefits to parents, are now seeing domestic birthrates trending below the replacement rate. Similarly, Germany has, in recent years, improved parental-leave policies, opened many more preschools, and increased financial support for families with children. But the effect on birthrates has turned out to be very minor—too small to make a real dent in projections about Germany's future population levels.

What's more, attempts to boost the birthrate have so far run into surprisingly resilient cultural obstacles. Polls show that many German women still feel that they would be failing their duties as mothers if they did not stay home with their children; according to a 2012 study, 63 percent of western Germans believe that "a young child will probably suffer if his or her mother works." A growing share of highly qualified women therefore decides not to have children in the first place.

Similarly, because prejudices against working mothers have long been very strong among Germany's conservatives, some policies that might make it easier for women to work while raising kids remain highly controversial. Most German children, for example, are only at school until about 1:00 p.m. on an average day. A longer school day would make it much easier for women to combine raising children with a professional career. Even so, most conservatives remain stridently opposed to lengthening school hours.

All in all, it therefore looks highly unlikely that rising birthrates could do enough to solve the problem. If Germany is to avoid rapid depopulation, it will have to replenish its shrinking populace through mass immigration.

In light of the country's depopulation crisis, there are three basic scenarios for Germany's future.

Germans could decide that, as Willy Brandt worried four decades ago, "the outer limit of our ability to absorb foreigners has been reached." This may well happen. Most Germans have never been in favor of mass immigration; now, they are arguably more tempted than at any point since the 1950s to close their country off to new arrivals. If Germans do choose to shutter their borders, nothing can stop them.

But the resulting drop in Germany's population would have disastrous social and economic consequences. If Germany lost close to a quarter of its population over the next fifty years, it would probably experience marked economic decline, slashed pensions, and an overstretched health-care system. If it lost even more, it would almost certainly experience precipitous economic decline, the utter collapse of its pension system, and rapidly declining levels of life expectancy. Ironically, such a horror scenario might not even guarantee full employment to those few remaining Germans who'd be young enough to work: since most mobile capital would flee from a country in such dire straits, even the greatly diminished number of working-age Germans would have to compete for scarcer and scarcer jobs.

In other words, Germany would pay for its unwillingness to welcome more immigrants with rapid economic decline. Though most Germans remain unaware of this, their choice against immigration would, to all intents and purposes, amount to a choice against economic growth and the welfare state.

Alternatively, Germans could grudgingly allow mass immigration, even as they retain their restrictive conception of membership in the nation. If responsible politicians manage to convince voters of the economic horrors that would await them if Germany's population were to plummet, they might temporarily put their deep-rooted worries about *Überfremdung*, or "over-foreignization," to one side. The country would then open its borders to a new wave of immigration—a wave that, if it is to prevent Germany's demographic decline, would have to be much bigger than the one it experienced in the 1960s.

But, as the history of the "guest workers" shows, the fact that Germany might open its doors to these immigrants does not necessarily mean that they will be truly welcome. Germans, in this second scenario, would continue to define true membership in the nation on ethnic, or at least on deeply cultural, lines. New arrivals would forevermore remain a group apart. At best, they would be tolerated with gritted teeth. At worst, they would be openly hated and mistreated.

Doomsayers like Brandt could then be proved right. Germans might prove able to open up their borders to scores of immigrants, yet unable to open up their hearts to them. The potential consequences of such a schizophrenic stance are easy to imagine. The greater the tensions between immigrants and natives, the greater the backlash against all supposed foreigners. The greater this backlash, the more alienated ethnically "foreign" children growing up in Germany will come to feel. And the more alienated the new generation of immigrant children, the more likely it is that existing tensions eventually lead to bloody clashes. In this vision of the future, relations between immigrants and natives could enter a vicious cycle—and it wouldn't be all too surprising if that cycle eventually ended in violence.

Economically, a Germany that has mass immigration but minimal integration might do well enough. But politically, culturally, and socially, the country would then enter the most dangerous and unhappy period of its postwar history.

Thankfully, a third alternative does exist. Germany can avoid the double specter of economic collapse or civil strife by turning itself into a genuine country of immigration. Copying what's best about the United States and Canada, such a changed Germany would finally embrace the right kind of multiculturalism: not a multiculturalism that sacrifices universalist values at the false altar of cultural relativism, but rather a pluralism that recognizes that universalist values consist precisely in treating everybody—residents of German, Turkish, or African origin; Christians, Muslims, and Jews—as full citizens, with equal rights to match equal responsibilities.

But all of this assumes that Brandt was wrong when he proclaimed that the "outer limits of our ability to absorb foreigners" had been reached long ago. Was he? Are Germans really capable of divorcing themselves from long-standing assumptions about what makes a true German?

I don't know the answer to these questions. What I do know is that Germany's prosperity, the fate of immigrants already in the country, as well as—last and probably least—the long-term future of Germany's Jews now depends on it.

•

In *Germany Is Abolishing Itself,* Thilo Sarrazin repeatedly implies that the real reason for the Turks' failure to integrate in Germany is genetic. In one particularly outspoken passage about the genes of Turkish immigrants, he writes:

> Whole clans have a long tradition of incest, and, correspondingly, many disabilities. It is known that the proportion of congenital disabilities among the Turkish and Kurdish migrants in Germany is far above average. But the topic is hushed up. Otherwise, some people might get the idea that genetic factors are responsible for the failure of parts of the Turkish population in German schools.

Given the Third Reich's penchant for racial pseudoscience, which led the regime to carry out horrific experiments in concentration camps and murder tens of thousands in a brutal program of eugenics, Sarrazin surely realized that this kind of talk might associate him a little too closely with Nazi ideas. He therefore needed a rhetorical shield to protect himself from such associations. Luckily, he soon found a perfect piece of armor: he had, he realized, but to enlist the Jews in his cause!

That, at least, seems to be the most obvious explanation for why Sarrazin's book is peppered with fawning references to Jews. There is nothing wrong with studying the IQ of different population groups, he argues, for the inventors of the field of study were themselves Jews. What is more, Sarrazin implies, his kind of racialist thinking about genetics couldn't possibly lead to anti-Semitism; after all, "early research about intelligence found the IQ of Jews to be fifteen points higher than that of other Europeans as well as their descendants in North America." And in case even that wasn't enough, Sarrazin, for no explicit reason, goes on to detail all kinds of Jewish achievements—from the number of Jewish Nobel Prize winners to the "far above average" success of Jews in present-day America—over the course of four long pages.

Sarrazin's tactic is ingenious. It's also pernicious, and increasingly widespread.

Especially when German politicians want to exclude Muslim immigrants and insist that, in a favorite phrase of the times, "Islam is not a part of Germany," they usually express their devotion to the country's "Judeo-Christian heritage." The rather mysterious *Leitkultur*, which immigrants should be required to follow, according to politicians like Merkel, is invariably characterized as Jewish as well as Christian. In fact, even Seehofer saw fit to start his polemical Seven Point Plan with the remark that integration would have to be built on the "shared foundation of the values enshrined in our constitution and the German lead culture, which has been shaped by our Christian-Jewish roots."

It is very generous—or, at any rate, rhetorically shrewd—of Merkel, Seehofer, and Sarrazin to include us in the coveted ingroup. How nice to be a part of Germany's "lead culture"! How gratifying to be told that our genes make us so intelligent that Germans will continue to welcome us with open arms!

But in my experience, the reality on the ground looks rather different. Whatever the public pronouncements of politicians, in truth this restrictive conception of citizenship excludes Jews as well as Muslims.

"Yascha Mounk . . . What kind of a name is that, anyhow?"

Stunned, I looked up at Volker Zastrow, a senior political editor at the *Frankfurter Allgemeine Zeitung* (FAZ), one of Germany's two leading dailies. His question didn't strike me as a particularly appropriate start to a job interview. But what, I asked myself, did he mean, anyway? Did he suspect, because of the Y in Yascha, that I might be Turkish? Or did he recognize the origin of my first name and was trying to figure out whether I was, as he already suspected, Jewish?

Zastrow visibly enjoyed my confusion. He flashed me the demonstrative smile of a chess player about to checkmate his opponent. Then he leaned forward a little, and added: "Yascha Mounk . . . That's not a *German* name, is it?"

I wasn't going to give Zastrow the answer he was looking for quite as easily as that. After a moment's tense silence, I launched into a diversionary tactic. "Well, that's a funny story, you know," I said brightly. "My name is actually made up."

Zastrow hadn't seen that one coming. "Made up?" he asked.

"My mother is a conductor. When she was starting her career she still went by the name of Skrzyposzek. Then she got her first permanent position at an opera house, and the general manager told her that there was only one condition: 'You have to change your name. Ski . . . Kshi . . . You'll never have a big career with that name. No one can remember it. No one can pronounce it. No one can spell it. So come back to my office tomorrow, tell me what name you've chosen for yourself, and we'll have you sign a contract.' And that's what she did."

"So you have your mother's name?"

"Well, yes . . ."

"What about your father?"

This was getting to be a little much for me. If Zastrow considered an interview to be a test of submission, I was only too happy to fail it. "I don't suppose that's any of your business, but if you care to know, they were never married."

We glared at each other in mute hostility for a few seconds.

"Oh. My condolences!" he finally offered.

In a separate interview later that afternoon, one of the publishers of the *FAZ*, after he, too, asked me what kind of a name Yascha Mounk was, started to interrogate me about my résumé. "So you were an undergrad at Cambridge and now you are going to do your Ph.D. at Harvard. Can you explain to me who is paying for all of that?"

Taken aback, I pointed out that fees at British universities had been minimal when I studied there, and that places in Ph.D. programs at top U.S. universities come with full funding. Then, though the question had been posed in a neutral enough tone, I tried to decipher its implications. Was it a surprise that an immigrant with a Turkish name could have the money to study abroad? Or was it some half-conscious set of cultural assumptions about Jews and money? Either way, I just cannot imagine that a "true German" would have been asked the same question.

In fairness, I should add that I was offered the internship I'd applied for. As so often in Germany, my predicament did not end up being exclusion. Rather, it consisted of the terms and conditions attached to my inclusion. Had I been willing to smile in silent submission as condolences were expressed about my being a bastard or my having a foreign name, even the *FAZ*, that embodiment of Germany's conservative establishment, may well have been willing to tolerate me. Given the alternative of making my way abroad without enduring such humiliations, I politely declined the offer.

Most middle-class Germans have a much higher opinion of Jews than they do of Turks. But, as my experience with the *FAZ* shows, German prejudices against immigrants ultimately affect us all.

Not only are a vast majority of Jews who currently live in Germany relatively recent immigrants; even those German Jews who were born in Germany or speak the language without a trace of an accent are often marked out as having foreign roots by their names.

That, to me, was the real takeaway from my interviews at the *FAZ*. I don't know whether the journalists who interviewed me thought I was a Jew or whether they thought I was a Turk. What I do know is that, though I was born in Germany, though I don't look any different from most Germans, though I speak the language without an accent, my name was enough to mark me out as somebody who didn't truly belong.

A few months ago, I was once again reminded how salient this simple fact of a foreign name can be to ordinary Germans. I used to write a weekly column on politics and culture for *The European*, a German magazine. The column was frequently picked up by various German websites, including the news section of

T-Online, the biggest German Internet provider. One week, I wrote an article critical of Thilo Sarrazin. Dozens of commentators on T-Online, who rushed to Sarrazin's defense, immediately latched on to my foreign-sounding name.

"We don't need any clever comments from a guy whose name already betrays that he's an immigrant, and who therefore cannot possibly be impartial about this subject," said one.

"This guy should be sent back to his country of origin," seconded another.

One thing, then, is clear: so long as Germans retain an ethnic conception of citizenship, they will think of anybody whom they know to be a Jew as a kind of immigrant. Jews who are neither immigrants nor have a foreign-sounding name might be able to pass as German so long as they don't mention that they are Jewish; but they, too, will be treated as outsiders as soon as they reveal this one fact about themselves.

A large part of why I came to feel less and less German as I grew up has to do with Germany's relationship toward its past, and its ongoing effects on daily interactions between Jews and Gentiles. But another reason for my exclusion stems from the fact that Germany has long told *all* children of immigrants that they aren't "really" German. From that perspective, it is hardly surprising that, along with so many Turkish immigrants, I still feel like a foreigner in what should, by now, have become my own country.

For all the fashionable rhetoric of including Jews the better to exclude Turks, in reality the current rebellion against pluralism is disastrous for us all. In the long run, only a multicultural Germany can accept Jews as an integral part of the country. If Jews are to feel German, Germans will have to shed their ethnic conception of nationhood. And that would also require them to accept that an ethnic Turk can truly become a part of the German nation.

Epilogue: No Longer a Jew

"Also, if I spent a year in Germany I'd be thinking of one thing only," he stated publicly (I was the only one listening). "For twelve months I'd be a Jew and nothing else. I can't afford to give an entire year to that." But I think a better explanation is that he was having a grand time being mad in New York.   —Saul Bellow, *Humboldt's Gift*

My little family has, in a way, been reunited once more.

As a child, I would frequently spend whole weeks with Leon in Frankfurt, where he'd retired from his job as a printer. Sometimes, Leon would take me to the Jewish community center, or to the old ghetto in the center of town. But much more often we would go to the city's beautiful palm garden. I would run around the luscious, expansive grounds. Once I'd tired myself out, Leon would take me by the hand and show me the exotic trees and plants in the arboretum. Then we'd go home, Leon would make me my favorite dish (a prawn omelet), and read to me—usually his favorite German poets, Heinrich Heine and Johann Wolfgang von Goethe.

In these happy days, I never had the impression that my grandfather held any kind of grudge against Germany. On the contrary. Despite his family's fate, he himself had chosen to live there when he might just as well have made his home in Israel. On the whole,

Leon knew, the Federal Republic was as decent a state as ever he had lived in.

That is not to say, however, that Leon's sense of belonging didn't have limits—limits that may have been ill-defined and intangible, but that were no less real for all of that.

So far as I remember, Leon had very few, if any, Gentile acquaintances. He preferred to spend his days on his own, or with friends from Frankfurt's sizable Jewish community. And while he accepted that he would likely die in Germany, he did not want his earthly remains to spend eternity in German soil: a few years before his death, he asked that he be buried in Sweden.

Leon died in a Munich hospital on August 18, 1999, at the proud age of eighty-six. A week later, on a lovely summer day, Roman, Ala, Rebecka, and I held traditional funeral rites for Leon at the Jewish cemetery in Malmö—about a mile from the police station where, some three decades earlier, his son had spent his first night in his new country.

Ewa, my grandmother, still lived in nearby Lund when Leon passed away.

In her first months in Sweden, Ewa had briefly worked at a local library. When she reached the official retirement age, soon after, she was given a small apartment in a public housing project to complement her minimal state pension. By most anybody's standards, Ewa had a modest end to her life.

But what struck me as remarkable, even when I was a kid, was that Ewa could not have been more grateful. Many times a day she looked around her apartment in wonderment, and gave a thoroughly contented sigh: "I never imagined that I would end my days amidst such luxury. Never could I have imagined that."

Ewa died in June of 2002. Like Leon, she was buried in Malmö, but it didn't quite seem appropriate to make a family grave for the two of them. "They fought enough when they were alive," Ala said. "Let them keep their distance from each other in death." And yet, although they each have a separate grave, no more than a few yards of cold Swedish earth keep them apart. And so, after spending the first half of their adult lives as husband and wife, and the second half of it separated by a good thousand miles, Leon and Ewa were posthumously reunited in a small Jewish cemetery in the largely Muslim neighborhood of Rosengård, in southern Sweden.

If Leon and Ewa are, in their peculiar way, reunited, so, too, are Ala, Roman, Rebecka, and I.

As a conductor, Ala frequently moved from job to job. Over the years, she lived in Detmold, Berlin, Cologne, Krefeld, Munich, Freiburg, Munich again, Kassel, Maulbronn, Laupheim, and Munich once more. (As a result, I went to four *Gymnasien*, three primary schools, and countless kindergartens.)

With Ala's future so uncertain much of the time, there was little point buying an apartment in any one place. But then, finally, everything conspired for Ala to make a more stable home for herself. In the late 1990s, she accepted a position as a tenured professor at the music university in Karlsruhe. Though she still gave occasional concerts as a freelancer, her itinerant years were over: it was clear that Ala would most likely remain in Karlsruhe until her retirement. Her friends advised that she should finally buy her own place.

But Ala didn't want to do it. In her mind, when you buy property in a place, it doesn't just come to belong to you; to some degree, you also come to belong to it. Owning a home in Germany would mean putting down real roots there. It would mean that, as the Jews of postwar Germany might have put it, Ala had unpacked her bags for good.

Though she seemed content enough in Germany, and made no concerted effort to pursue her career elsewhere, this was not a commitment Ala was ever quite willing to make. Karlsruhe, in particular, just wasn't a place where she could envisage spending the rest of her life. Better, she decided, to continue to rent, to hold firm to the fiction that, at any moment, she could up and leave.

Once the idea of calling a nice dwelling her own had entered her mind, however, Ala did quietly start to dream. The idea of owning a place in Karlsruhe might have frightened her. But, after a whole life on the go, was there not some other corner of the world where she would delight in intertwining her future with a few rocks and a modest patch of land?

Put like that, the answer slowly became obvious. Ala would buy a place in Tuscany—that charmed region she'd first gotten to know when she won a scholarship to spend a month at the Accademia Musicale Chigiana in Siena as a young music student, and which she had come to love on her many visits since.

When Ala first told me about her idea, I couldn't have been more enthusiastic. I'd been to Tuscany once when I was six years old; I'm told that I'd loved it even then. But the first visit I clearly remember came in 1995, when I was thirteen.

I was off from school for the Easter holiday, and Ala had dragged me from familiar Munich, where I would have preferred to stay, playing eventless days of soccer by the river Isar, to faraway Tuscany. We arrived in Montepulciano when it was already pitch-dark. The few lights I saw through the windows of our beat-up Fiat Panda made the surroundings look industrial to me. The prospect of endless hours in churches and museums—there were many of these here, Ala had been foolish enough to warn me—did the rest. Once we arrived at the basement apartment where we were going to stay for the next two weeks, I curled up in a comfortless bed and surrendered to the fast sleep of a surly teenager.

The next morning, still in a bad mood, I woke up at the crack of dawn, far earlier than usual. To my confusion, I discovered that the basement apartment had a window, and that window—so steep is the hilltop on which Montepulciano is built—offered up a stunning view over vast stretches of land. The roof of a lower, neighboring house formed a kind of makeshift terrace. I climbed through the window, sat on the terrace, and started to look out in earnest.

The landscape I stared at remained incomprehensible for seconds, for minutes, for a whole hour. There were little circles of land: steep, green fields leading up to small groups of fairy-tale houses, each arrangement topped with one church tower, the whole ensemble bathed in bright orange sunlight. Below the isolated circles of land, there appeared to be a cold, gray sea.

As the minutes went by—the first-ever minutes of true aesthetic contemplation in my life—the sea slowly retreated. Was this the ebb, I wondered?

Then I realized. The gray sea was fog. It was retreating ever so slowly, ever so coquettishly, to reveal Tuscany's breathtaking fields and valleys to my admiring eyes. I was stunned.

Over the next two weeks, with the peculiar obsession of a teenage boy, I immersed myself in every detail of this landscape, this history, this people. When I had to go back to Munich—despondent to return to the place I had so recently been despondent to leave—I vowed to learn Italian. In the years since then, I have spent a part of virtually every summer in Tuscany.

So, back in Karlsruhe, when Ala told me that we might just have enough money to look for a place to call our own in that wonderful part of the world, I was overjoyed.

We did not have to search for long. That summer, while we were visiting close family friends in Tuscany, we looked up a local real estate agent. The first village to which he took us was the most beautiful we had ever seen. Built in the eleventh century as a castle town, Montelaterone was never meant to look inviting. Its streets and alleyways are steep and narrow. Its houses are simple. There are only a few, huddled piazzas. The castle that stands at its top has been in ruins for decades, perhaps centuries. But what

Montelaterone lacks in twee opulence, it makes up for with its unvarnished authenticity, its labyrinthine layout, and its dramatic views on neighboring valleys and villages.

When we saw a house at the lowest edge of the village's historic part, we immediately fell in love with it. Because the hill on which it is built is so steep, it gives the impression of being in the town and the country all at the same time. Its front entrance is located alongside a little, narrow street. To get to it in the summer, you have to pass old grandmothers sitting on their plastic chairs outside their homes, chatting with one another for hours on end and merrily detaining anyone who passes. But while the front of the house is at street level, its back gives the impression of hovering above the countryside. Its small garden, its narrow balcony, and its every window afford commanding views over the soaring Monte Amiata, the ancient olive trees that line its slopes, the wheat fields and haystacks that dominate the gentler, lower hills, and the lush vineyards that guide the eyes in the direction of distant Siena.

We loved the village and the landscape at first sight. Over time, we have developed an even greater affection for its people.

Montelaterone—this poor and remote village of a few hundred aging inhabitants—has welcomed us into the fold with uncanny warmth. When we first met our neighbors, they asked us a few halfhearted questions about our origins. But, really, our answers didn't seem to matter very much. Soon enough, they treated us much like anyone else—not as though we'd been born into this tight-knit community, of course, but about as well as any newcomer who might have moved to Montelaterone from Florence or Rome. In the years since we first turned up there, the extent of their open-mindedness toward all kinds of difference has surprised us over and over again.

One of my friends there, Ale, is a trainee electrician by day and a death metal rocker by night. With his long beard, his unremittingly black clothes, and his many earrings and piercings, he does not exactly look like a grandmother's idea of a polite young man. One day, I was taking a walk around the village with him when we passed his next-door neighbor, a rather pious and elegant older lady.

"I heard you practicing this morning," Neda said to him.

"I'm so sorry," Ale said. "Does the music bother you?"

"No, no," she said, with a smile. "To be honest, I don't quite understand your music. But, you know, it's so nice to have a little life in the village. Practice whenever you like, *caro*."

Another time, Heinz and José, good friends of my mother's, stayed with us in the village for a couple of nights. After they had left, Rosemma, an unfailingly cheerful old lady who must once have been a great beauty, stopped Ala in the street.

"I was going to ask . . ." she said, uncharacteristically hesitant. "Your friends. Are they . . . ?"

"Oh, well, Heinz is German and José is Spanish," Ala quickly replied.

"No, I mean . . . Are they, well, together?"

Ala hesitated for just a moment. "Yes, Rosemma. They're gay."

"Oh," she exclaimed happily, "they make such a nice couple!"

That is not to say that Montelaterone, let alone Italy as a whole, is always a model of tolerance. It is enough to watch TV or listen to the radio to know that xenophobia is increasingly widespread in the country. Right-wing populists, from Silvio Berlusconi to the Lega Nord (Northern League), have long been strong. As Italy's economic troubles deepen, more and more people are tempted to look for scapegoats.

But somehow, whenever we might have reason to doubt how we are perceived, the place conspires to make us feel at ease. One morning, for example, I heard a politician from Berlusconi's party make particularly racist remarks on the radio. That same afternoon, I was chatting with Dolores, one of our neighbors, in her garden, which overlooks the striking towns that are precariously perched on the western slopes of the Monte Amiata. The conversation turned to some of the Moroccan immigrants who had recently moved to the region.

"What would you say," I asked Dolores offhandedly, "if your grandson married a Moroccan girl?"

"Oh, I don't know anything about the Moroccans," Dolores replied after giving my question some thought. "Nothing at all. But, you know, if she's a nice girl, why not?"

My heart melted a little. But Dolores hadn't finished quite yet.

"I'll tell you one thing, though," she said in a conspiratorial tone, pointing to the village just across the valley. "The people of Castel del Piano. Them I do know." She shook her head sadly. "Them you mustn't trust."

Dolores's mistrust of the good people of Castel del Piano is, obviously enough, absurd. Even so, there was something in her attitude that I found winning, even admirable.

Dolores has had ample experiences with people from Castel del Piano. For whatever idiosyncratic reason, she has decided that she cannot trust them. But, right or (probably) wrong, that's still a local judgment, one rooted in personal experiences and concrete interactions; it is the same logic by which she arrived at her perfectly commonsensical judgment about the people of Morocco— not knowing them, what reason could she possibly have to think ill of them?

This preference for the personal over the abstract might lie at the root of why Ala and I have, in many ways, found it easier to feel at home in Montelaterone than in the much bigger, much more diverse German cities where we have lived. It's not just that Ala and I remained exotic outsiders in Germany. More than that, abstract notions about who we were actually seemed to change how some people treated us. Since they had thought so much about the role that Germany's past should play in the present, yet met so few Jews, it was all but inevitable that they would turn us into an object for their projections.

In Montelaterone, too, most of our neighbors see us as exotic outsiders; it would be ridiculous to pretend that they are unaware of our foreign accents, or the fact that we have never made an appearance in the village church. But, somehow, interactions in the village are so personal, so rooted in particular judgments about who is nice and who isn't, who is a good neighbor and who is inconsiderate, that these abstract notions seem to matter a whole lot less. As a result, what had been so elusive in Germany for so long has, strangely, caught up with us far more quickly than we might ever have imagined in remote Montelaterone: a feeling of home.

The unexpected feeling that Montelaterone was becoming a real home to us was only amplified a few years later. Ala casually mentioned to her brother that our next-door neighbor was looking to sell her house. Roman immediately decided to make an offer on it. He hadn't even seen the house from the inside—the opportunity to move next door to his sister, he realized, would not present itself again.

For a good part of every year, Ala and Roman now live in adjacent houses, their lives miraculously transformed into some kind of goofy family sitcom, with minor fights, and minor plot twists, and many a heartwarming moment. On most mornings, Ala leans out of the kitchen window. "Rooooman. Breakfaaast," she calls to her long-lost neighbor, and another episode begins.

As the seasons grow in number, so, too, does the cast of supporting characters. Marian, a good friend of Ala's from primary school, recently bought a house in nearby Montegiovi; Irena, Ala's best friend from high school, just moved into a house a hundred yards or so down the road. Slowly, a set of childhood friends from Warsaw, long dispersed to the four corners of the world, is being reassembled in this—in our—idyllic village.

Ala, for now, remains a professor at the Hochschule für Musik in Karlsruhe. Even when she retires next year, she will likely spend a part of every year in either Munich or Berlin. Similarly, Roman still spends most of his time in southern Sweden. His dental practice is thriving. His lifelong friends—those aging men and women who, back in 1968, when they had barely finished high school, were granted visas by a generous Swedish consular officer after sending him their report cards—live close by in Lund or Malmö. He will likely keep a place there.

No matter. For the first time since Roman, all on his own, boarded that night train to a foreign land on the evening of his eighteenth birthday, he and Ala are no longer separated by thousands of miles. Against the odds, our little family has found a kind of second home.

●

When people ask me where I'm from nowadays, I never quite know how to respond.

At first, I simply used to say: "I'm from various places in Europe." But this would only annoy people. "I know Europe," more than one person has said to me, visibly irritated. "*Where* in Europe?"

So, instead, I tend to resort to an awkward list of places. "My parents are Polish, I was raised in Germany, my family's now sort of at home in Italy, and I went to college in England."

But that, too, elicits an impatient response. "I see," people tell me. "So you're Polish?"

"No, not really."

"German?"

"Well, it's a bit more complicated than that."

"Fine," they conclude. "So you're some kind of a cosmopolitan."

But that isn't quite true either. As understood by Diogenes, a cosmopolitan is somebody who makes the whole world—literally speaking, the whole cosmos—his home. He feels the same allegiance to every place, every culture, every ethnic group.

That is an admirable attitude to try to cultivate. But it also bears a serious risk: in the end, a universalized sense of allegiance may be so diluted as to be altogether ineffective. Somebody who tries to feel as passionately about every place may end up not feeling particularly passionately about any place. And then he would have no reason for the great virtues that—along with the undoubted dangers—have often been inspired by a sense of civic belonging: charity, community spirit, public service, a genuine concern for the common good.

So I honestly admire true cosmopolitans, those supremely empathetic men and women who are viscerally struck by all suffering, however remote it might be in time or place, as though it were the suffering of their own relatives. But they are rare creatures. As for myself, I have no illusions: I could never aspire to their goodness.

No, I am no cosmopolitan. The only difference between me and most people is that whereas they have only one town or country to call their own, for me there are a number of places in the world that give me that special fondness only a home can evoke. Montelaterone is one of these. Cambridge, where I went to college, is another. New York, where I now live, is perhaps the most important.

From this list, I realize, Germany is conspicuously absent. This has long been, and even now remains, rather puzzling to me. After all, I was born and grew up there. In the sixty-odd years since the Federal Republic's gray beginnings, Germany has become a vastly more diverse and democratic country. Jewish life in Germany is now more widespread, varied, and visible than it has been at any time since World War II. As the number of Jews in Germany continues to grow, so do daily interactions between Jews and Gentiles. And though a new generation's determination to make Germany a "normal" country has so far been more rhetoric than reality, their ever-repeated prophecies may, eventually, prove self-fulfilling.

Once ethnic or religious identities become a site of conflict in society, it becomes difficult to imagine how their divisiveness might ever subside. But sometimes, unexpectedly, a wound that has festered for decades, a wound everybody expected to fester for decades more, suddenly heals. Tensions between Protestants and Catholics in most parts of Europe, or the wide gulf that divided *Mayflower* folk from more recent Irish, Italian, or Jewish immigrants to the United States—all of these divisions were hugely important before they lost their salience with unforeseen rapidity. Retrospectively, they seem so implausible as to appear altogether quaint.

It's perfectly possible that some similar process of spontaneous regeneration will finally heal tensions between Germany's Jews and Germany's Gentiles. Many of the necessary preconditions are already in place. So I cannot rule out that I might not, at some point in the future, when the seemingly interminable process of forgiveness and reconciliation has finally played itself out, return to Germany, and come to feel at home in the place where I was born. For now, though, the stubborn fact remains what it is: I simply do not feel German.

Germany is a place to which I continue to have real ties. My mother still works and lives there for half of every year. German is still the only language I speak without an accent. I frequently write for German papers. In many ways, I always have been, and now remain, very fond of the country.

And yet, all things told, Germany just doesn't feel to me like the place I am *from* in anything other than the most factual sense. With every year I spend abroad, it seems less and less likely that this might one day change.

Am I being too tough on Germany?

After all these years of philo-Semites tormenting themselves, after all those contradictory attempts by 68ers to right the wrongs of the past, I still find fault with the country. Germans can deny the past, for which I will call them cowardly. They can obsess about it, for which I will call them misguided. Or they can try to move on from it, for which I will call them delusional. How can anybody safely navigate this minefield? What more do I want? If I am so discontented, what solution do I have to offer?

These are very legitimate questions, so let me be crystal clear: none of what I've written is intended as an accusation. Nor do I mean to take the moral high ground. Quite the contrary. I am fully aware that, were I not Jewish, I'd most probably treat Jews just as awkwardly as Franz, Marie, and Markus do.

My point, rather, is that the ardent wish to leave behind the mistrust, guilt, and suspicion that still persist between Jews and Gentiles is not strong enough to do so in practice. Even if everybody now alive has only the best of intentions, historical injustices continue to cast long shadows. To say that the state of German-Jewish relations is still poor is not necessarily to blame anybody who is now alive—but neither is it to promise that things will soon get better.

In other words, I openly admit that I have no solution to offer. That's because, on reflection, I do not believe that there is an easy solution.

If no amount of willpower can wish away the lasting neuroses from which both the descendants of perpetrators and the descendants of their victims suffer, then the desire that there should be an immediate solution to the ongoing awkwardness is not just futile; it may itself prove dangerous. What we need is not a determination to right the wrongs of the past at any cost—nor even an obsession with declaring that now, finally, Jews and Gentiles can resume normal relations. We've had more than enough of both. What we actually need is a lot of patience.

This patience is in increasingly short supply. Most people are genuinely acting as best they can. Yet they soon notice that the situation is not improving as quickly as they had hoped. Far from receding into the past, controversies and misunderstandings between Jews and Gentiles only seem to multiply: over the last year alone there have been media storms about Grass's poem; a lower court ruling outlawing Jewish circumcision rites; the question whether Jakob Augstein, a leading German journalist (and Martin Walser's illegitimate son), is a virulent anti-Semite; and much, much more.

For those who are frustrated with this interminable strife, a natural reaction is to blame the other side. Jews and Gentiles alike are tempted to say: "I know that *we* are doing our best, so if things aren't getting any better, *they* must be at fault."

If we indulge in this kind of blame game, however, we risk reopening wounds that had only just begun to heal. That's why only a greater understanding of each other's difficulties can facilitate the patience that's necessary to avoid the danger of relapsing into mutual recrimination. The first step in that direction would be to appreciate just how easily, in such a charged situation, genuine misunderstandings can arise without it being anybody's fault.

A recent exchange between Renate Künast, a Green Party politician, and Thomas Hemberger, a political activist, is a good example of such a genuine misunderstanding. On the afternoon of July 2, 2009, in the middle of a federal election campaign, Renate Künast was leaving her offices in the Bundestag. Just as she was about to get into her limousine, Hemberger, an activist for Stop the Bomb, an organization opposing the Iranian nuclear program, tried to enlist her support.

A winningly outspoken woman with short, dirty-blond hair, Künast has always been feared for her sharp tongue. On this particular occasion, though, her rhetorical talent was to backfire. Instead of politely declining the request, Künast was so displeased that she went on an impromptu rant. According to the activist (Künast denies this part of the exchange), she even went so far as to say: "You are a front operation of Mossad!"

In many countries, the incident might not have been noticed. In the German context, however, an unintended side effect of philo-Semitic political correctness kicked into action. Remarks that are openly hostile to Jews are, quite rightly, generally shunned. As a result, clever anti-Semites never voice their opinions openly. They realize that to be heard at all they have to speak in codes. So they issue thinly veiled populist appeals that hint at their true intent, yet studiously leave what they really mean to the imagination of their audience. It's a kind of "anti-Semitism by insinuation."

Hemberger, attuned to this strange discourse, interpreted Künast's superficially rather innocuous remark as just such a sly instance of anti-Semitism by insinuation, and said so to several reporters. A big scandal ensued, with Künast's critics blasting her for anti-Semitism, and her defenders attesting to her good intentions.

I must say that I felt a little sorry for Künast during the ensuing media frenzy. In her long years in public life, she has never engaged in the kind of dog-whistle politics of which she now stood accused. I doubt that she really meant to invoke anti-Semitic stereotypes, or to stoke some pernicious form of populism, when she suggested that Stop the Bomb is financed by the Mossad.

But if Künast was not particularly blameworthy, this does not mean that Hemberger was necessarily at fault either. While he could not be sure that Künast's remark was meant to be anti-Semitic, as a concerned citizen, he was certainly within his rights to report what he had good reason to suspect might be a defamatory insinuation. After all, if nobody ever protested against statements that sound like anti-Semitism by insinuation, no politician would ever be sanctioned for stoking populist sentiments against Jews.

It is unfortunate that anti-Semitism by insinuation allows anti-Semitic content to be expressed in public. What is much worse, however, is that it displaces the space of what *can* be spoken even further. True anti-Semites twist words that are not literally anti-Semitic to make their despicable point. They largely fall on deaf ears. But now normal people making normal points can't use those normal phrases anymore—lest they, too, end up sounding as though they were secretly anti-Semitic. In this way, the problem of anti-Semitism by insinuation gives rise to a second problem: anti-Semitism by attribution. The ultimate outcome is a discourse about Jews in which every sentence is potentially suspect and every speaker is perpetually nervous about what he says.

As a result, some Germans are growing resentful of the tense public discourse regarding all things Jewish. They worry that, like Renate Künast, they might end up the victim of a witch hunt just because they inadvertently used words that are open to misinterpretation.

To a large degree, I sympathize with their complaint. However, many Germans, in turn, overlook that the outcome is as pernicious for Jews as it is for Gentiles. Just as Gentiles are unsure which words to speak, so Jews are nervous about how to interpret the words they hear. Anxiously, they end up scouring perfectly normal utterances for their hidden meanings.

Both Jews and Gentiles are thus captives in a vicious cycle they would love, but are unable, to escape. As the clash between Hemberger and Künast shows, this is a "negative sum" game— one in which all players are likely to lose from the start.

I may be pessimistic about the future of German-Jewish relations. But I do not mean to suggest that Germany's problems are unique. On the contrary, I sometimes fear that the United States suffers from some remarkably similar neuroses.

After graduating from college, I spent some time in Munich, Paris, and London; but eventually I gravitated to the United States, and especially New York. When I spent a year as an exchange student at Columbia University, I fell in love with the city; though I eventually decided to pursue a Ph.D. in political science at Harvard, I've been splitting my time between New York and Boston (as well as, in the summers, Montelaterone) ever since.

I love living in the United States. But during the years I've spent here, the hunch I had during that discussion group about the situation of African-Americans has never left me: one could, I think, draw a very illuminating, if limited, parallel between German-Jewish relations, on the one hand, and the relations between white and black Americans, on the other.

Just as an old legacy of anti-Semitism persists in parts of Germany, some Americans still give credence to the crudest, most disgusting types of racial hatred. White supremacist groups still exist; so does the Ku Klux Klan. In certain parts of the country, racists boast a depressing amount of influence. And other parts of the country aren't always as much better as we might like to think: even in supposedly liberal, supposedly tolerant circles, pernicious stereotypes persist.

There is another parallel. In the same way that many well-meaning Germans are trying to overcome the legacy of historical injustice by cultivating a special love for klezmer and Yiddish, there are liberal Americans who, just a tad too conspicuously, profess their special appreciation for hip-hop—or, indeed, white teenagers who, in a vain attempt at coolness, copy the speech patterns of black urban youth.

Perhaps because my ample experiences with awkward philo-Semites has made me particularly sensitive to the false tones of self-conscious admiration for African-American culture, I have, over the years, seen dozens of instances of this. But the funniest example of "philo-African-American" tropes I've come across is a fictional one, to be found on a satirical website by the name of blackpeopleloveus.com. Ostensibly a venue for "Sally" and "Johnny" to show how "psyched" they are to have "real life friends" who are black, it features testimonials that sound eerily similar to Markus, Franz, and other characters I thought I'd left behind when I moved away from Germany.

"Sally and Johnny are always going on and on about how Tiger Woods changed the face of golf, and the Williams Sisters changed the face of tennis!" one of their made-up friends says, echoing Franz's comments about Woody Allen.

"Sally's always saying: 'You go, girl!' while 'raising the roof' to mainstream hip-hop tracks at cheesy bars," another seconds, channeling Markus. "That's fun! I relate to that."

Last, there is even an American version of the movement for a "finish line." Just as a new generation of Germans is impatiently announcing that, sixty-odd years after the Holocaust, the time for "normality" has finally arrived, their American counterparts insist that, 150-odd years after the end of slavery, whites should finally stop giving blacks special treatment.

All too often, this resentment takes a comparably passive-aggressive tone: many Germans fear that Jews are exploiting their guilt, turning them into the true victims; similarly, many whites have convinced themselves that they are suffering from the consequences of "reverse racism."

Even the trope that most people aren't allowed to say what they really think exists on both sides of the Atlantic: in Germany, advocates of the finish line complain that all criticisms of Israel will be denounced as anti-Semitic; in the United States, blowhards on Fox News claim that the mainstream media routinely shuts down any criticism of blacks by labeling it racist.

Alongside these similarities, there are, of course, deep and important differences. For starters, the socioeconomic status of black Americans is much lower than that of German Jews; as a result, the prejudices from which they suffer combine to form a much greater obstacle to their lives and their careers. Perhaps even more important, most Germans are bad at telling who is an Aryan; to some degree, Jews can therefore pick their battles. African-Americans, by contrast, do not have the luxury to remain inconspicuous whenever they choose.

Nevertheless, it is hardly a coincidence that the controversies that arise between white and black Americans can be strikingly similar—in both tone and substance—to those between Jews and Germans. Two weeks to the day after Thomas Hemberger accused Renate Künast of anti-Semitism, for example, Sgt. James Crowley created an even bigger controversy by arresting Henry Louis Gates, Jr., a tenured professor at Harvard University, outside his home in Cambridge, Massachusetts.

Gates had just returned home from a research trip to China. When he got out of his cab, he found his front door jammed. With the help of his cabbie, he managed to force it open. Unfortunately, a concerned neighbor had seen Gates and his cab driver, and feared that a break-in might be in progress.

"I don't know if they live there, and they just had a hard time with their key," the neighbor cautioned when she called 911, "but I did notice that they had to use their shoulders to try to barge in." Sergeant Crowley was dispatched to Gates's residence.

As in the confrontation between Künast and Hemberger, there are competing accounts of what happened next.

According to Sergeant Crowley, he politely asked Professor Gates for identification to check that he was the rightful occupant of his residence. But Gates grew belligerent, engaging in "very loud" and "tumultuous" behavior. Eventually, Sergeant Crowley had no choice but to arrest Gates for disorderly conduct.

According to Professor Gates, it was Sergeant Crowley who was needlessly aggressive.

> I said "Officer, can I help you?" And he said, "Would you step outside onto the porch." And the way he said it, I knew he wasn't canvassing for the police benevolent association. All the hairs stood up on the back of my neck, and I realized that I was in danger. And I said to him no, out of instinct. I said, "No, I will not."

According to Professor Gates, he firmly but politely requested that Sergeant Crowley tell him his name and badge number. But instead of complying with this request, one of the "ocean of po-lice" who by this time had gathered on his front porch handcuffed and arrested him. For Professor Gates, it was clear what was going on. As he was walked to the police car, he asked: "Is this how you treat a black man in America?"

Over the next days, the story of Skip Gates's arrest dominated the American news cycle. A fierce debate erupted. Who was lying, Gates or Crowley? Had Crowley mistreated and then arrested Gates for no better reason than that he is black? Or was Gates play-ing the "race card" to get a free pass for his disorderly conduct?

Like in the case of Hemberger and Künast, we don't have all the facts, so there's no way of giving a definitive answer. But in my mind these are, in any case, the wrong questions. They assume that one person must be good, and the other evil; one forthright, and the other disingenuous. But isn't it possible that both Gates and Crowley were acting reasonably (if a little rashly)?

I think so. It is certainly understandable that Sergeant Crow-ley would initially confront Professor Gates in a sharp tone. He had been dispatched to investigate what he'd been told was a seri-ous crime in progress. When he arrived at the scene, he wasn't expecting to face a Harvard professor; he was expecting to face a hardened criminal, who might well be carrying a gun. Under those circumstances, it is easy to understand why his request for Professor Gates to step out onto the front porch wouldn't have sounded as though he were "canvassing for the police benevolent association."

But if Sergeant Crowley's initial rudeness is forgivable, so is Professor Gates's wrath at being treated rudely. He was in his own home. He hadn't broken the law. And yet, here was a policeman who, for no reason that was apparent to him at the time, seemed to doubt that he, a black man, could possibly be the rightful occu-pant of this nice a home; a cop who, despite everything Professor Gates had achieved in his life, had the temerity to talk to him as if he were a common criminal. Sure, he couldn't know that this cop would have been less rude to a white man—but, then, few cops would be foolish enough to give proof positive of being racist. So, from what Professor Gates knew at the time, wasn't his assumption reasonable enough?

As in many confrontations between Jews and Germans, then, our instinct to pick sides in a controversy as fraught with history and ambiguity as this one is likely to lead us astray. To explain the situation, we don't have to imagine either that Gates was the victim of Crowley's racism or that Crowley was the victim of Gates's cynical desire to use his race for some advantage.

By far the more likely explanation is that both were victims of a situation they did little to create, and were powerless to resolve. As in Germany, a very real history of injustice makes it difficult for members of groups with opposing historical experiences to get along, even in situations where both sides are doing their best to act fairly.

So, however pessimistic, this is one lesson I think we can draw about societies, like Germany and the United States, where the descendants of perpetrators and the descendants of victims are frustrated that they do not get along better: a pure heart and an ardent wish to overcome are powerful weapons in the fight for social change. But to assume that they can overcome all obstacles, or make the past disappear, is to believe in magic.

The United States suffers from its own share of seemingly insurmountable tensions. But for all of my encounters with these neuroses, the fact remains that, as a white immigrant from Europe, they affect me in, at most, a rather superficial manner.

I don't mean to be glib about this: injustices and their long-term legacies have a way of affecting every member of a society, even those who are lucky enough to escape the most direct consequences much of the time. If any American readers have allowed themselves to feel a little smug when they were reading about Germany's ongoing problems, I hope they are sobered by the thought that comparable issues exist close to home.

Even so, the degree to which I myself am affected by these kinds of problems in my everyday life does matter to me. In deciding where to spend my life, I didn't ask myself whether the United States of America has fewer flaws than the Federal Republic of Germany; I wouldn't know how to begin addressing so sweeping and elusive a question.

Rather, I asked myself where I might one day come to feel at home. That question, I did know how to answer. Given who I happen to be, I feel much more at home in New York City than in Munich or Berlin.

●

There is, I realize, one question I have overlooked, ignored, perhaps deliberately dodged. It is simple, yet fundamental. Now, at the close of this book, it is finally time for me to tackle it head on: Am I really a Jew?

Growing up, my identity as a Jew was incompatible with my identity as a German. The seemingly innocuous fact of being Jewish, I write, explains my increasing alienation from the country where I grew up. But by my own admission, I am not religious. I never go to synagogue, didn't have a bar mitzvah, and rarely notice when Yom Kippur or Pesach come around. So what, if anything, makes me a Jew?

For a long time, I've relied on two handy subterfuges to banish doubts about my Jewish identity from my own mind. The first was to tell myself that I'm a cultural Jew. It wasn't too difficult to make myself believe that lie. I do enjoy a good whitefish bagel, love *Seinfeld*, and have even been known to make mildly self-deprecating jokes. Isn't that enough?

Well, actually, no, it probably isn't.

It's obvious enough why, like so many other people of my generation, I was tempted to call myself a cultural Jew. Nobody wants to admit to what extent they have lost touch with their family traditions or heritage. To lay claim to the remnants of my origins allowed me to latch on to *something*, at least; in a world in which "who you are" is to a large degree a question about your heritage, any excuse for an identity was welcome—even though, deep down, I knew mine to be rather flimsy.

After a while, though, I found it increasingly difficult to ignore just how flimsy that excuse really was. I came to fear that to lay claim to Jewish culture for no better reason than bagels, *Seinfeld*, and a half-decent sense of humor was to treat the very heritage I was claiming with disrespect.

I still don't know whether or not it's truly possible to separate Jewish culture from Jewish religion. But one thing I do know: if it is possible, then what's left of Jewish culture once you've taken religion out had better be more substantive than food and stand-up comedy. People who speak Hebrew, say, or play klezmer, or observe the rituals of their ancestors, or have some other form of serious and sustained engagement with Judaism may truly be culturally Jewish. I, for one, am not.

The second subterfuge was to tell myself that, in some vague and oddly reassuring sense, I did, after all, belong to something like a Jewish ethnicity.

The possible sources of my belief are many. The Jews of the Old Testament, described as a people and subdivided into twelve tribes, sound rather like an ethnic group to a modern reader. The Jews of Eastern Europe, I knew, were largely confined to their shtetls, mixing genes with Gentiles only as a result of secret liaisons or rapes. Finally, when I was growing up, it quickly became clear to me that, in the minds of those around me, what it meant to be a true German was to have German genes; since I did not qualify, I naturally assumed that I must be defined by having Jewish genes instead.

It's not clear to me that any of this is particularly wrong. If (and this is a reasonably big if) there is something like a coherent understanding of what a Spanish, Italian, or German ethnicity consists in, then I don't see why there might not be a Jewish ethnicity as well. But is it meaningful to call somebody Spanish by mere virtue of their descent—even though they don't live in Spain, don't speak Spanish, and don't even have any particular knowledge of Spanish culture? More important, would I *want* to identify as Spanish, Italian, or German for the sole reason that such is the "blood" that "courses through my veins"?

The honest answer is no. To say that I'm ethnically Jewish may well be correct. Even so, it remains far from clear why I should choose to invest that biological fact with any particularly deep meaning.

This leaves me with one last possible source for my Jewishness: the cold fact that my grandparents, and even my parents, have been defined, hated, and persecuted as Jews; and the additional fact that many of my supposed countrymen ceased thinking of me as a real compatriot as soon as I mentioned these ancestors to them.

In a sense, this was enough. I love my parents and my grandparents. If to speak honestly about their life stories is to become, in the eyes of most beholders, a Jew—and if being a Jew, in turn, means not being a true German—then, so long as I lived in Germany, my family history made me a Jew. That's why, even in hindsight, I think I was right to internalize the categories other people employed to describe me: that of being a Jew; that of not being a German.

To say that I don't regret having self-identified as a Jew while I lived in Germany does not, however, mean that I want to continue thinking of myself as a Jew for the rest of my life. So long as I could avoid thinking of myself as a Jew only by deceiving myself about the world around me (or by deceiving others about my family history), I was right to embrace being a Jew. But being a

Jew was an external imposition. My acceptance of that label remained contingent: something I tolerated, but also something that could not—or, at any rate, did not—grow into a wholehearted expression of my inner self. One thing therefore became increasingly clear to me as I reflected on whether or not I truly am a Jew: in a place where people wouldn't label me a Jew even if they knew about my family history (or in a place where that label, even if it were applied to me, would be irrelevant in my everyday life), I'd no longer need to define myself by the words of others. I'd be free not to be a Jew. For me, that place—the place where I can cease to be a German and cease to be a Jew and come to be at home—is New York City.

Some, of course, would insist that being Jewish still makes you a kind of outsider in the United States.

It's only natural that American Jews should at times feel nervous about their position. After all, their acceptance into the highest echelons of American society is still relatively recent. Though anti-Semitism has never been as visceral in North America as in most parts of Europe, the United States does have a long history of discrimination against Jews. Not so long ago, Ivy League universities had de facto quotas to stop Harvard and Princeton from going "too Jewish." Many country clubs would not admit Jews as members. Jewish politicians were a rarity.

It's hardly a coincidence, then, that the Jews' precarious state of inclusion is such a dominating theme of twentieth-century American literature—most obviously in famous Jewish authors like Philip Roth and Saul Bellow, but just as interestingly in the works of arch-Gentiles like F. Scott Fitzgerald (think of Meyer Wolfsheim in *The Great Gatsby*) or Shirley Jackson ("A Fine Old Firm").

It would be highly surprising if the questions and anxieties so evocatively portrayed in these brilliant works had completely vanished from the thoughts and fears of American Jews within the short span of one or two generations. Thus, some Jews—even some young, extremely successful Jews—dutifully ask themselves the same old searching questions from time to time. Despite their success, isn't there some sense in which they still do not belong? Even though most people around them don't seem to care one bit whether they are Jewish, Christian, or Buddhist, isn't there always the possibility that they will suddenly be made to feel like outsiders?

I suppose that everyone has to answer that question for himor herself. So far as I am concerned, though, being Jewish in the United States is blissfully straightforward. Whenever I have mentioned to an American that my family is Jewish, they have shrugged and moved on with the conversation. I cannot recall a single instance when I had the impression that this fact—which was laden with so much significance for me when I was growing up—changed how they saw or treated me.

If I am confident that my being a Jew, or my growing up in Germany, wouldn't be a big obstacle to my inclusion in most parts of the United States, I am doubly confident about that fact in the city I hope to call home for the rest of my life.

Part of the reason, of course, is that Jews are so numerous in New York. It may be ironic that it takes living in a city with well over a million Jews to stop feeling like a Jew—but, really, it's obvious enough why the fact of being Jewish is so much less salient in a place where so many other people are Jewish, too.

I suspect, however, that another reason is even more important. It is that, as E. B. White remarked in his luminous essay on that most luminous of cities, New York is defined by its newcomers much more than by its natives.

There are, White wrote, roughly three New Yorks. The first is the city of those who were born there. But a native New Yorker "takes the city for granted and accepts its size and turbulence as natural and inevitable."

The second is the city of commuters. White's disdain for

them is palpable: "Except in rare cases, the man who lives in Mamaroneck or Little Neck or Teaneck, and works in New York, discovers nothing much about the city except the time of arrival and departure of trains and buses, and the path to a quick lunch." Finally, there is the third New York, the New York of those who were born elsewhere and came to the city "in quest of something."

> Of these three trembling cities, the greatest is the last—the city of final destination, the city that is a goal. It is this third city that accounts for New York's high-strung disposition, its poetical deportment, its dedication to the arts, and its incomparable achievements. Commuters give the city its tidal restlessness; natives give it solidity and continuity; but the settlers give it passion. And whether it is a farmer arriving from Italy to set up a small grocery store in a slum, or a young girl arriving from a small town in Mississippi to escape the indignity of being observed by her neighbors, or a boy arriving from the Corn Belt with a manuscript in his suitcase and a pain in his heart, it makes no difference: each embraces New York with the intense excitement of first love, each absorbs New York with the fresh eyes of an adventurer, each generates heat and light to dwarf the Consolidated Edison Company.

A true Berliner is one whose ancestors are German. A true Parisian is one whose parents—or, better still, whose grandparents—were born inside the Boulevard Périphérique. A true New Yorker is one who has come to the city in quest of something.

Whether he is a farmer arriving from Italy, a young girl arriving from a small town in Mississippi, a boy arriving from the Corn Belt, or a German Jew who no longer wants to be either a German or a Jew, he embraces New York with the intense excitement of first love—and, without a thought for who he may be, is embraced by it in turn.

It is because of this wonderful quality that New York has become my final destination.

Here I can talk all I want about who I am or where I come from. It makes little difference. My identity is no longer that of a Jew or a German. It is that of a seeker who has found; that of a stranger who has come to be at home; that of, simply and immeasurably, a New Yorker.

Notes

All translations into English, unless otherwise indicated, are by the author.

PRELUDE: AN UNLIKELY REFUGE

7 *In 1960, General Wojciech Jaruzelski*: Susanne Starecki, "Remedying Past Abuses of Governmental Power—Legal Accountability for the 1968 Events in Poland," *Hastings International and Comparative Law Review*, vol. 26, 2002, p. 482.

8 *To diffuse popular resentment and rescue their authority*: Gomułka had let loose the opening salvo of this new wave of persecution even earlier, in June 1967, when Israel won a decisive victory against its Arab neighbors in the Six Day War. Speaking in the war's immediate aftermath, he announced in his address to the Sixth Trade Union Congress:

> The Israeli aggression on the Arab countries was met with applause in Zionist circles of Jews . . . We cannot remain indifferent toward people who in the face of a threat to world peace, and thus also to the security of Poland and the peaceful work of our nation, come out in favor of the aggressor, the wreckers of peace, and imperialism. Let those who feel these words are addressed to them, irrespective of their nationality, draw the proper conclusions. We do not want a Fifth Column to be created in our country.

(Quoted in Starecki, "Remedying Past Abuses," p. 483; translation by Dariusz Stola.)

20 *According to a family story (beloved by Christian but probably apocryphal)*: Wlodzimierz Nechamkis: "Vom Ender einer 'Zielgerichteten humanistischen Mission': Zum Freitod des Exilschriftstellers Christian Skrzyposzek," Deutschlandfunk, 4/10/2001.

1. A BOY NAMED JEW

29 *In 2011, 811 anti-Semitic crimes*: These figures are compiled by the German government in quarterly installments in response to inquiries by the
parliamentary faction of DIE LINKE. The figures for 2011 are available at
www.petrapau.de/17_bundestag/dok/down/2011_zf_antisemitischen
_straftaten.pdf (accessed on 6/28/2013).

29 *As former government spokesman Uwe-Karsten Heye admitted*: For Heye's
controversial remarks about "no-go areas," see, for example: www.spiegel
.de/politik/deutschland/rassismus-debatte-selbst-die-polizei-hat-mancher
orts-aufgegeben-a-417861.html (accessed on 12/13/2012).

30 *According to a 2012 study*: Oliver Decker, Johannes Kiess, and Elmar
Brähler, *Die Mitte im Umbruch: Rechtsextreme Einstellungen in Deutsch-
land 2012* (Bonn: Verlag J.H.W. Dietz Nachf. Gmbh, 2012), pp. 29–30.
Available online at www.fes-gegen-rechtsextremismus.de/pdf_12/mitte
-im-umbruch_www.pdf (accessed 12/12/2012). Please note that there are
five distinct categories of answers: "I fully disagree," "I mostly disagree,"
"I partly agree and partly disagree," "I mostly agree," and "I fully agree."
The figures I use represent the sums of the latter three categories.

30 *A study commissioned by the German government*: "Bericht des unab-
hängigen Expertenkreis Antisemitismus: Antisemitismus in Deutschland—Erscheinungsformen, Bedingungen, Präventionsansätze." Available
at: http://dipbt.bundestag.de/dip21/btd/17/077/1707700.pdf (accessed on
12/11/2012).

30 *Hatred of immigrants is even more widespread*: See Decker, Kiess, and
Brähler, *Die Mitte im Umbruch*, p. 19.

30 *a staggering 58 percent believe*: This figure stems from an earlier study by
the Friedrich-Ebert-Stiftung. For media coverage, see www.publikative
.org/2010/10/13/mehrheit-will-religionsfreiheit-fur-moslems-einschranken
(accessed on 7/13/2012).

30 *even highbrow German papers referred to these tragic events as the* "Döner-
Morde": For some of the many uncritical uses of this term, see, for example: www.faz.net/aktuell/politik/doener-morde-mutmasslicher-komplize
-festgenommen-11527576.html; www.sueddeutsche.de/panorama/ermittler
-finden-tatwaffe-bombenbauer-moerder-rechtsextremisten-1.1187136;
www.spiegel.de/politik/deutschland/doener-morde-sie-nannten-ihn-den
-kleinen-adolf-a-798035.html; and www.bild.de/news/inland/news-inland
/11-tote-polizei-prueft-weiteren-doener-mord-20993648.bild.html (all accessed on 11/15/2012). Note, however, that there was an eventual backlash
against the term, especially after an organization that annually chooses
what they consider the worst term of the past year chose it as the "Un-
wort" of 2011 (see www.spiegel.de/kultur/gesellschaft/sprachkritik-doener
-morde-ist-unwort-des-jahres-a-809512.html; accessed 4/27/2013).

37 *a majority of the population endorses these views*: See Decker, Kiess, and Brähler, *Die Mitte im Umbruch*, pp. 68–86.

2. THE REMNANT

42 *Nearly 600,000 Jews lived in Germany*: Depending on the precise criteria, there are slightly different estimates about the number of German Jews both when the Nazis took power and at war's end. I follow the figures used by the Central Council of Jews in Germany (see, for example, www.zentral ratdjuden.de/de/topic/17.html; accessed on 9/12/2012). The figures for the number of German Jews killed in the Holocaust also vary slightly. The United States Holocaust Memorial Museum, for example, concludes that "between 160,000 and 180,000 German Jews" were killed in the Holocaust (www.ushmm.org/wlc/en/article.php?ModuleId=10005469; accessed on 9/12/2012).

44 *"this became an unexpected moment in Jewish history"*: Ruth Gay, *Safe Among the Germans: Liberated Jews After World War II* (New Haven: Yale University Press, 2002), p. xi.

45 *the birthrate among Jewish DPs was, according to some estimates*: German Historical Institute of Washington, D.C.: http://germanhistorydocs.ghi-dc .org/sub_image.cfm?image_id=1084 (accessed on 3/13/2010).

45 *the parting consul, Chaim Yachil, reaffirmed his expectation*: Michael Brenner, *Nach dem Holocaust: Juden in Deutschland 1945–1950* (München: Beck'sche Reihe, 1995), p. 100.

46 *In the evocative description of Amos Elon*: Amos Elon, *The Pity of It All: A History of Jews in Germany, 1743–1933* (New York: Metropolitan Books, 2002), pp. 1–12.

48 *German Democratic Republic (GDR)*: The GDR's German name was Deutsche Demokratische Republik (DDR).

49 *a "share of the guilt is borne by all those"*: "Aufruf des ZK der KPD vom 11. Juni 1945," in *Dokumente und Materialien zur Geschichte der deutschen Arbeiterbewegung*, Reihe III, Bd. I (East Berlin, 1959), p. 15.

50 *"even in a show trial with an anti-Semitic component"*: Mario Kessler, *Die SED und die Juden—zwischen Repression und Toleranz. Politische Entwicklungen bis 1967* (Berlin: Akademie Verlag, 1995), p. 89.

3. SILENCE, REVERBERATING

54–55 *By the early 1950s, Allied involvement in bringing Nazi war criminals*: The Allies' change of course brought on some real injustices. For practical reasons, the denazification campaign had begun by investigating mid-ranking Nazis. Eventually, it had been supposed to work up to trying more high-ranking criminals. But the Allies' political will lost steam long before that stage. As a result, only a small, random subsection of mid-level Nazis was singled out for punishment—while many of the most heinous culprits got off scot-free. For a recent narrative history, see Frederick Taylor, *Exorcising Hitler: The Occupation and Denazification of Germany* (London: Bloomsbury, 2011).

55 *"Tell me the year in which a war criminal"*: Personal communication with Devin Pendas.

56 *"the world's Jewry is a great power"*: As Tobias Jaecker points out, this Adenauer quote was still being invoked in debates between Jews and Gentiles over three decades later. (See Tobias Jaecker, "Die Wasler-Bubis-Debatte: Erinnern oder Vergessen?" Available at: www.antisemitismus.net/deutsch land/walser-bubis.htm; accessed on 1/12/2013).

56 *"The power of the Jews"*: For video footage of this interview, see www.you tube.com/watch?v=2wbs6Elfme8 (accessed on 2/12/2012).

57 *Public opinion . . . remained resolutely opposed to the reparations*: Elisabeth Noelle and Erich Peter Neumann, *Jahrbuch der Öffentlichen Meinung, 1947–1955* (Allensbach: Verlag für Demoskopie, 1956), p. 130.

57 *three out of every five bureaucrats appointed to leading positions*: Edgar Wolfrum, *Die geglückte Demokratie: Geschichte der Bundesrepublik Deutschland von ihren Anfängen bis zur Gegenwart* (München: Pantheon Verlag, 2007), p. 58.

59 *By 1976, only 20 percent of Germans were dissatisfied*: Christopher Duggan, *A Concise History of Italy* (Cambridge, U.K.: Cambridge University Press, 1994), p. 274.

60 *"Father could not permit sorrow, only anger"*: Uwe Timm, *Am Beispiel meines Bruders* (Köln: Kiepenheuer & Witsch, 2003), p. 78.

62 *"My teachers simply avoided the subject"*: Judit Yago-Jung, "Growing Up in Germany: After the War; after Hitler; 'Afterwards,'" in *New German Critique*, no. 19, Winter 1980, p. 75.

64 *Filbinger had him imprisoned*: In keeping with the Geneva Convention, the Allies allowed German troops to administer justice within their own ranks independently according to their own rules and standards.

64 *"what was just then cannot be unjust now"*: In the original German ("Was damals rechtens war, kann heute nicht Unrecht sein"), it remains ambiguous whether Filbinger meant for "just" and "unjust" to have a primarily legal or a primarily moral meaning.

64 *At his state funeral in 2007*: In the relevant passage of the speech, Öttinger claimed: "In contrast to what one could read in some obituaries, we need to say for the record: Hans Filbinger was no National Socialist. On the contrary: he was an opponent of the Nazi regime." A transcript of his speech is available online at: www.spiegel.de/politik/deutschland/dokumentation -hans-filbinger-war-kein-nationalsozialist-a-476898.html (accessed on

3/19/2011). On Walter Nachmann's defense of Hans Filbinger, see Lynn Rapaport, *Jews in Germany after the Holocaust: Memory, Identity, and Jewish-German Relations* (Cambridge, U.K.: Cambridge University Press, 1997), p. 34.

68 *No longer called Carl-Laemmle-Gymnasium*: After a controversial campaign, which culminated after we had left Laupheim for Munich in 1994, the school was eventually renamed Carl-Laemmle-Gymnasium.

4. SWEET SURRENDER

79 *the Third Reich had been an* "Unrechtsstaat": Claudia Fröhlich, *Wider die Tabuisierung des Ungehorsams: Fritz Bauers Widerstandsbegriff und die Aufarbeitung der NS-Verbrechen* (Frankfurt/Main: Campus Verlag, 2006), pp. 97–100.

80 *"Auschwitz was not hell"*: Martin Walser, "Unser Auschwitz," in Hans Magnus Enzensberger (ed.), *Kursbuch*, no. 1 (June 1965), pp. 189–200.

81 *The people of Göppingen were only too happy*: Hans Georg Frank, "Lügen für ein neues Leben," *Südwest Presse*, 12/8/2012 (www.swp.de/ulm/nach richten/suedwestumschau/Luegen-fuer-ein-neues-Leben;art4319,1759852; accessed on 1/10/2013).

85 *"The 1968 movement in Germany challenged"*: Yascha Mounk, "Contagious Utopianism," *The Utopian*, 5/14/2008 (available at: www.the-utopian.org /post/2411719137/contagious-utopianism; accessed on 4/12/2011).

87 *"My gesture was symbolic"*: Beate Klarsfeld, "J'ai giflé le Chancelier Allemand Kiesinger," *Paris Match*, 08/17/2009 (available at: www.parismatch .com/Actu-Match/Monde/Actu/Gifle-Kiesinger-Beate-Klarsfeld-nazi -120738; accessed on 4/14/2011).

87 *"Esteemed ladies and gentlemen; dear Negroes"*: This line has been extensively quoted, both in the German press and in numerous books. However, there does not appear to be an authoritative source for it. One newspaper article that tried to verify its authenticity ultimately concluded that it may be no more than an apt invention: Christoph Drösser, "Stimmt's? Lübke und die Neger," *Die Zeit*, no. 14, 2002.

88 *"Some are still invested in the authoritarian state"*: Quoted in Edgar Wolfrum, *Die geglückte Demokratie* (München: Pantheon Verlag, 2007), p. 290.

92 *Marcel Reich-Ranicki, a Polish Jew who survived*: Video interview with Marcel Reich-Ranicki, available at: www.histoclips.de/video_clip_liste -205-47-5-0-1970_-_Der_Kniefall_von_Warschau (accessed on 11/14/2012).

92 *"Ladies and Gentlemen, I interrupt our session"*: For video footage of the announcement, see www.youtube.com/watch?v=cRy-NzyLDBk (accessed on 1/8/2013).

94 *Franz Josef Strauss, Bavaria's far-right prime minister*: Martine Thiele, "Publizistische Kontroversen über den Holocaust im Film," Dissertation zur

Erlangung des Doktorgrades der Mathematisch-Naturwissenschaftlichen Fakultäten der Georg-August-Universität zu Göttingen, 2001, p. 310 (available at http://webdoc.sub.gwdg.de/diss/2001/thiele/thiele.pdf; accessed on 9/14/2012).

94 *Even so, the show's impact proved overwhelming*: "Holocaust: Die Vergangenheit kommt zurück," *Der Spiegel* no. 5, 1979 (1/29/1979).

94 *According to polls taken after the broadcast*: Wolfrum, *Geglückte Demokratie*, p. 398.

95 *"Earlier, I thought that the Jews must have committed some kind of a crime"*: "Vergangenheit kommt zurück," *Der Spiegel*.

96 *"Most Germans had thought that they were fighting and suffering"*: A recording of the speech in the original German is available online at: www.youtube.com/watch?v=twOsY-Zag7c; accessed on 9/15/2012.

5. THE SILENT JEW

98 *"because he married his stepdaughter"*: Unbeknownst to Franz and Marie, Soon-Yi was not, strictly speaking, Woody Allen's stepdaughter. She was an adopted daughter of Mia Farrow and her former husband André Previn. Though Allen and Farrow were a couple before he began a relationship with Soon-Yi, they had never been married, and Allen had never formally adopted Soon-Yi.

98 *"his Jew humor is admirable"*: The German term Franz used is *"Judenhumor,"* a term no less strange than the English translation I chose.

102 *a large number of Jews decided to come to Germany*: Barbara Dietz, "German and Jewish Migration from the Former Soviet Union to Germany: Background, Trends and Implications," *Journal of Ethnic and Migration Studies*, vol. 26 (4), 2000.

102 *the real number of ethnic Jews living in Germany today is probably higher still*: However, it is probably lower than the high number of Jewish immigrants might suggest. This has various reasons. Some of these immigrants eventually moved on to Israel or the United States, or returned to Russia. Some of them were the Gentile spouses of Jewish immigrants. Others still were not Jewish at all but had cajoled or bribed local officials to get a visa as a *Kontingentflüchtling*.

103 *a recent study found that about 40 percent of highly qualified Jewish immigrants*: Quoted in Julia Smilga, "Geste der Wiedergutmachung: 20 Jahre jüdische Einwanderung aus der ehemaligen Sowjetunion," *Deutschlandradio Kultur*, 1/7/2011. (Available at www.dradio.de/dkultur/sendungen/ausderjuedischenwelt/1358527; accessed on 12/13/2012.)

107 *"so long as Germans refuse to say anything negative about Jews"*: Peter Zadek, *My Way: Eine Autobiographie, 1926–1969* (Köln: Kepenheuer & Witsch, 1998), p. 315.

107 *"Philo-Semites are really something very German"*: Birgit Lahann, "'Shakespeare hätte mich nicht verstanden,'" *Die Zeit*, no. 33, 2009. (Available at www.zeit.de/2009/33/Interview-Zadek/komplettansicht; accessed on 12/11/2012.)

108 *"Even forty years after the end of World War II, Richter's attitude toward Jews"*: Marcel Reich-Ranicki, *Mein Leben* (Stuttgart: Deutsche Verlags-Anstalt, 1999), p. 411. Interestingly, on another occasion Richter reports that there was a widespread feeling in the group that Reich-Ranicki "just doesn't belong to the clique, belongs to it as little as Hans Mayer [another Jew]." (Cited in Uwe Neumann, "Deckname Marcel—Uwe Johnson und Marcel Reich-Ranicki," in Ulrich Fries, Holger Helbig, and Irmgard Müller (eds.), *Johnson-Jahrbuch*, vol. 10, 2003, p. 47.)

108 *"But it could frequently be found in the rabble-rousing press"*: Reich-Ranicki, *Mein Leben*, p. 472.

6. FAILED FRIENDSHIPS

112 History as Making Sense of the Senseless: Theodor Lessing, *Geschichte als Sinngebung des Sinnlosen* (Munich: C. H. Beck, 1921).

113 *Hindenburg, he claimed, seemed like a harmless "zero" in his old age*: Theodor Lessing, "Hindenburg," *Prager Tageblatt*, 4/25/1925. Reprinted in Theodor Lessing, *Ich warf eine Flaschenpost ins Eismeer der Geschichte: Essays und Feuilletons* (Darmstadt: Edition Luchterhand, 1986), pp. 65–69.

113 *triumphantly announced that he had "cast off that yoke"*: Ursula Homann, "Die Waffe der Kritik vortrefflich genutzt: Vor siebzig Jahren wurde Theodor Lessing ermordet" (available at: www.ursulahomann.de/DieWaffe DerKritikVortrefflichGenutztVorSiebzigJahrenWurdeTheodorLessing Ermordet/komplett.html; accessed on 5/3/2008).

114 *"Conscious control of all births on earth"*: Theodor Lessing, *Europa und Asien*, 4th edition, 1927, pp. 124–25. (My emphases.)

115 *"announce to the world the well-known teachings"*: Theodor Lessing, *Deutschland und seine Juden* (Prague: Neumann, 1933), p. 15.

115 *"by and large, Lessing shared his ideology with his murderers"*: Thomas Mann, *Tagebücher 1933–1934* (Frankfurt/Main: S. Fischer Verlag, 1977), entry for 7/15/1934, p. 474.

115 *"the history of his public reputation is, above all else, to be understood"*: Rainer Marwedel, *Theodor Lessing. 1872–1933. Eine Biographie* (Darmstadt: Edition Luchterhand, 1987), p. 10.

117 *as Hans Kundnani convincingly argues*: Hans Kundnani, *Utopia or Auschwitz: Germany's 1968 Generation and the Holocaust* (New York: Columbia University Press, 2009). Some material in the following pages is drawn from "A Moral Baseball Bat," a review I wrote for *n+1* (available at

www.nplusonemag.com/a-moral-baseball-bat; accessed on 1/16/2012). My argument in these pages is indebted to Kundnani's excellent book.

120 *According to Reich-Ranicki, whom she interviewed in the mid-1960s*: Reich-Ranicki, *Mein Leben*, pp. 459–60.

120 *She now spoke of Auschwitz and the Allied bombings of German cities*: Kundnani, *Utopia or Auschwitz*, p. 111.

120 *As Wolfgang Kraushaar, a German historian, has argued*: Wolfgang Kraushaar, *Die Bombe im jüdischen Gemeindehaus* (Hamburg: Hamburger Editionen, 2005).

120 *"On the 31st anniversary of the fascist Kristallnacht"*: Cited in Timo Stein, *Zwischen Antisemitismus und Israelkritik: Antisemitismus in der deutschen Linken* (Wiesbaden: VS Verlag für Sozialwissenschaften, 2011), p. 50.

122 *"Israel is shedding crocodile tears"*: Sarah Colvin, *Ulrike Meinhof and West German Terrorism: Language, Violence, and Identity* (Rochester, N.Y.: Camden House, 2009), p. 158.

122 *"I am no Nazi," he declared. "I am an idealist!"*: David Tinnin, "Like Father," *Time*, 8/8/1977.

123 *"And so you alleviate your anguish by transposing the dispute"*: Henryk M. Broder, "Ihr bleibt die Kinder eurer Eltern," *Die Zeit*, 2/27/1981 (available at: www.zeit.de/1981/10/ihr-bleibt-die-kinder-eurer-eltern/komplettansicht; accessed on 12/12/2012).

7. THE CLOSED SEASON ENDS

131 *he inquired whether the names were arranged in alphabetical order*: Monika Köpcke, "Helmut Kohl trifft in Israel ein und spricht von der 'Gnade der späten Geburt,'" Deutschlandradio Berlin, 1/24/2004 (available at www.dradio.de/dlr/sendungen/kalender/227514; accessed on 1/17/2013).

132 *"I know German history very well"*: "Kohl's History Lesson," *Newsweek*, 2/6/1982, p. 38.

132 *"I am speaking to you as somebody who could not come to guilt"*: Mathias Berek, *Kollektives Gedächtnis und die gesellschaftliche Konstruktion der Wirklichkeit. Eine Theorie der Erinnerungskulturen* (Wiesbaden: Harrassowitz Verlag, 2009), p. 97 (note).

133 *Reagan visited the Bitburg cemetery on May 5, 1985*: Bernard Weinraub, "Reagan Joins Kohl in Brief Memorial at Bitburg Graves," *New York Times*, 5/6/1985.

133 *"The demand that is gaining more and more support in West Germany"*: "Dispute over Cemetery Visit Angers Many West Germans; 'Forty Years Are Enough,' Newspaper Says," *Washington Post*, 4/27/1985.

134 *According to Nolte, a "conspicuous shortcoming"*: All quotes from Nolte in the following pages are from Ernst Nolte, "Vergangenheit, die nicht verge-

hen will. Eine Rede, die geschrieben, aber nicht gehalten werden konnte,"
Frankfurter Allgemeine Zeitung, 6/6/1986.

135 *Jürgen Habermas fired the opening salvo*: Jürgen Habermas, "Eine Art
Schadensabwicklung. Die apologetischen Tendenzen in der deutschen
Zeitgeschichtsschreibung," *Die Zeit*, 7/11/1986.

135 *Left-leaning historians and journalists like Hans Mommsen*: The most important texts from this year-long debate are collected in Rudolf Augstein
(ed.), *Historikerstreit: Die Dokumentation der Kontroverse um die Einzig-
artigkeit der nationalsozialistischen Judenvernichtung* (München: Serie
Piper, 5th ed., 1987).

138 *In the 1970s, commentators in the major national papers*: Sigrid Meu-
schel and Benjamin Gregg, "The Search for 'Normality' in the Relationship between Germans and Jews," *New German Critique*, no. 38, special
issue on the German-Jewish controversy (Spring–Summer 1986),
pp. 39–56.

139 *"membership of several representatives of Jewish capital"*: *Frankfurter Rundschau*, 11/5/1986.

139 *a phrase that Rühle, according to multiple witnesses, proclaimed*: Günther
Rühle later denied saying that the "closed season is over," insisting instead
that he had talked of an end to Jewish "no-hunting zones," "areas," or
"reservations." For contemporary articles on the subject, see "German
Drops Anti-Semitism Suit," *New York Times*, 12/12/1986, and Hans
Schueler, "Schonzone und Schonzeit," *Die Zeit*, 10/5/1986.

141 *"A routine of accusation has arisen in the media"*: Martin Walser, "Erfah-
rungen beim Verfassen einer Sonntagsrede." (Available at: www.hdg.de
/lemo/html/dokumente/WegeInDieGegenwart_redeWalserZumFrie
denspreis; accessed on 12/5/2012.)

143 *opinion polls revealed that 63 percent of Germans were in favor*: Tobias
Jaecker, "Die Walser-Bubis-Debatte: Erinnern oder Vergessen?" (Available at: www.hagalil.com/antisemitismus/deutschland/walser-1.htm; accessed 1/18/2012.)

143 *"The wind left the trees naked"*: From Heinrich Heine, *Deutschland. Ein
Wintermärchen*, Caput I, "Im traurigen Monat November war's . . ." Translation by Sam Munson.

145 *"What would you do if Germany were occupied?"*: "Möllemann-Affäre:
Die Zitate, die die Republik bewegen," Spiegel Online (available at: www
.spiegel.de/politik/deutschland/moellemann-affaere-die-zitate-die-die
-republik-bewegen-a-199445.html; accessed on 1/11/2013).

145 *"I fear that hardly anybody feeds the anti-Semitism"*: Ibid.

146 *a practical joke played on the party by* Titanic: All the quotes in this section stem from: "'Asoziale Rattenfänger!' Wie TITANIC und FDP ein-
mal gemeinsam in Thüringen einen antisemitischen Spaßwahlkampf
führten," *Titanic*, 7/2002 (available at www.titanic-magazin.de/archive

/heftarchiv00-06/?f=0702%2Ffdp1&cHash=b7f83ec0b8eaf37b4a07536ce d4b97cf; accessed on 5/20/2013).

150 *Walser followed that speech up with a roman à clef*: Martin Walser, *Tod eines Kritikers* (Frankfurt: Suhrkamp Verlag, 2002).

150 *Frank Schirrmacher, a publisher of the* Frankfurter Allgemeine Zeitung: Frank Schirrmacher, "Der neue Roman von Martin Walser: Kein Vorabdruck in der F.A.Z.," *Frankfurter Allgemeine Zeitung*, 5/29/2002 (available at www.hagalil.com/antisemitismus/bgaa/walser-roman.htm; accessed 1/20/2012); reprinted in *Wer schweigt, wird schuldig! Offene Briefe von Martin Luther bis Ulrike Meinhof*, ed. Rolf-Bernhard Essig and Reinhard M. G. Nickisch (Göttingen: Wallstein Verlag, 2007), pp. 243–47.

151 *an inconclusive historical debate about whether Grass volunteered for the SS*: In a sworn affidavit, Grass insists that he did not volunteer for the SS. However, he also admits, in his autobiography, that he did not find the prospect of carrying the uniform of the SS to be "objectionable" at the time. See Günter Grass (trans. Michael Henry Heim), *Peeling the Onion* (Orlando, Fla.: Harcourt, 2007), and Thorsten Dörting, "Streit um Biografie: Günter Grass klagt gegen SS-Vorwurf," Spiegel Online, 11/23/2007 (available at: www.spiegel.de/kultur/literatur/streit-um-biografie-guenter -grass-klagt-gegen-ss-vorwurf-a-518926.html; accessed on 1/20/2012).

152 *In nine brief, rhymeless, meterless verses, Grass identified an easy culprit*: The quotes that follow are from Günter Grass, "Was gesagt werden muss," *Süddeutsche Zeitung*, 4/10/2012 (available at www.sueddeutsche.de/kultur /gedicht-zum-konflikt-zwischen-israel-und-iran-was-gesagt-werden-muss -1.1325809; accessed on 5/6/2012).

154 *hostility to his poem was owed to a* "Gleichschaltung *of opinion"*: The video of the interview is available at: www.ndr.de/kultur/literatur/grassgedicht103 .html (accessed on 5/6/2012).

8. POISONING THE WELL

159 *As Sigmund Freud argued in* The Psychopathology of Everyday Life: Sigmund Freud (trans. Anthea Bell), *The Psychopathology of Everyday Life* (New York: Penguin, 2003), pp. 70–71.

160 *a golden garden gnome raising his right arm in the Hitler salute*: See www.bild.de/news/2009/nuernberg/nazi-zwerg-schockt-nuernberg-904 5026.bild.html and www.spiegel.de/kultur/gesellschaft/posse-um-nazi -gartenzwerg-heil-heinzelmann-a-636617.html (both accessed on 1/12/2013).

161 *"it is true that ethnically Turkish Muslims in Germany"*: "Zentralrat der Juden nimmt Faruk Sen in Schutz," *Die Welt*, 6/30/2008 (available at: www.welt.de/politik/article2162691/Zentralrat-der-Juden-nimmt-Faruk -Sen-in-Schutz.html; accessed on 1/20/2012).

166 *"Out of the crooked timber of humanity"*: Immanuel Kant, "Idea for a Universal History with a Cosmopolitan Purpose," Sixth Proposal. See *Kant: Political Writings*, ed. H. S. Reiss, trans. H. B. Nisbet (Cambridge, U.K.: Cambridge University Press, 1970), p. 46. The translation I use stems from Isaiah Berlin, *The Crooked Timber of Humanity: Chapters in the History of Ideas*, ed. Henry Hardy (New York: Alfred A. Knopf, 1991), p. 48.

167 *"He never did anything to me, it's true, but"*: Quoted in James Wood, *The Irresponsible Self: On Laughter and the Novel* (New York: Farrar, Straus and Giroux, 2004), p. 61.

168 *"I won't mention that Holocaust and you won't mention Michel Friedman"*: Michel Polak, *Ich darf das, ich bin Jude* (Köln: Kiepenheuer & Witsch, 2008), p. 11.

169 *"At the beginning of the eighties, there were only two kinds of Jews"*: Maxim Biller, *Der gebrauchte Jude: Ein Selbstporträt* (Köln: Kiepenheuer & Witsch, 2009), p. 11.

9. THE NEW GERMAN QUESTION

181 *"those who emphatically set themselves apart from National Socialism"*: Quoted in Hans Kundnani, *Utopia or Auschwitz: Germany's 1968 Generation and the Holocaust* (New York: Columbia University Press, 2009), p. 136. (Kundnani's translation.)

181 He didn't just learn *"Never again war"*: For video of Joschka Fischer's impassioned speech, see: www.youtube.com/watch?v=7jsKCOTM4Ms (accessed on 1/15/2012).

182 *"if not to forget, then to fade out"* Germany's guilt: Quoted in Micha Brumlik, Hajo Funke, and Lars Rensmann, *Umkämpftes Vergessen: Walser-Debatte, Holocaust-Mahnmal und neuere deutsche Geschichtspolitik* (Tübingen: Verlag Hans Schiler, 2004), p. 108.

183 On another occasion, declaring his outright opposition to the looming war: Susanne Scheerer, "SPD-Wahlkampfauftakt: Schröders 'deutscher Weg,'" *Frankfurter Allgemeine Zeitung*, 8/5/2002. (Audio of the relevant parts of the speech available at: www.faz.net/aktuell/politik/spd-wahlkampfauftakt -schroeders-deutscher-weg-170241.html; accessed on 1/16/2012.)

190 As Otmar Issing, a former member of the board: Christian Grimm, "'Man darf Deutschland nicht mit seiner Vergangenheit erpressen,'" *Wall Street Journal Deutschland*, 8/9/2012 (available at: www.wallstreetjournal.de /article/SB10000872396390443404004577578990832865830.html; accessed on 1/14/2013).

191 *"In 1960, Adenauer's government doled out 115 million deutschmarks"*: Paul Ronzheimer and Ralf Schuler, "Warum machen die Griechen uns zum Buhmann?" *Bild*, 6/21/2011 (available at: www.bild.de/politik/ausland

/griechenland-krise/deutschland-zahlt-und-wird-dafuer-beschimpft-1845
2080.bild.html; accessed on 1/26/2012).

191 *69 percent of Germans favoring a Greek exit from the euro zone*: "Mehrheit
der Deutschen plädiert für Euro ohne Griechen," DPA, 6/13/2012 (available at www.handelsblatt.com/politik/international/umfrage-mehrheit-der
-deutschen-plaediert-fuer-euro-ohne-griechen/6745962.html; accessed on
1/16/2013). Note that as the euro crisis has calmed somewhat and Greece
has made progress, support for Greece remaining in the euro zone has
markedly increased in some polls.

191 *Germany's economic growth slowed to a snail's pace*: Michael Steen,
"Bundesbank Cuts German Growth Forecast," *Financial Times*, 12/7/2012
(available at www.ft.com/intl/cms/s/0/8e845114-4045-11e2-8f90-00144fe
abdc0.html#axzz2IR5KSv6l; accessed on 12/8/2012).

192 *Berlin "followed its own instincts"*: John Vinocur, "German Reunification: From Rejection to Inevitability," *International Herald Tribune*,
11/8/2009.

10. THE REBELLION AGAINST PLURALISM

197 *"who feel that somebody who is called Cem Özdemir cannot be a German"*:
"Cem Özdemir—Politics Beyond Ethnic Terms." Available at: www.bbc.co
.uk/languages/germany_insideout/berlin3.shtml; accessed on 1/16/2013.

197 *multiple studies have shown that, when making decisions about children*:
A good summary of recent research on discrimination in the German
school system is given in Mechthild Gomolla, "Institutionelle Diskrimi-
nierung im Bildungs- und Erziehungssystem: Theorie, Forschungsergeb-
nisse und Handlungsperspektiven," in *Heinrich-Böll Stiftung: Schule mit
Migrationshintergrund*, dossier, pp. 20–29 (available at: www.migration
-boell.de/web/integration/47_1451.asp; accessed on 4/28/2013).

198 *But after age nine I rarely encountered them as peers*: Academic studies
suggest that this was hardly a coincidence. According to one study, for example, 40 percent of "autochthonous" youths aged between sixteen and
twenty-five were either attending *Gymnasium* or had already graduated
from one. The same was true of only 13 percent of second-generation
Turkish immigrants. See Susanne Worbs, "The Second Generation in
Germany: Between School and Labor Market," *International Migration
Review*, vol. 37 (4), 2003, p. 1020.

201 *only about 13,000 Turks gained German citizenship*: Records of the Statistisches Bundesamt, obtained in private communication with its press office. (Please note that data for 1967, 1968, and 1969 are not available, but,
from the preceding and succeeding period, can be surmised to be roughly
consistent with those years.)

201　5 *million Germans signed a petition against dual citizenship*: "CDU: Fünf
Millionen Unterschriften gegen Doppel-Paß," Spiegel Online, 5/20/1999
(available at: www.spiegel.de/politik/deutschland/cdu-fuenf-millionen-unter
schriften-gegen-doppel-pass-a-23661.html; accessed on 1/17/2013).

202　*Sarrazin once said about Josef Goebbels*: "Test-Talkshow: Sarrazin ver-
zettelt sich mit Goebbels," Spiegel Online, 10/9/2010 (available at: www
.spiegel.de/kultur/tv/test-talkshow-sarrazin-verzettelt-sich-mit-goebbels
-a-716749.html; accessed on 1/13/2013).

202　*Why would more than one and a half million Germans*: "Thilo Sarrazin
sprengt alle Rekorde," Media Control, 10/29/2010 (available at: www.media
-control.de/thilo-sarrazin-sprengt-alle-rekorde.html; accessed on 1/13/2013).

203　*"To say 'Let's have some multiculturalism in our country'"*: "Kanzle-
rin Merkel erklärt Multikulti für gescheitert," *Die Welt* 10/16/2010 (available at: www.welt.de/politik/deutschland/article10337575/Kanzlerin-Merkel
-erklaert-Multikulti-fuer-gescheitert.html; accessed on 1/12/2013).

207　*that number is set to fall to at most 73.8 million by 2040, and 64.7 million
by 2060*: These figures stem from variant 1-W1, in the twelfth coordinated population projection by the Statistisches Bundesamt, Germany's
statistics office. They are calculated on the basis of a birthrate of 1.4 children per woman and annual net migration of 100,000 people. They are
available online at: www.destatis.de/bevoelkerungspyramide; accessed
on 6/29/2012.

208　*Germany's population would shrink even more quickly*: According to
"Modellrechnung W0 AG" by the Statistisches Bundesamt, under the
assumption of a birthrate of 1.4 children per woman and zero net migration, the number of Germans would shrink to 58.2 million by 2060.
But the main difference between the two scenarios does not consist
in a population that is lower by approximately 8 million, but rather in
the much bigger adverse impact it would have on the—in any case very
unfavorable—age distribution projected for 2060. (Data drawn from
"Bevölkerung Deutschlands bis 2060: Ergebnisse der 12. koordinierten
Bevölkerungsvorausberechnung" [Wiesbaden: Statistisches Bundesamt,
2009]. Available as an Excel document online at: www.destatis.de/DE
/ZahlenFakten/GesellschaftStaat/Bevoelkerung/Bevoelkerungsvoraus
berechnung/Tabellen/VorausberechnungDeutschland.xls?__blob
=publicationFile. See worksheet "Modellrechnung W0 AG"; accessed on
6/29/2012.)

209　*"the outer limit of our ability to absorb foreigners has been reached"*:
Bundeskanzler Brandt, "Regierungserklärung des zweiten Kabinetts Brandt/
Scheel vom 18. Januar 1973," Presse- und Informationsamt der Bundes-
regierung, p. 46 (available at: http://library.fes.de/pdf-files/netzquelle/a88
-06578.pdf; accessed on 6/30/2012).

212 *"Whole clans have a long tradition of incest"*: Thilo Sarrazin, *Deutschland schafft sich ab: Wie wir unser Land aufs Spiel setzen* (München: Deutsche Verlags-Anstalt, 2010), p. 316.

212 *Luckily, he soon found a perfect piece of armor*: As Sarrazin puts this point: "I have talked in a little more detail about the German-Jewish roots of research about intelligence because discussions about its genetic component often meet great emotional resistance" (Sarrazin, *Deutschland schafft sich ab*, p. 97).

213 *"shared foundation of the values enshrined in our constitution"*: "Integration: Seehofer legt Sieben-Punkte-Plan nach," Focus Online, 10/16/2010 (available at: www.focus.de/politik/deutschland/integration-seehofer-legt -sieben-punkte-plan-nach_aid_562723.html; accessed on 5/12/2011).

216 *"We don't need any clever comments from a guy whose name"*: Yascha Mounk, "Der Stil schafft sich ab," *The European* (available at: http:// nachrichten.t-online.de/sarrazins-populismus-der-stil-schafft-sich-ab/id _44054152/index; accessed on 1/19/2011).

EPILOGUE: NO LONGER A JEW

230 *A recent exchange between Renate Künast*: Veit Medick, "Streit mit Israel-Bündnis: Künast, der Mossad-Vorwurf und das Dementi," Spiegel Online, 7/14/2009 (available at: www.spiegel.de/politik/deutschland/streit-mit -israel-buendnis-kuenast-der-mossad-vorwurf-und-das-dementi-a-636151 .html; accessed on 1/25/2012).

235 *"I don't know if they live there"*: Peter Schworm and John Ellement, "Gates Tapes Show Confrontation, Don't Answer Question of Blame," *Boston Globe*, 7/28/2009 (available at: www.boston.com/news/local/massachusetts /articles/2009/07/28/gates_arrest_audio_indicates_race_was_not_factor _at_start; accessed on 1/25/2012).

235 *"very loud" and "tumultuous" behavior*: Cambridge Police Department, incident report no. 9005127, 7/16/2009 (available at: www.samefacts.com /archives/Police%20report%20on%20Gates%20arrest.PDF; accessed on 12/10/2012).

235 *"I said 'Officer, can I help you?'"*: Dayo Olopade, "Skip Gates Speaks," *The Root*, 7/21/2009 (available at: www.theroot.com/views/skip-gates-speaks ?page=0,1; accessed on 12/10/2012).

242 *There are, White wrote, roughly three New Yorks*: The following quotations are all taken from E. B. White, *Here Is New York* (New York: The Little Bookroom, 2011), pp. 25–27.

Acknowledgments

In the process of writing this book I have incurred countless debts, both personal and intellectual. The ritual of thanking friends, colleagues, and mentors in a long public list is an inevitably inadequate expression of my gratitude. But it's the best I can do, and it gives me great pleasure to at least acknowledge their contribution.

Sydelle Kramer has been a fierce advocate, a forthright critic, and an incredibly patient adviser since the very beginning. This book would have been a lot less good, and my nerves a lot more frayed, without her help. Eric Chinski has been supporting, demanding, and incisive in just the right measure—I couldn't have hoped for a more helpful, or more genial, editor. Working with the incredible team at Farrar, Straus and Giroux has been a real pleasure since the moment I first stepped into the offices. Particular thanks go to Gabriella Doob, Ed Cohen, Mareike Grover, Jeff Seroy, Lottchen Shivers, Amanda Schoonmaker, Amber Hoover, and Devon Mazzone.

Tom Meaney has been my literary consigliere since I first arrived in the United States. Without his support and his advice, I would never have dreamed of becoming a writer. The idea for this book comes from a night of drinking with Rebecca Nagel and Sam Munson. Without their encouragement to write down my story—and Rebecca's patient advice on the proposal—this book wouldn't exist.

Carly Knight, Sabeel Rahman, Emma Saunders-Hastings, Matt Landauer, and Justin Reynolds have read early drafts of the book and given extensive comments. I have done my imperfect best to incorporate their excellent suggestions.

When I first arrived at Cambridge University as an undergraduate, my English was shaky, and my average sentence five lines long. For teaching me how to write idiomatic, clear, and (hopefully) concise English, I owe a lifelong debt of gratitude to Hazel Pearson, William Seward, Martin Ruehl, and Richard Serjeantson.

For the generous advice they have given me over the past years, I would also like to thank Sadie Stein, Eleni Arzoglou, Thierry Artzner, Amy Hempel, Sara Bershtel, Charles Petersen, Michael Wachsmann, Gabriele Bodenstein, Unhee Do, Dina Gusejnova, Manuel Hartung, Miles Pattenden, Alessandra Heinemann, Mark Krotov, Chantal Clarke, Peter Gordon, Stanley Hoffmann, Bret Johnston, Darcy Frey, Christopher Caldwell, Wesley Yang, Aleksandra Dier, Lucas Stanczyk, Roberto Foa, Alexander Lee, Bernardo Zacka, Mathilde Unger, Gideon Lewis-Kraus, Ed Baring, Katja Guenther, Al Prescott-Couch, Caleb Crain, Giles Harvey, Rachel Reilich, Rahawa Haile, Johann Frick, Henry Midgley, Karan Mahajan, Francesca Mari, and Alexander Benaim.

While working on the manuscript for this book, I had the privilege of passing an idyllic and productive month at Yaddo in a space called, for complicated reasons involving Philip Roth and a curvaceous ceiling, "The Breast Room." A big thank-you goes to Yaddo's staff and trustees, as well as to my wonderful fellow residents.

In writing this book, I have drawn on articles I have published in *Slate*, *Foreign Affairs*, and the blog of the *London Review of Books*. A few passages may bear substantial similarity to this previously published work. I have also drawn on a review of Hans Kundnani's *Utopia or Auschwitz: Germany's 1968 Generation and the Holocaust,* which I wrote for *n+1*, and I am indebted to Kundnani's excellent work.

The memoiristic elements of this book describe encounters with real people. Since I do not wish to embarrass anybody, I decided to protect their identity. While the names of members of my family, as well as those of public or historical figures, are real, many others appear in altered form.

Part of this book tells the story of my family. For providing me with the facts and anecdotes that allowed me to reconstruct, however imperfectly, the unrecorded past—and for accepting so cheerfully to feature in a book they never asked to be a part of—I owe immense gratitude to Helka, Roman, Andrzej, Alex, Witek, Daniel, Casper, Tom, Rebecka, and Olek. The greatest thank-you goes to the person whose wonderful qualities I have always admired—but who, as is a son's wont, I am nevertheless in danger of underappreciating at times: my incomparable mother, Ala.

Finally, for giving such tireless advice on innumerable drafts of this book, and for having been a wonderful friend, companion, and intellectual ally: thank you, Carly.

Printed in the USA
CPSIA information can be obtained
at www.ICGtesting.com
LVHW091140150724
785511LV00005B/443